T0305088

Teaching Post Keynesian Economics

Teaching Post Keynesian Economics

Edited by

Jesper Jespersen

Professor of Economics, Roskilde University, Denmark

Mogens Ove Madsen

Associate Professor of Economics, Aalborg University, Denmark

Edward Elgar

Cheltenham, UK • Northampton, MA, USA

Published by
Edward Elgar Publishing Limited
The Lypiatts
15 Lansdown Road
Cheltenham
Glos GL50 2JA
UK

Edward Elgar Publishing, Inc.
William Pratt House
9 Dewey Court
Northampton
Massachusetts 01060
USA

A catalogue record for this book
is available from the British Library

Library of Congress Control Number: 2013932988

This book is available electronically in the ElgarOnline.com
Economics Subject Collection, E-ISBN 978 1 78254 700 6

ISBN 978 1 78254 699 3

Typeset by Servis Filmsetting Ltd, Stockport, Cheshire
Printed and bound in Great Britain by T.J. International Ltd, Padstow

Contents

Figures and tables

FIGURES

TABLES

Contributors

Angel Asensio, CEPN, University Paris 13, France

Victoria Chick, University College London, UK

Allin Cottrell, Wake Forest University, USA

Andy Denis, City University London, UK

Sheila Dow, University of Stirling, UK

Jesper Jespersen, Roskilde University, Denmark

Marc Lavoie, University of Ottawa, Canada

Bruce Littleboy, University of Queensland, Australia

Mogens Ove Madsen, Aalborg University, Denmark

Poul Thøis Madsen, Aalborg University, Denmark

Marco Missaglia, Universidad Nacional de Colombia, Bogotà, Colombia

Finn Olesen, Aalborg University, Denmark

Roy J. Rotheim, Skidmore College, USA

Michael J. Salvagno, University of Cambridge, UK

Introduction

Jesper Jespersen and Mogens Ove Madsen

The year 2011 marked 75 years since the publication of *The General Theory of Employment, Interest and Money*. It was published on 4 February 1936 in the middle of an economic depression, a time in which politicians were groping in the dark with little help from the field of economics. People were queuing to buy the book as soon as it was released, and expectations were high.

There are many similarities between then and now, including unemployment, low growth and mounting public debt. Unfortunately, nobody is talking about a new 'General Theory' being on the way, which gives us all the more reason to re-read and reconsider Keynes's seminal book.

At the brink of the 21st century, a number of academic economists were asked which economist they considered to have had the greatest impact on the 20th century. Most named Keynes, many referring directly to *The General Theory*; but this vote was about influence in the past. One hardly sees references to Keynes in macroeconomic textbooks any more – perhaps a passing remark related to the case of rigid wages in the labour market (which only demonstrates that the author has not read *The General Theory*). Given the number of similarities between the economic crisis of the 1930s and the present one, we considered this an obvious time to gather Keynes scholars from around the world to discuss and exchange views on the 'relevance and perspectives' of *The General Theory* for this century.

The theme of this volume is the teaching of the economics of Keynes. This theme is important as much of the original 'message' of *The General Theory* is no longer present in the syllabuses taught in most universities. In many ways, questions can be raised as to whether the original elements in *The General Theory* have ever truly been a part of the syllabus in macroeconomics, even in the 1950s and 1960s. The so-called 'Keynesian Economics', as we know it from Paul Samuelson's textbook *Economics*, first published in 1948, is not really the economics of *The General Theory*. The methodology, the emphasis on equilibrium and the role of the inflexibility of prices and wages in explaining unemployment are features which

Samuelson, together with many other neoclassical synthesizers, developed in the 1950s and 1960s with inspiration from Hicks's ISLM diagram. This macroeconomic teaching was easy to explain in the classroom and to use for constructing the new macroeconometric models which dominated the macroeconomic debate for some time and represented mainstream macroeconomics at that time. In the 1980s, this approach in macroeconomics was swept aside by the claim that it was not 'scientific', because a rigorous microeconomic foundation was lacking and the theory of expectations was *ad hoc* – not grounded in rational choice theory. In fact, this is where the teaching in macroeconomics stands today. Only textbooks assuming general equilibrium and using the microeconomic foundation of rational choice theory are widely available. This version of macroeconomics is of little help towards understanding the present economic crisis: what caused it, why it is dragging on and how to get out of it. These are questions which cannot be answered within a general equilibrium model, where crises are caused by exogenous shocks and the macroeconomic system assumed to be self-adjusting. This teaching situation is, of course, especially embarrassing for the macroeconomists who hold that Keynes and *The General Theory* possess indispensable insight which would give students a better understanding of the world economy in which they live.

At this stage, we feel tempted to quote directly from Keynes, who anticipated this difficult situation with teaching new ideas. In his time, he was up against what he called Ricardian Theory, which was represented in Cambridge by the only professor in economics, Arthur Cecil Pigou, who had just published his view of macroeconomics in a book entitled *Unemployment* (1933). In *The General Theory*, Keynes asked how it was possible that:

> Ricardo conquered England as completely as the Holy Inquisition conquered Spain . . . The completeness of the Ricardian victory is something of a curiosity and a mystery. It must have been due to a complex of suitabilities in the doctrine to the environment into which it was projected. That it reached conclusions quite different from what the ordinary uninstructed person would expect, added, I suppose, to its intellectual prestige. That its teaching, translated into practice, was austere and often unpalatable, lent it virtue. (Keynes, 1936: 32–3)

TEACHING POST KEYNESIAN ECONOMICS

Marc Lavoie, in his chapter 'Teaching post Keynesian economics in a mainstream department', describes how he came into contact with post Keynesian economics early in his studies at Carleton University in the 1970s. He describes how the students had a hard time making sense of the Cambridge capital controversies. One of the seminars was given by T.K. Rymes at a point when Lavoie had been attracted to post Keynesian economic theory but had yet to be convinced – although the survey chapter by Eichner and Kregel (1975) had made quite an impression on him. He later followed a course in advanced macroeconomics at the University of Paris 1 and was confronted with various forms of Keynesian theory, notably disequilibrium theory and monetary circuit theory. One of the main lecturers was Alain Parguez. Lavoies' dissertation was essentially inspired by monetary circuit theory and many of the new and important books at the time.

In 1979 Lavoie began his academic career at the University of Ottawa, and he and Mario Seccareccia were awarded tenure-track positions in 1981. Today they are the only two remaining heterodox economists in their department. It is against this background that Lavoie gives his thoughts as to the options for teaching post Keynesian economics in a mainstream department.

According to Lavoie, the most successful option is undoubtedly a full heterodox course when the economy is in a recession or with a high rate of unemployment, much like the current situation with the subprime financial crisis and its aftermath. Students will be looking for alternative explanations of the crisis. Other strategies include either an introduction to elements of heterodoxy in orthodox modules or courses, or teaching orthodox and heterodox economics in parallel.

There are three possible paths to follow if the strategy with an independent course is established. The first is to use existing course titles, the second to create a new course with explicit titles, and the third is to create a new course with an ambiguous title. Examples are given.

The extent to which it is possible to teach a fully heterodox course also depends on which textbooks are available. Godley and Lavoie's brilliant 2007 book, which presents a stock-flow consistent approach, gave post Keynesian economics new opportunities to assert themselves.[1] Another way is to introduce elements of heterodoxy in orthodox textbooks. A successful example of this is the adaption of the US Baumol and Blinder textbook, which was in its 10th edition. Much to Lavoie's surprise, it was much easier to introduce eclectic or heterodox elements in the micro part of the textbook than in the macro section, but overall a very satisfactory result.

In his chapter, 'The economist who mistook his model for a market' *Roy Rotheim* emphasizes the didactic aspect of and limitations of any teaching; the discrepancy between what the teacher intends the students to learn and what they learn. Of course, the focus point of post Keynesian teaching is to give students an insight into real-world processes in time and space. This is ambitious and difficult because we do not really know the real world; but with inspiration from Keynes's path-breaking contribution in *The General Theory* there is at least a starting point for post Keynesian teaching. Whatever is told in the class-room is at best a vague mirror picture of reality. Roy Rotheim points at a number of obstacles: lack of understanding, of language, of metaphors and (ab)use of mathematics. But, at least, good post Keynesian teachers know these limitations and attempt to avoid falling into the trap of mixing the pedagogic model with reality. Exactly for that reason, the author claims, post Keynesian economics will never be a part of teaching in a mainstream department. Here it is expected that teaching in economics is without ambiguities. Economics is an exact science and the teaching has to be undertaken in accordance with this scientific principle. Hence, in that case mathematics is the preferred language: exact, deductive and without ambiguity. In that case there is no reason to differentiate between model and reality – the model is the best possible understanding of the market. Therefore, the author sees no possible bridging in mutual understanding between mainstream and post Keynesian economics either in economic analysis or in teaching. One has to be realistic about this lack of mutual research and teaching agenda.

THE BASICS: OPEN SYSTEMS, PLURALISM AND RHETORIC

The chapters that follow focus on a number of methodological considerations required to support the teaching of post Keynesian economics. They are about the choice between closed and open models in economic thinking. It will be argued that pluralism and the rhetoric used are crucial to how powerful post Keynesianism will work.

Victoria Chick, in her chapter 'The future is open: on open-system theorizing in economics', stresses that open systems should form the core of economics teaching on the grounds of their superior relevance. However, there is some psychological difficulty related to this approach. Modern economics is often attributed to its formalism, particularly its reliance on mathematics and how it encourages a closed-system approach to theory construction from a methodological point of view.

There can be many types of openness, but no system can be completely open – boundaries must exist. Four dimensions of openness are identified: subject matter, the object of study, the level of analysis (micro and macro), and time.

Chick is very aware that open systems will cause problems beyond the usual ones of doing something which is not mainstream. Principal among these is an adverse reaction to the lack of definiteness or certainty. All this goes against the Cartesian mode of thought which has dominated Western thinking for a very long time.

Open systems are obviously created by open minds and require open minds to understand them, but this requires experiences, and learners can become increasingly open in their belief systems. The chapter demonstrates a description of progression from closed to more open forms of learning – the so-called 'stages of student maturation'. A way of developing this is getting students to realize that they are responsible for their own learning.

Sheila Dow argues in a similar manner in her chapter, 'Teaching open-system economics', favouring use of an open-system approach when teaching economics. Again, an open system is not the opposite of a closed system since there are many possibilities for open-system approaches to economics. A system is open if any one of the conditions for a closed theoretical system is not met. Closed system economics is based on classical logic and therefore on a deductivist methodology often presented in mathematical terms. Conversely, an open system calls for a different kind of logic: human or ordinary logic. According to Dow, a closed-system approach poses tremendous challenges in its application to an open-system economy. Experience shows, however, that internal consistency is given higher methodological priority within mainstream economics than applicability to the real world. On the contrary, open-system thinking is specifically designed to recommend a critical realist approach to addressing open-system subject matters. Uncertainty is an inescapable part of realistic economics and therefore an argument for using open-system analysis. Social phenomena are evolving over time in an unpredictable manner that must deal with mechanisms and structures partly unknowable to the researcher.

Even if there is some psychological (and methodological) aversion to handling uncertainty in the teaching of economics, post Keynesian economics has indicated a willingness to engage with it. This requires a special kind of economics thinking such as that which Keynes expressed in *The General Theory* – that the object of the analysis is not to provide a machine or method of blind manipulation, but rather that we are to provide ourselves with an organized and orderly method of thinking out particular problems. The actual financial and economic crisis could call forth a range of competing explanations and theories on which to base policy solutions, drawing on different approaches. At the very least it is a wonderful case study for teaching post Keynesian economics.

A challenge for teaching open-system analysis is that it leaves the outcome open-ended, meaning that students must learn the art of independent thinking and judgement in addition to a large body of material. Open-system learning thus develops different skills from closed-system learning. The teaching of any models should therefore be embedded in a broader discussion of the factors left out of the model in order to teach how models can be useful as well as to demonstrate their limitations.

Andy Denis, in his chapter 'Pluralism in economics education', argues that pluralism should be a central part of economics. Basing the teaching of economics on controversy will be to the benefit of students, staff, employers and polity alike. It is emphasized that every science is rhetorical and the social sciences doubly so: there is a body of knowledge and an image of knowledge. The latter part in particular concerns economics due to its proximity to policy-making, and in particular the economic policy-making process. But it is important to notice that while the field of economics is inevitably plural, many contributions have not been refuted; instead, they are simply ignored. This long, drawn-out process of squeezing the history and methodology of the subject out of the curriculum is part of an organic process of quarantining and sequestering heterodox thought in the discipline.

What we have today is monism, or the hegemony of a particular approach. The alternative, then, is pluralism, or a tolerant, critical conversation. Pluralism can either be permissive or assertive. The lower grade of pluralism is permissive as a permission to introduce different kinds of schools. Assertive pluralism requires the mutual engagement of different schools of thought.

By viewing the phenomena in question from multiple perspectives, pluralism raises the issues of uncertainty, complexity and context. In this manner, pluralism helps students learn to become life-long learners; it gives them the ability to make judgements in the context of uncertainty and a commitment to questioning one's own purposes, evidence, implications, assumptions and standpoint.

In his chapter 'Truth and beauty in macroeconomics', *Allin Cottrell* takes issue with Paul Krugman's notion that Keynesian economics is the best macro-theory that we have, but is somewhat messy and unclear. This is refuted and it is documented how Keynes's theory, when correctly interpreted, exhibits an elegance and coherence that Krugman somehow misses. In Cottrell's optic, neoclassical macro-theory may be internally consistent from a purely logical point of view, but there is a gross discrepancy between the epistemology of the theory and the ontology of the domain it claims to be theorizing on. To the contrary, the relevance of Keynes' *General Theory* lies in how he is able to build a powerful engine of analysis capable of illuminating a wide range of macroeconomic phenomena on the parsimonious basis of a few very general facts about the macroeconomic reality in 'which we happen to live'. An example of this scientific relevance is found in Keynes's analysis of the role of 'wage flexibility' in the labour market. Nothing can be said about the macroeconomic outcome if the money wage level were assumed to be perfectly flexible until uncertainty is taken deliberately into the argument, including its impact on planned investments. If there is a fall in the volume of saving, full employment will not be obtained at any money wage level.

According to Cottrell, there is a trade-off between detail and conceptual clarity, and the desirable point in that trade-off depends on the particular question we are trying to address. In this manner, Keynes offers a clear conceptual account of the problem of demand-deficient unemployment in a capitalist economy.

Bruce Littleboy takes a different, less exegetical and critical direction into rhetoric in his chapter 'Rhetoric in the spirit of Keynes: metaphors to persuade economists, students and the public about fiscal policy'. In his opinion, the economics of Keynes has been too aggregated for too long. What used to be simplified has become simplistic. But debating the merits of a metaphor helps us probe what we are really talking about. A metaphor has three clear uses: it inspires new hypotheses, it offers a means of education and spreading ideas, and it tests causal reasoning by permitting critical thought experiments.

To provide an example, Littleboy shows how wastefulness is not sufficient for providing a demand stimulus. It makes better rhetorical sense to focus on how markets can waste resources through idleness than to advocate wasteful activity by government. Littleboy finds it striking that Keynesian ideas once regarded as routine and introductory are now widely regarded as being fallacious at best and dangerously imbecilic at worst. Littleboy gives an example of recent debates over the suitability of fiscal policy that in part reflects the Austrian critique of the Keynesian approach. The chapter offers a first step as to how the debate barely extends beyond assertion and crude metaphor. The different intuitions are in collision; they are not yet in exploratory engagement.

TEXTBOOKS

The macroeconomics of Paul Davidson is the economics of the real world. This is what *Finn Olesen* highlights in his chapter: 'Teaching macroeconomics – seeking inspiration from Paul Davidson'.

The chapter examines two of Davidson's economics textbooks, *Post Keynesian Macroeconomics Theory* (2011) and *Aggregate Supply and Demand Analysis* (1964; together with Eugene Smolensky). The latter was originally presented and designed to be the ultimate post Keynesian macroeconomics textbook. Both books are meant to be seen as clear alternatives to the prevailing mainstream interpretation of macroeconomics by using 'the principle of effective demand' as the pivotal part of their teaching model.

Throughout almost all of his writings, Davidson has repeatedly argued that to understand the relevant economics processes of a modern monetary entrepreneurial macro economy you have to acknowledge and take Keynes's fundamental conclusions into account. Consequently, Davidson's interpretation of Keynes holds that money is never neutral in the sense that money actually does affect real economic variables in the short run as well as in the longer run. According to Davidson, Keynes also rejected the axiom of gross substitution – all markets are not going to clear simultaneously. And as a final and fundamental viewpoint, Keynes understood the macroeconomic system as a system that was functioning in a non-ergodic manner.Davidson's macroeconomic universe is, according to Olesen, quite different from the modern macroeconomic mainstream of today. Davidson proposes an alternative to the mainstream by focusing, as Keynes did, on 'time, money and uncertainty'.

In *Poul Thøis Madsen*'s chapter, 'What about the mainstream critique of American principles of economics textbooks?', it is made clear that the criticism of economics textbooks goes back a long way. It is a minor debate that has been going on for decades but especially in the period 1987–93. However, the author identifies a number of factors that make it difficult to find the mainstream debate on textbooks.

The critical points contained in the publications can be divided into three major problems. First, the so-called 'fundamental problem', such as the relationship between the textbook and actual economic reality. Less and less contextual and historical knowledge and fewer ideas drawn from the history of economics are to be found in textbooks. Disagreements among economists are thrown out together with a perceived bias towards neoclassical Keynesianism. Secondly, leading textbooks are tending to become increasingly similar. Thirdly, important issues have been handled inadequately.

The author sets out to discover what has happened to the mainstream critique of textbooks. He concludes that its decline could be ascribed either to the fact that there is little merit in criticizing textbooks or that textbook authors and their publishers believe they have found a winning formula not in need of any change – even if relevant criticism leaves plenty of space for improving the textbooks.

CONFRONTATION AND COMPARISON

In a chapter entitled 'Teaching Keynes's theory to neoclassically formed minds', *Angel Asensio* argues that setting uncertainty at the centre of the methodological debate reveals the very reason for the theoretical oppositions between neoclassics and post Keynesians. The aim of the chapter is to offer an exposition of the macroeconomics of competitive equilibrium based on both a deconstruction of the neoclassical theory and a restatement of *The General Theory* proper, meaning a proper articulation of concepts at every level. It implies, among other things, the way both approaches deal with uncertainty and rational decisions, and it is argued that modern theory of decision-making under uncertainty supports Keynes's approach. *The General Theory* revolutionized macroeconomics because it renewed the microfoundation, the result being a transmutation of competitive equilibrium analyses and detection of the failure of competitive forces to eradicate unemployment. The chapter also reviews a number of potentially destabilizing forces of competitive markets.

Compared with mainstream economics, Keynes did adopt the widest approach to uncertainty. That is also why *The General Theory* is basically more general and realistic than mainstream economics. Keynes's equilibrium accordingly involves both a wider role for institutions and a richer concept of equilibrium, which admits the possibility that all markets do not clear. Unfortunately mainstream thinking dominates students' first years of study. 'Post Keynesian' teaching therefore requires that the concepts are first deconstructed. Otherwise, it will be difficult to break through with broader Keynesian thinking.

Confrontation between the neoclassical and Keynesian macro models is also the topic in *Marco Missaglia*'s chapter, 'Neoclassical and Keynesian macro models: thinking about the "special case"'. This chapter argues that Keynesian models are the general case, whereas neoclassical models constitute the special one. It is also shown that the reason why the opposite belief has been dominating the scene for decades is to be found in the overemphasis Keynes himself placed on his theory of 'liquidity preference'.

What makes Keynesian ideas regarding macroeconomics much more general than neoclassical views is not related to what money is for, but rather to how money is created and introduced into the system. The theory of endogenous money developed by the post Keynesians is the analytical tool through which Keynesian causality – from investment to savings – is to be explained. This chapter also emphasizes that all sorts of Keynesian models may be written in a 'complementarity format', which is a way of showing the formal similarities between the neoclassical and Keynesian macro models.

Throughout the chapter it is argued that the most important Keynesian idea – that aggregate demand is the engine which moves the economic system – is not a 'special case', as neoclassical economists otherwise claim. The special case is the neoclassical one in which any increase in investment expenditure is to be accompanied by a reduction in consumption expenditure.

The last chapter, 'Economists on the 2008 financial crisis: genuine reflection; or constructing narratives to re-affirm the profession's authority?' by *Michael Salvagno* provides an analysis of a sample of initial writings by leading economists and financial journalists in the financial press. They primarily focus on their efforts to evaluate both the performance of the profession and the suitability of the project of modern economics.

These writings capture a series of debates in what could only be described as a period of distress in the discipline. The writings are assessed in order to determine how to identify the role and performance of the economics profession leading up to and during the crisis, as well as the suggested proposals for reforming the discipline.

It has been argued that the unreal assumptions of the leading models – the efficiency of the market and the rationality of individuals – led to poor understanding of the economy and therefore inadequate management, which can paradoxically serve to re-affirm the authority of empirically divorced theoretical ideas. So the question then becomes how to develop analysis of the economy from rationality of individuals and markets to establish a range of signals for identifying new risks to both the economic system and the financial sovereignty of states. It is suggested that this transformation would require a new foundation for economic theory.

But while it may seem as though genuine reform or a critical review of the profession's performance is taking place, the analysis presented in this chapter contends that from the authors listed, and with the exception of the institutionalist reformers, this process has barely begun.

NOTE

1. See e.g. Bezemer (2009) for an analysis presenting evidence that accounting or flow-of-fund macroeconomic models helped anticipate the credit and economic recession.

REFERENCES

Bezemer, Dirk J. (2009): *'No One Saw This Coming': Understanding Financial Crisis Through Accounting Models*, MPRA (Munich Personal RePE Archive), Paper No. 15892, June.

Eichner, A.S. and Kregel, J.A. (1975): 'An essay on post Keynesian theory: a new paradigm in Economics', *Journal of Economic Literature*, 13 (4), December, 1293–1311.

Godley, Wynne and Lavoie, Marc (2007): *Monetary Economics – An Integrated Approach to Credit, Money, Income, Production and Wealth*, Palgrave, New York.

Keynes, J.M. (1936): *The General Theory of Employment, Interest and Money*, Macmillan, London.

1. Teaching post-Keynesian economics in a mainstream department[1]

Marc Lavoie

INTRODUCTION

The outline of this chapter is the following. First, I will provide some background information about how I became interested in post-Keynesian economics. This will be followed by a short discussion on the various strategies that can be adopted to teach heterodox economics, in particular in a mainstream department. One of these strategies, creating entire alternative courses, will then be dealt with in more detail, as this was the main strategy that I pursued with some of my colleagues. There are three possible ways in which entire new courses can be created, and these three sub-strategies will be considered in turn, since all three were pursued. Finally, my more recent experience in adapting a first-year textbook will be discussed in the last section, before the conclusion.

I have no particular expertise in pedagogy, and so my comments will be limited to elements of autobiography, some history of recent economic thought, the description of some of the courses that I have taught over the years, and a little analytical content.

BACKGROUND INFORMATION

I was an undergraduate student in economics and mathematics (the latter for three years) at Carleton University in 1972–1976. Carleton University is the rival English-speaking university of my current employer, the University of Ottawa, which is itself a bilingual university. My first indirect encounter with post-Keynesian economics was when I took a one-year tutorial reading course in 1975–1976 with Gilles Paquet, who was an eclectic scholar, a prolific writer and a busy administrator. Paquet gave me a list of various classic papers to read, among which were some writings by G.L.S. Shackle and Sraffa's famous 1926 article in the *Economic Journal*. Paquet warned me not to be overly seduced by the mesmerizing prose of

Shackle and his convincing description of fundamental uncertainty, since this could only lead to nihilism. As to Sraffa's article on the contradictions of the Marshallian analysis, I only remember that I found the arguments difficult to follow and that my interpretation of them did not seem to make much sense to Gilles Paquet, so I presume that his interpretation was different.

My second encounter with post-Keynesian economics occurred at the same time in the Honours Seminar in Modern Classics, given during the whole academic year of 1975–1976 by Thomas K. Rymes.[2] This seminar covered an incredible amount of ground and introduced its students to a wide range of highly diversified literature, including consumer theory, the theory of the firm, general equilibrium theory and Keynesian macroeconomics. We were asked to read the 1937 *Quarterly Journal of Economics* paper written by Keynes as a response to some of the reviews of his *General Theory*, which gave me a second opportunity to encounter the concept of fundamental uncertainty and its impact on rational behaviour. Rymes always remained fascinated by Keynes's *General Theory* and his breakaway from neoclassical analysis, and he is well known for having been the editor of *Keynes's Lectures 1932–35* (Rymes, 1989).

Rymes also spent a couple of weeks on growth theory and another couple of weeks on the Cambridge capital controversies. I very much remember being fascinated by Robinson's (1962) banana diagram, which shows the relationship between investment and realized profit rates, and between expected profit rates and desired investment. I was also very much enthusiastically puzzled by Pasinetti's (1962) reinterpretation of Kaldor's (1956) macroeconomic profit equation, where the profit rate, in the long run, only depends on the growth rate and the propensity to save of the capitalist class, regardless of the propensity to save of the working class. All of us, however, in the class, had a hard time making sense of the Cambridge capital controversies, to which Rymes (1971) had himself contributed. At that stage I had been seduced by post-Keynesian economic theory but not yet convinced, although the survey article by Eichner and Kregel (1975) had made quite an impression on me.

As an honours student I had applied for all kinds of scholarships to study in a graduate programme abroad. I ended up going to the University of Paris 1, in part because Paris was the right place to pursue the sport of fencing, in which I was very much engaged. I was accepted in the Advanced Macroeconomics field unit (*Macroéconomie approfondie*), which was essentially devoted to various forms of Keynesian theory, notably disequilibrium theory and monetary circuit theory. The latter was being advocated by young assistants there, with whom I became friends, notably Frédéric Poulon and Alain Parguez, who, as most readers will know, became the editor of the French series *Monnaie et production* within the monthly *Économies et Sociétés* journal, a series which for nearly a decade, starting in 1984, provided an outlet for the writings of both French- and English-speaking post-Keynesian and other heterodox economists.

I had to take four full-year courses for my graduate studies, and hence chose the minimally required three courses in my major field unit, and the fourth in international finance. This fourth course was given by Paul Coulbois, who was a stern expert in international finance and who, with the help of a foreign exchange trader, had developed an alternative theory of forward exchange rates. I always thought that this explanation of forward exchange rates, based on the assumption that the forward rate is simply the result of a markup over the current exchange rate, with the markup determined by interest rate differentials, made more sense than the supply and demand academic theory that presumed that the forward rate was some unbiased estimator of future exchange rates. I used this theory in my own teaching at graduate level, and I tried to make it known to the post-Keynesian audience (Lavoie, 2000, 2002–2003).

The course in international finance replaced the fourth course in Advanced Macroeconomics, the one that was given by Alain Barrère, who for a long time had been the main French advocate of Keynesian economics. I regret not having taken the course, but did not do so because of force majeure, as the course clashed with my fencing training schedule.[3] The first of the other three courses in the field unit was a course devoted to a study of flow-of-funds and input–output theory, given by Miss Jacqueline Fau, who was in my view a highly original thinker, as can be seen from her book *Le circuit économique national* (Fau, 1974), although she was considered almost a crank by her colleagues. The second course was all about disequilibrium Keynesian theory. It was offered by Pierre-Yves Hénin, who later became the President of the university. It dealt with the fashionable theories of the day in macroeconomics, those of Clower and Leijonhufvud, as well as Barro and Grossman, Ostroy and Starr, and Bénassy, just before Malinvaud burst onto the disequilibrium scene. Finally, there was a third course, offered by Bernard Ducros, devoted to a critique of these disequilibrium theories and an introduction to the theory of the monetary circuit. A large number of its lectures were given by Alain Parguez.

Ducros eventually became my doctoral advisor, but he had little interest in providing over-guidance, and so I wrote what I wanted in the dissertation, essentially being inspired by the emerging monetary circuit theory as well as the many new important post-Keynesian books that were being published at the time. These included Harcourt (1972), Davidson (1972), Kregel (1973), Pasinetti (1974), Minsky (1975), Wood (1975), Koutsoyiannis (1975), Eichner (1976) and Weintraub (1978), all of which

I read many times over. Ducros, Parguez and Barrère were on the jury of my doctoral dissertation.

In 1979, I was hired as replacement professor in the Department of Economics at the University of Ottawa, thanks to reference letters by Paquet and Rymes which, I was told, were highly enthusiastic. In 1979, nearly half of the members of the department were 'heterodox' or non-mainstream economists. There was a newly converted Marxist, an econometrician who was highly critical of the methodology of neoclassical economics, a Keynesian who was a former student of Sidney Weintraub, a follower of the François Perroux tradition, a newly converted Sraffian, and two post-Keynesians – Mario Seccareccia, who had also been hired as a replacement professor in 1978, and myself, with both of our positions being turned into tenure-track positions in 1981. The department was thus fairly eclectic, and at the time did not seem to care too much about the theories being held by its members. Thus, initially there was no problem in teaching what we wanted or in creating new courses with heterodox content.

Unfortunately, this situation did not last for very long. A new joint PhD programme, with the more mainstream economics department of our sister university, Carleton University, was launched in the early 1980s, and this seemed to be the signal that induced the senior members of the department, including some of the heterodox ones, to launch an offensive to cleanse the department of its least productive and weakest elements, meaning, to start with, members without tenure! A new chair was brought in, Anna Koutsoyiannis, after an unsuccessful half-hearted attempt to attract Jan Kregel, who then wanted to leave Belgium. Koutsoyiannis should have been sympathetic to heterodox economists (us), since she had been a close colleague of P.W.S. Andrews at Lancaster University and given the contents of her remarkable textbook in intermediate microeconomics (Koutsoyiannis, 1975), but this did not turn out to be so, because she had been brainwashed by some of the senior members. Getting tenure, for me and Mario Seccareccia, was a long, arduous battle, with no support from the department tenure committee, the chair or the dean, but finally reason prevailed at the highest levels. Unfortunately, as in many other departments in economics, things became much more ideological over the following years, as were many of the new colleagues who were hired at the time. I was told that they were annoyed at being teased during conferences about how post-Keynesian their department had become!

This is certainly not the case anymore. Mario Seccareccia and I are the only two remaining heterodox economists in the department, out of a staff of about 20 members, although there are a couple of heterodox-friendly economists in neighbouring departments, such as public affairs and international affairs. This happened through attrition (retirements and deaths), as we were given no access to recruitment committees. This justifies the title of the present chapter, 'Teaching post-Keynesian economics in a mainstream department'. While our newest members are certainly less concerned about theoretical rectitude, I doubt we would be able to create new explicit heterodox courses. Indeed, at one stage we tried unsuccessfully to create a new MA programme in political economy, and we failed to convince our colleagues of the necessity of a course on currents in modern economic theory. This said, we are still able to do 'our thing' within the existing course offering.

STRATEGIES IN TEACHING HETERODOX ECONOMICS

Here I refer readers to the excellent article written by Andrew Mearman (2007). Mearman says that there are three main strategies for teaching heterodoxy. The first is to introduce elements of heterodoxy in orthodox modules or courses. This we have done in first-year introduction courses. This will be discussed more specifically in a further section. The second main strategy is to teach orthodox and heterodox economics in parallel: we have done this in the Honours course in macroeconomics. Finally, the third main strategy is to create an entire course devoted to an alternative approach. This we have done by creating or adapting four courses in post-Keynesian economics. I can thus say that we have tried all three strategies at different stages. I may also add that there are courses in the history of economic thought and methodology, but, as has been the case in many departments around the world, their numbers have been shrunk from three to one at the graduate level. The history of economic thought is still a compulsory requirement at the undergraduate level, something that cannot be said for many North American economics departments.

Let us start with the second strategy, that of teaching orthodox and heterodox theories in parallel. Mearman (2007, p. 8) defines this as 'a series of topics of interest or theoretical concerns [that] are taught first from one perspective, then from the other, allowing comparison'. Still, according to Mearman, pedagogically, this option 'is the most beneficial, because it is based on comparative, critical treatments of both orthodox and heterodox. Also, by committing to comparative treatment, the parallel perspectives approach can prevent the confusion which can occur when students are faced with different perspectives only occasionally' (2007, p. 8).

Mario Seccareccia and I did this in the Honours Macroeconomics course, in turn, for about 15 years, after which this compulsory fourth-year course was given to someone more mainstream. Personally, I did not find that this approach was particularly successful. As a result of the required comparison, fewer topics are covered in a module, and at the end of the course, students do not seem to have learned much about heterodox economics. These are feelings, not backed by hard numbers, but I rarely felt that the students enjoyed this approach. This, of course, could be my own fault, and so other teachers could find the method highly useful. I should point out that there exists a first-year textbook that precisely follows the teaching in parallel method. This is *Microeconomics in Context*, written by Goodwin et al. (2009), in which each chapter contains a mainstream view and a critical one. I reviewed the book in Lavoie (2009), arguing that the critical sections require better thinking and reading skills.

The third strategy is to create an entire alternative course. As Mearman (2007, p. 8) says, 'this option means that justice can be done to heterodox ideas, but is often restricted to specialist, optional "ghetto" modules, where the development of a critical understanding may be limited'. It was nevertheless our favourite option. The option of a full heterodox course was most successful when the economy was in a recession or with high rates of unemployment. The interest in heterodox courses was particularly high during the subprime financial crisis and its aftermath, as students were looking for some alternative explanations of the crisis, with some (of the more audacious and bright) students even questioning our colleagues as to why alternative theories were not being discussed in other courses, in particular in the compulsory macro courses.

In the process of creating an entire alternative course, there are three possible paths. The first path is to use an existing course, keeping its title and transforming it into a heterodox course. One can do this with a course with a generic name, such as 'Macroeconomic Theory' or 'Theory of Growth', only presenting heterodox content. This tactic can also be useful if your chair is asking you to teach a large-enrolment compulsory course that you do not wish to take: you then threaten only to teach heterodox material in that course, invoking academic freedom. It worked in my case on a couple of occasions.

The second path, and no doubt the most obvious one, is to create a new course with an explicitly heterodox title, such as 'Post-Keynesian Economics', which leaves no ambiguity. It was possible for us to do this in the early 1980s, as the department then was still eclectic. Finally, the third path to the creation of a heterodox course is the creation of a new course, with some ambiguous title, such as 'Explorations in Monetary Economics'. I now discuss in more detail the evolution and content of these three paths, as they were followed at the University of Ottawa.

FIRST SUB-STRATEGY: USING EXISTING COURSE TITLES

When I arrived at the University of Ottawa in the summer of 1979, I was given the option of teaching a graduate course on the 'Theory of Growth'. The contents of the initial course included:

- Keynesian growth theories: Harrod–Domar;
- neoclassical growth theories: Solow;
- technical progress: Robinson (1956), Kaldor (1957), Rymes (1971), Näslund and Sellstedt (1978);
- post-Keynesian growth theory: Shapiro (1977), Kaldor (1956), Pasinetti (1962);
- the Cambridge capital controversies: Harcourt, Robinson, Samuelson and Modigliani, and then Solow, Pasinetti, Garegnani, Petri, Eatwell, Hahn (1975), Spaventa (1970), Harris (1978);
- growth and finance: Kaldor (1966), Moore (1973), Eichner (1973), Harcourt and Kenyon (1976), Wood (1975).

After a few years, the unofficial subtitle of the course became: 'Growth, Income Distribution and Capital'. The course gradually evolved into a manuscript, with roughly the content given above, that was called 'Macroéconomie: Théories et controverses postkeynésiennes'. It was eventually published (Lavoie, 1987) in a prestigious collection, which at that time only included six titles, by authors such as Debreu, Benassy, Denizet and Pasinetti. I learned afterwards that the referee had been Gilbert Abraham-Frois, a well-known Sraffian from Paris 10.[4] Ironically, as I was finishing the book, around 1986, a colleague asked me why I was still bothering to write about growth theory when obviously growth theory was a dead science and business-cycle theory was the 'in thing'. This was at the same time that Lucas and Romer were publishing their articles on growth theory, which propelled growth theory back to the front stage. From this I certainly learned that fashion and fads should not dictate one's teaching or research agenda!

The 1987 book contained a chapter discussing what happens when production increases or growth speeds up. What if profit margins or shares do not rise, as described by the Cambridgians, a mechanism which is sometimes called the Cambridge hypothesis? I argued in the book that rates of capacity utilization in the Kaldor–Robinson growth models were assumed to remain at their normal levels. The chapter also argued, however, that in reality, following an increase in demand, rates of utilization would first rise over their normal levels in the short run, and that this would bring about a higher share of profits, despite a constant markup over direct costs, because of the fixed labour costs associated with supervisory work (Kaldor, 1964; Asimakopulos, 1970; Harris, 1974). It was also claimed that, in the long run, prices would rise relative to wages, to finance faster growth, and that rates of utilization would return to normal, but no mechanism was being provided. At the time, I was not aware of the existence of the neo-Kaleckian model based on flexible rates of capacity utilization (Rowthorn, 1981; Taylor, 1983; Dutt, 1984; Amadeo, 1986). I only discovered this literature when I stumbled upon Dutt's (1987) critique of Marglin's (1984) survey article. These neo-Kaleckian models were introduced in the course outline of autumn 1987. All this was a rather frustrating experience for me, as I had realized, but too late, that I had not kept track appropriately of the relevant heterodox literature.

Eventually, the growth course was taken over by a mainstream colleague who had suddenly discovered endogenous growth theory, becoming highly enthusiastic about a huge survey article written by Frédéric Lordon (1991a, 1991b), not realizing that Lordon was a heterodox economist. After having himself done some work on endogenous growth, he absolutely wanted to teach the growth theory course, which the chair graciously granted.

SECOND SUB-STRATEGY: CREATE A NEW COURSE WITH EXPLICIT TITLES

In October 1978, a neoclassical-turned-Sraffian tenured colleague at the University of Ottawa, Jacques Henry, proposed in a memo to create a new course that would be called 'Elements of Neo-Ricardian Economics'.[5] In 1981, Henry and Seccareccia (1982) organized a small conference on post-Keynesian theory (with Vicky Chick, who was then visiting at McGill University, Eichner, Asimakopulos, Dostaler, Davenport, Seccareccia and myself). Incidentally, the paper by Paul Davenport, whose author unfortunately went on to do administrative work and become the President of two universities, made me realize for the first time that nearly all growth models assumed the absence of path-dependence, that is, the path taken during the transition has no impact whatsoever on the final equilibrium path of the economy. The equilibrium growth rate is entirely determined by supply-side parameters in neoclassical economics and by the parameters of the behavioural equations in other models – something that is taken for granted once we have been sufficiently brainwashed by our teachers, but something that certainly looks whimsical to most naive observers, who would think that the transition path would affect the final outcome. As with many other discoveries of mine, I did nothing about this until about 15 years later (Lavoie, 1996).

Following on the footsteps of the conference, we decided to move on and propose the creation of two courses in post-Keynesian economics. Both courses were to be called 'Post-Keynesian Theory', but initially the first was to cover flex-price systems in the long period, and the second was to cover fix-price systems in the short period. Then, following a suggestion by Edward Nell, made when he gave a stunning lecture at the University of Ottawa in 1980 on how to formalize the principle of effective demand (Nell, 1978), we decided to split the two courses along Sraffian and more traditional post-Keynesian lines. The Sraffian course, considered to be tougher, was set at the graduate level, and was called 'Post-Keynesian Theory: Value and Production'. The other course was set as a fourth-year undergraduate course, taking the name 'Post-Keynesian Theory: Money and Effective Demand'. These two courses still exist today, but while the undergraduate course is being taught every year, the graduate course is taught more rarely. The graduate course was at first offered by Jacques Henry, and the course description was the following:

> Historical perspective on the theory of the surplus. Characteristics of the post-Keynesian approach. Sraffa's contribution. Price and value theory. Theory of production and capital. Rent. Joint production. Analysis of the traverse. Applications and policy implications: international trade and public finance.

Unfortunately, Jacques Henry passed away in 1989, when he was only 55 years old. This was obviously a terrible blow, first to our heterodox economics teaching, but also because Henry was part of a small group of post-Keynesian and Sraffian thinkers who, along with Hicks, were concerned with an analysis of the traverse rather than the popular comparisons between steady states (Henry and Lavoie, 1997). Henry also held views of his own about the directions that the post-Keynesian research programme should be taking (Henry, 1993). Henry used to argue that time was the only scarce commodity and that what was really interesting to an economist ought to be the transition path between equilibrium states, since this was where all the action was, a view which is certainly akin to Joan Robinson's historical time. As a result of Henry's absence, I have occasionally given the 'Value and Production' course. The last time I did so, I followed the outline below, which contains many elements of the previous 'Theory of Growth' course as well as new elements based on Pasinetti's (1981) book and an analysis of the Hicksian and the Kaleckian traverses (in two-sector models), the first one being at full capacity (and full employment) while the other occurs at less than full capacity (Lavoie and Ramírez-Gastón, 1997):

- general introduction to post-Keynesian economics;
- the neoclassical parables;
- prices of production in a stationary state, in a growing economy;
- direct, indirect and hyper-indirect labour;
- consequences for trade theory, for the measure of technical progress and for empirical production functions;
- the quantity traverse in the two-sector Sraffian model;
- the convergence or gravitation towards prices of production;
- models with endogenous rates of capacity utilization;
- the traverse in Kaleckian two-sector models;
- traverses towards normal rates of utilization.

As mentioned earlier, we created a second course in post-Keynesian economics, this second course being focused on money and effective demand. This course has been given occasionally by Mario Seccareccia, and I taught it most of the time. Here is the initial course outline when 'Post-Keynesian Theory: Money and Effective Demand' was created in the early 1980s, with the description being split into a micro and a macro part:

- The firm: markup theory; degree of monopoly and capacity utilization; the megacorp: power and objectives; managerial theories of the firm: the valuation ratio and financial constraints; growth and investment of the firm as determinants of the markup.
- The economy: normal prices and wages, endogenous money supply, effective demand; investment, expectations, uncertainty, speculation, financial instability, economic cycles and growth; the aggregate markup and income distribution; stagflation and income policies.

A quick read of the description certainly shows that the micro course content was being influenced by managerial theories of the firm, such as those of Robin Marris (1964), as well as the Eichner–Wood–Harcourt view of pricing, based on the investment financial requirements of firms. In the macro part, the wording reflects a strong Minskyan influence, as well as the influence of Sidney Weintraub (1978), with his views of a near constant aggregate markup, and the need to contain the strong inflationary forces of the early 1980s with wage and incomes policies or tax-based incomes policies. As one would guess, the course outlines and descriptions changed over a period of 30 years. Below is the current description of the course. Among the changes and additions, there is a concern about whether managerial theories of the firm are still appropriate in a world of financialization. There is more emphasis on the neo-Kaleckian model of employment and growth, and also an obvious reference to the work of John McCombie and Tony Thirlwall (1994) on balance-of-payments constraints. The policy emphasis has switched from inflation to financial instability.

- Key presuppositions of heterodox and post-Keynesian economics.
- The firm: managerial versus finance capitalism, objectives and financial constraints of growing firms, empirical studies of cost curves, pricing theories and normal prices.
- Theories of employment: effective demand, Keynes's view and Kaleckian models.
- The financial system: the monetary circuit, endogenous money supply, stock–flow coherence.
- Expectations, fundamental uncertainty, speculation, financial fragility, economic cycles.
- Growth, investment, income distribution, capacity utilization, balance-of-payments constraints.
- Policies to deal with economic and financial instabilities.

This 'Money and Effective Demand' course gave rise to a textbook, *Foundations of Post-Keynesian Economic Analysis* (Lavoie, 1992), which was designed for fourth-year undergraduate students, but which, so I am told, is a better read for graduate students.[6] As a consequence, I had planned to write a simpler version, in French, and after a couple of unsuccessful offers, I thought about asking Gilles Dostaler if he could help me get in touch with some French publishers that specialized in small, inexpensive books. This turned out to be a good move, because Dostaler had himself just received an informal offer to write such a book on post-Keynesian economics, and so he quickly proposed my name as an alternate author. The course thus gave rise to a second textbook, a simpler and shorter one, *L'Économie postkeynésienne* (2004), in a series for a large readership, the *Repères* series, which has very strict rules, obviously regarding the maximum number of words but also rules such as being required to have a title, subtitle, graph, table or box on each page, so as to break the monotony of the text. The book was then translated into English by Louis-Philippe Rochon, who had taken the course as a student in the mid 1980s, becoming *Introduction to Post-Keynesian Economics* (2006).[7] The outlines of the two books, as shown below, are identical. I tried to modify the outline for the second book, but the experienced series editor, without being aware of the contents of my first book, turned down my proposed outline and ended up suggesting an outline that was similar to that of the 1992 *Foundations*. I thus came to the conclusion that the 1992 outline must have been the better one and ought to be kept!

- methodology;
- micro: consumer theory and agent behaviour;
- micro: theory of the firm;
- macro: money and credit;
- macro: employment, short run;
- macro: growth, long run (the Kaleckian model);
- macro: inflation.

I have not yet discussed the possible pedagogical difficulties involved with teaching an entire course devoted to heterodox theories. I have found that the main problem is that students have been exposed to three years of intensive brainwashing, having been given no indication whatsoever by my colleagues that there exist economic theories or economic traditions alternative to the neoclassical view. Some students would get angry at me, because I would criticize, either directly but mostly indirectly – since the intent of these two courses is to present a positive alternative – all the models that they had spent so much time comprehending in earlier years.[8] I now warn students on the first day of class that if they do not wish to hear direct or indirect criticisms of mainstream economics, then they ought to register on another course. As a result, thanks to this warning, I don't get any feelings of animosity anymore. At worst, students act in a schizophrenic way, putting this course in a small compartment of their brains, perhaps never to be opened again once the exams are over. However, as pointed out earlier, the subprime financial crisis has brought a lot of credibility to alternative views, which now seem more relevant and more realistic to current students. It has also generated some positive feed-back from past graduates, from whom I received emails during the crisis, demonstrating that their 36 hours of post-Keynesian economics had not been entirely wasted.

THIRD SUB-STRATEGY: CREATE A NEW COURSE WITH AN AMBIGUOUS TITLE

In the late 1980s, our joint PhD programme was revamped, and a new field, Monetary Economics, was added to the existing fields. Mario

Seccareccia and I were asked to participate in the new field and to design one of the new courses. Initially we wanted to call this course 'Alternative Theories in Monetary Economics', but finally we were encouraged to adopt a more ambiguous and diplomatic title, 'Explorations in Monetary Economics'. The course held up without any blips until 2011, when there was another revamping of the PhD programme. This was the occasion for some Carleton staff members to question the existence of the course, but at the end of a heated meeting, the course was kept as is, hopefully for some time.

Graduate students are usually more receptive overall to this heterodox graduate course than are undergraduates. The reason is that many of our graduate students come from abroad, and hence either they have already been exposed to alternative theories or, ironically, they know less about economics than many of our undergraduates, and hence are less brainwashed. For some of these students, many coming from China, all theories are created equal and hence they hold no prejudices. The problem, however, when these students write PhD theses, is that their knowledge of the literature, orthodox or heterodox, is rather slim, and does not equate with their technical skills.

During the first two years, I gave this new graduate course in tandem with Mario Seccareccia; then I offered the course every year or nearly every year. The contents of this course changed considerably over the years, even if it did not change that much from one given year to another. The first course outline covered the following topics:

- Features of neoclassical monetary theory, the natural rate of interest and the impact of the Sraffian critique (Rogers, 1989).
- The finance motive, the monetary circuit (Graziani).
- Money supply and its causality (Kaldor, Moore, Dean).
- The determination of interest rates (Pasinetti, Davidson, Pivetti).
- The instability of velocity (Rousseas).
- Monetary policy (Niggle).
- Financial instability (Minsky, Dow).
- International endogenous money (Coulbois).

Various other topics were then introduced at various stages, either following fads or my own research interests, giving rise or being inspired by research papers, on topics such as:

- The horizontalist versus structuralist debate.
- Credit rationing and creditworthiness.
- Kaleckian growth models incorporating interest payments.

- The operating procedures of central banks and the clearing and settlement system.
- The 'New Consensus' model.
- Neo-chartalism and the fiscal–monetary links.
- The subprime financial crisis.

As well as the above changes and additions, there was a major change in the contents of the course in the early 2000s, as a consequence of a meeting with Wynne Godley, who was then working at the Levy Institute, and whom we had invited to give a lecture at the University of Ottawa in December 1999. Godley and I worked together on a paper for a week during the summer of 2000. As we found that we got along well, this led to a more ambitious collaboration – expanding and finishing a manuscript that Godley had been thinking about for a long time – giving rise eventually, after several stop-and-go episodes, to our book on the stock-flow consistent approach (Godley and Lavoie, 2007). For a while, as I was over-enthusiastic with this new approach that allowed us to go beyond overly vague heterodox assertions about money, most of the course was devoted to the chapters and models of the book, probably boring to death many of the students. However, this was corrected later, with no more than half of the course dealing with the stock-flow consistent approach. Initially, the students were asked to reproduce and simulate a model of the manuscript on software of their choice. Then, as the models became available in Eviews on the website of Gennaro Zezza, a collaborator of Godley, their life became easier as students were only asked to take any one electronic version of these models, modify it somehow, and perform simulations. As many of us would expect, these hands-on experiments help the students understand the logic and meaning of these stock-flow consistent monetary models and the implications of endogenous money.

FIRST TEACHING STRATEGY: INTRODUCING ELEMENTS OF HETERODOXY IN ORTHODOX TEXTBOOKS

For a long time, Mario Seccareccia and I had played around with the idea of writing a principles of economics textbook. But this is a huge endeavour and it requires a substantial amount of financial resources, so we never went ahead. In 2005, however, the publisher Nelson Thomson wanted to launch a new introductory textbook on the Canadian market, and was looking for a more eclectic textbook than its successful Mankiw Canadian edition. We were asked to make an adaptation of the US

Baumol and Blinder textbook (the creators of the famous aggregate supply and aggregate demand model, the AS/AD model), which was then in its 10th edition.[9] Because we thought that this was a golden opportunity to transmit some of our ideas to a much wider audience, we accepted the offer. Our task was to 'canadianize' the textbook (i.e. provide Canadian examples and discuss Canadian institutions), taking the opportunity to introduce some heterodox elements, but without antagonizing potential adopters of the textbook. As David Colander has mentioned a number of times, there is a lot of pressure on textbook writers not to introduce too many innovations, with the publishers reminding the authors that their ideas will only get across as long as their books are sold!

The Baumol and Blinder textbook was chosen as a proper alternative to the Mankiw textbook because it is one of the few remaining pro-Keynesian textbooks on the American market, and it is also very much oriented towards policy issues. We took this as a departure point, attempting to display even more intellectual scepticism, or less arrogance, with regards to so-called 'economic laws' or overly broad generalizations. This we do in the very first chapter, where we reproduce on the first page a quote from Joan Robinson which now seems to have gained some recognition: 'The purpose of studying economics is not to acquire a set of ready made answers to economic questions, but to avoid being deceived by economists' (Robinson, [1955] 1980, p. 17). In the same chapter we attempt to promote pluralism, pointing to what we call a sophisticated view of social sciences, where theories not only arise from the observation of stylized facts but also depend on opinions and values, and where theories are not necessarily rejected because new facts do not give support to the theory. Furthermore, we provide numerous definitions of economics, and not only the standard definition based on the analysis of scarcity.

Although the microeconomics textbook is not much different from other introductory textbooks, we have tried to de-emphasize the generality of competitive markets.[10] There are a number of sections or boxes that question the relevance of assuming profit maximization instead of profit satisficing and that ask whether businesses do pursue profit objectives without any regard for ethical goals. There is some discussion of linear production relations, which then leads to a chapter that introduces constant marginal costs, decreasing average costs, cost-plus pricing, sticky prices, and the overwhelming presence of unused capacity. These features reappear in various chapters, including those discussing natural monopolies, taxation, business choices, and so on.

In the macroeconomics textbook, we have tried to emphasize that microeconomic behaviour may lead to macroeconomic consequences that are fundamentally different from what one might expect by making analogies to the individual. The paradox of thrift, which has been removed from many introductory textbooks, is given pre-eminence in ours. We also emphasize that market mechanisms do not necessarily bring about equilibrium or optimum positions. For instance, while we reproduce the standard AD/AS analysis, where falling wages bring about a downward shift in the aggregate supply curve which eventually leads to lower prices and a full-employment equilibrium, through the cash-balance or wealth effect, we also present an alternative possibility. In this alternative world, the aggregate demand curve is upward sloping rather than downward sloping, because debt effects à la Tobin and Fisher overcome wealth effects. As a consequence, falling wages and the downward shift in the aggregate supply curve drive the economy away from the full-employment position, as lower wages and lower prices raise the real debt burden of those households and firms that have a fixed nominal debt.

The three chapters devoted to money and banking and to the central bank are completely different from the original US textbook. The quantity theory of money is given a reverse causation interpretation. The chartalist view and the commodity views on the origins of money are opposed. The banking system is presented as relying essentially on confidence and trust. Again, there is reverse causation, with loans giving rise to deposits, without any role being played by reserves. In other words, money is shown to be created *ex nihilo*, based on the creditworthy demand of borrowers, as assessed by the bankers, while the money multiplier mechanism, so dear to lecturers and textbook writers, is totally eliminated. The implementation of monetary policy at the Bank of Canada, with its corridor system and its reaction function relying on interest rates rather than any measure of the money supply, is also presented in some detail. We show how reserves are being transferred from one bank to another through the clearing and payments system, and how payments occur between the government and the private banking system, thus leading to the conclusion that a government deficit, all else equal, leads to an increase in bank reserves and therefore downward pressures on the overnight rate – the exact opposite of the mainstream crowding-out argument. Thus this gave rise to a rather critical assessment of the possibility of crowding out and lack of sustainability in the chapter on government deficits and debt.

Other macro chapters also include heterodox features that can however be discussed within the standard AS/AD framework, such as a discussion of the Dutch disease, or the particular problems that arise in a developing country faced with a devaluation of its currency when its foreign debt is expressed in a foreign currency. In the chapter on the Phillips curve, the possibility of a flat Phillips curve is entertained, as is the possibility of persistence and hysteresis of the natural rate of unemployment.

To our surprise, we discovered that it was much easier to introduce eclectic or heterodox elements in the micro part of the textbook than it was in the macro part. Each draft of a chapter was read by about five first-year instructors. Chapters that generated controversial comments were assigned additional readers. Our changes in microeconomics, especially those on cost-plus pricing and constant marginal costs, were accepted without any interference. By contrast, there was a lot of reluctance to accept our changes in macroeconomics, both in form and in content. We had initially relied on a version of the Romer (2000) graphical apparatus, based on output and inflation, with a monetary policy reaction function. But under the pressure of the readers and the publisher, we had to backtrack to the AS/AD model, realizing in the process however that the AS/AD framework was more flexible than we had initially thought and could be used to present many heterodox issues and claims. There were also strong pressures to reintroduce the money multiplier, with readers begging to have it at least in an appendix, apparently not realizing that the money multiplier was in complete contradiction to our description of the clearing and settlement system. However, we remained impervious to these pressures.

Our experience with the third strategy, that of introducing heterodox elements in an overall orthodox textbook, has been, on the whole, satisfactory.[11] And so has been our teaching experience with such a textbook. The story line that I offer to students, both in microeconomics and in macroeconomics, is that there are two groups of economists out there: the bad guys, who are the majority of economists, and the good guys. In micro, the bad guys believe in the laws of supply and demand, because they assume that markets are free and competitive, and that power plays no role; the good guys believe otherwise. The story line in macroeconomics is that the bad guys rely on the market-clearing view, believing that the market is intrinsically stable and government actions are destabilizing or inefficient; the good guys are the Keynesians, who believe that markets must be tamed. As one would suspect, this kind of presentation generates contrasted reactions: most of our first-year students come from the management school and thus some of them are reluctant to accept any critique of capitalism; however, other students are quite happy to be given the two sides of the story.

CONCLUSION

In going over what I have so far written, I have noticed that I have said very little about methodology in post-Keynesian economics. It is easier to remember influential models than influential papers on fundamental uncertainty or weak rationality. I should point out, however, that both my 1992 and 2006 textbooks on post-Keynesian economics start with methodological concerns, in particular what I call the pre-suppositions of the orthodox and heterodox paradigms, thus showing the importance that I accord to these questions. I cleared this up in my own mind in 1989 when I was asked to introduce post-Keynesian economics to a University of Montreal research group in the philosophy of science, and then further asked to provide a short four-page summary of my findings, which forced me to focus on the really important distinguishing features.

As I think about methodology and as I prepared for the lecture that gave rise to this chapter, I realized how closely intertwined has been my teaching and the writing of books, and even the writing of some scholarly papers. It is unfortunate that articles in scholarly journals are given so much importance relative to books in the modern evaluation of scholarly activity, as it undermines pedagogical efforts. There is a controversy in education regarding the respective merits of a university system where teaching and research are closely related, and another model where the two streams of university work are separated, being assumed that good teaching does not require field research but only the acquisition of good pedagogical tools and skills as well as some updated knowledge of the field. Personally, I tend to agree with what was said by Ib Poulsen, the rector of Roskilde University, in his opening remarks of the 5th 'Dijon' post-Keynesian conference: research and teaching go hand in hand! This is particularly true in the case of heterodox and post-Keynesian economics.

NOTES

1. A version of this chapter was published in Spanish as: 'La enseñanza de Economía post-Keynesiana en un departamento ortodoxo', *Revista de Economía Crítica*, December 2011, pp. 180–198.
2. Unfortunately, Tom Rymes passed away on 13 May 2011, exactly one year to the day after the death of my former co-author, Wynne Godley.
3. Edwin Le Heron, who is now the President of ADEK (the Association des Économistes Keynésiens), took it one or two years later, and thus became himself a disciple of the Keynesian ideas professed by Barrère.
4. The manuscript was typed by secretaries at the Faculty, but as this was the beginning of word processors, the publisher never managed to read the floppy disks that I had sent, so that the son of a colleague from another department, who was travelling to Paris around Christmas, delivered the paper manuscript to the publisher. This young fellow, James Hyndman, then became a famous Quebec TV and movie star.
5. As an anecdote, it is intriguing to note that Henry, who was into international trade and development economics, decided to reject neoclassical theory and look for an alternative following a study trip in the Sahel, where he discovered that neoclassical rationality and models could not explain the wise behaviour of the Bedouins in the desert.

6. Readers of the 1992 book may have noticed that there is not a single footnote: the reason was that, at the time, having little experience with (DOS) word processors, I did not yet know how to introduce footnotes. I should also note that I have been under contract for a long time to Edward Elgar to write an enhanced second edition, but, to my despair, only recently have I found the time and the energy to start doing it!
7. The book was also translated into Spanish, Japanese and Chinese.
8. Some years I push my luck, based on Lavoie (2008), by spending two or three hours on the critique of the neoclassical production function and the neoclassical labour demand function, showing that their apparent empirical success relies on their reproduction of the national account identities, as shown in several papers by Anwar Shaikh, John McCombie, Jesus Felipe and even Herbert Simon.
9. As the question has been put to me many times, let me say that the original authors, Baumol and Blinder, have no say on the contents of the Canadian edition (Baumol et al., 2009, 2010).
10. We certainly have not gone far enough. Thompson (1999, p. 231) recommends removing the supply and demand analysis from the earlier chapters, introducing it only after chapters dealing with monopoly and oligopolistic markets. Hill and Myatt (2007) make a similar recommendation, pointing out that the analysis of a single monopoly is easier than that of perfect competition, which relies on a dual analysis of the firm and of the market. It would certainly help to de-emphasize the mainstream world-view according to which markets solve all problems if one were to introduce perfect competition as well as supply and demand analysis after chapters on monopolies and oligopolies.
11. Although our sales have been no better than those of more recent competitors to the three main introductory textbooks, which in Canada are those of Lipsey, Parkin and Mankiw.

REFERENCES

Amadeo, E.J. (1986), 'The role of capacity utilization in long-period analysis', *Political Economy: Studies in the Surplus Approach*, **2**(2), 147–185.

Asimakopulos, A. (1970), 'A Robinsonian growth model in one sector notation – an amendment', *Australian Economic Papers*, **9**, December, 171–176.

Baumol, W.J., A.S. Blinder, M. Lavoie and M. Seccareccia (2009), *Microeconomics: Principles and Policy*, Toronto: Nelson Education.

Baumol, W.J., A.S. Blinder, M. Lavoie and M. Seccareccia (2010), *Macroeconomics: Principles and Policy*, Toronto: Nelson Education.

Davidson, P. (1972), *Money and the Real World*, London: Macmillan.

Dutt, A.K. (1984), 'Stagnation, income distribution and monopoly power', *Cambridge Journal of Economics*, **8**(1), March, 25–40.

Dutt, A.K. (1987), 'Alternative closures again: a comment on growth, distribution and inflation', *Cambridge Journal of Economics*, **11**(1), March, 75–82.

Eichner, A.S. (1973), 'A theory of the determination of the mark-up under oligopoly', *Economic Journal*, **83**(332), December, 1184–1200.

Eichner, A.S. (1976), *The Megacorp and Oligopoly: Micro Foundations of Macro Dynamics*, Cambridge: Cambridge University Press.

Eichner, A.S. and J.A. Kregel (1975), 'An essay on post-Keynesian theory: a new paradigm in economics', *Journal of Economic Literature*, **13**(4), December, 1293–1311.

Fau, J. (1974), *Le circuit économique national*, Paris: Éditions Cujas.

Godley, W. and M. Lavoie (2007), *Monetary Economics: An Integrated Approach to Credit, Money, Income, Production and Wealth*, Basingstoke: Palgrave/Macmillan.
Goodwin, N., J.A. Nelson, F. Ackerman and T. Weisskopf (2009), *Microeconomics in Context*, 2nd edition, Armonk, NY: M.E. Sharpe.
Hahn, F.H. (1975), 'Revival of political economy: the wrong issues and the wrong arguments', *Economic Record*, **51**, September, 360–364.
Harcourt, G.C. (1972), *Some Cambridge Controversies in the Theory of Capital*, Cambridge: Cambridge University Press.
Harcourt, G.C. and P. Kenyon (1976), 'Pricing and the investment decision', *Kyklos*, **29**(3), 449–477.
Harris, D.J. (1974), 'The price policy of firms, the level of employment and distribution of income in the short run', *Australian Economic Papers*, **13**, June, 144–151.
Harris, D.J. (1978), *Capital Accumulation and Income Distribution*, Stanford, CA: Stanford University Press.
Henry, J. (1993), 'Post-Keynesian methods and the post-classical approach', *International Papers in Political Economy*, **1**(2), 1–26.
Henry, J. and M. Lavoie (1997), 'The Hicksian traverse as a process of reproportioning: some structural dynamics', *Structural Change and Economic Dynamics*, **8**(2), June, 157–175.
Henry, J. and M. Seccareccia (1982), 'Introduction: la théorie post-keynésienne: contributions et essais de synthèse', *Actualité Economique*, **58**(2), January–June, 5–16.
Hill, R. and A. Myatt (2007), 'Overemphasis on perfectly competitive markets in microeconomics principles textbooks', *Journal of Economic Education*, **38**(1), 56–77.
Kaldor, N. (1956), 'Alternative theories of distribution', *Review of Economic Studies*, **23**, March, 83–100.
Kaldor, N. (1957), 'A model of economic growth', *Economic Journal*, **67**, December, 591–624.
Kaldor, N. (1964), 'Introduction', *Essays on Economic Policy*, vol. 1, London: Duckworth.
Kaldor, N. (1966), 'Marginal productivity and the macro-economic theories of distribution', *Review of Economic Studies*, **33**(4), October, 309–319.
Koutsoyiannis, A. (1975), *Modern Microeconomics*, London: Macmillan.
Kregel, J.A. (1973), *The Reconstruction of Political Economy: An Introduction to Post-Keynesian Economics*, London: Macmillan.
Lavoie, M. (1987), *Macroéconomie: Théorie et controverses postkeynésiennes*, Paris: Dunod.
Lavoie, M. (1992), *Foundations of Post-Keynesian Economic Analysis*, Aldershot: Edward Elgar.
Lavoie, M. (1996), 'Traverse, hysteresis, and normal rates of capacity utilization in Kaleckian models of growth and distribution', *Review of Radical Political Economics*, **28**(4), 113–147.
Lavoie, M. (2000), 'A Post Keynesian view of interest parity theorems', *Journal of Post Keynesian Economics*, **23**(1), Fall, 163–179.
Lavoie, M. (2002–2003), 'Interest parity, risk premia and Post Keynesian analysis', *Journal of Post Keynesian Economics*, **25**(2), Winter, 237–249.
Lavoie, M. (2004), *L'Économie postkeynésienne*, Paris: La Découverte (Repères).

Lavoie, M. (2006), *Introduction to Post-Keynesian Economics*, Basingstoke: Palgrave/Macmillan.
Lavoie, M. (2008), 'Neoclassical empirical evidence on employment and production laws as artefact', *Rivista Economía Informa*, **351**, March–April, 9–36.
Lavoie, M. (2009), 'Book review of Goodwin et al.', *Intervention: European Journal of Economics and Economic Policies*, **6**(2), 315–316.
Lavoie, M. and P. Ramírez-Gastón (1997), 'Traverse in a two-sector Kaleckian model of growth with target return pricing', *Manchester School of Economic and Social Studies*, **55**(1), March, 145–169.
Lordon, F. (1991a), 'Théories de la croissance: quelques développements récents. Première partie: la croissance cyclique', *Observations et diagnostics économiques*, **36**, 159–211.
Lordon, F. (1991b), 'Théories de la croissance: quelques développements récents. Deuxième partie: la redécouverte des rendements croissants', *Observations et diagnostics économiques*, **37**, 193–243.
Marglin, S.A. (1984), 'Growth, distribution, and inflation: a centennial synthesis', *Cambridge Journal of Economics*, **8**(2), June, 115–144.
Marris, R. (1964), *The Economic Theory of Managerial Capitalism*, New York: Free Press of Glencoe.
McCombie, J.S.L. and A.P. Thirlwall (1994), *Economic Growth and the Balance-of-Payments Constraint*, London: Macmillan.
Mearman, A. (2007), 'Teaching heterodox economics concepts', http://www.economicsnetwork.ac.uk/handbook/heterodox/, last accessed 23 February 2013.
Minsky, H.P. (1975), *John Maynard Keynes*, New York: Columbia University Press.
Moore, B.J. (1973), 'Some macroeconomic consequences of corporate equities', *Canadian Journal of Economics*, **6**(4), November, 529–544.
Näslund, B. and B. Sellstedt (1978), *Neo-Ricardian Theory*, Berlin: Springer-Verlag.
Nell, E.J. (1978), 'The simple theory of effective demand', *Intermountain Economic Review*, Fall, 1–32.
Pasinetti, L.L. (1962), 'Rate of profit and income distribution in relation to the rate of economic growth', *Review of Economic Studies*, **29**(4), October, 267–279.
Pasinetti, L.L. (1974), *Growth and Income Distribution: Essays in Economic Theory*, Cambridge: Cambridge University Press.
Pasinetti, L.L. (1981), *Structural Change and Economic Growth*, Cambridge: Cambridge University Press.
Poulon, F. (1982), *Macroéconomie approfondie: équilibre, déséquilibre, circuit*, Paris: Cujas.
Robinson, J. ([1955] 1980), 'Marx, Marshall, and Keynes', *Collected Economic Papers II*, Cambridge, MA: MIT Press.
Robinson, J. (1956), *The Accumulation of Capital*, London: Macmillan.
Robinson, J. (1962), *Essays in the Theory of Economic Growth*, London: Macmillan.
Rogers, C. (1989), *Money, Interest and Capital: A Study in the Foundations of Monetary Theory*, Cambridge: Cambridge University Press.
Romer, D. (2000), 'Keynesian macroeconomics without the LM curve', *Journal of Economic Perspectives*, **14**(2), Spring, 149–169.
Rowthorn, B. (1981), 'Demand, real wages and economic growth', *Thames Papers*

in Political Economy, Autumn, 1–39. Reprinted in *Studi Economici*, (1982), **18**, 3–54.
Rymes, T.K. (1971), *On Concepts of Capital and Technical Change*, Cambridge: Cambridge University Press.
Rymes, T.K. (1989), *Keynes's Lectures, 1932–35: Notes of a Representative Student*, London: Macmillan.
Shapiro, N. (1977), 'The revolutionary character of post-Keynesian economics', *Journal of Economic Issues*, **11**(3), September, 541–560.
Spaventa, L. (1970), 'Rate of profit, rate of growth and capital intensity in a simple production model', *Oxford Economic Papers*, **22**(2), July, 129–147.
Taylor, L. (1983), *Structuralist Macroeconomics: Applicable Models for the Third World*, New York: Basic Books.
Thompson, G.F. (1999), 'Strategy and tactics in the pedagogy of economics: what should be done about neoclassical economics?', in R.F. Garnett Jr (ed.), *What do Economists Know?*, London: Routledge, pp. 223–235.
Weintraub, S. (1978), *Capitalism's Inflation and Unemployment Crisis*, Reading, MA: Addison-Wesley.
Wood, A. (1975), *A Theory of Profits*, Cambridge: Cambridge University Press.

2. The economist who mistook his model for a market

Roy J. Rotheim*

'Just to amuse myself, and keep the good people busy, I ordered them to build this City, and my Palace; and they did it all willingly and well. Then I thought, as the country was so green and beautiful, I would call it the Emerald City; and to make the name fit better I put green spectacles on all the people, so that everything they saw was green.'

'But isn't everything here green?' asked Dorothy.

'No more than in any other city,' replied Oz; 'but when you wear green spectacles, why of course everything you see looks green to you. The Emerald City was built a great many years ago, for I was a young man when the balloon brought me here, and I am a very old man now. But my people have worn green glasses on their eyes so long that most of them think it really is an Emerald City, and it certainly is a beautiful place, abounding in jewels and precious metals, and every good thing that is needed to make one happy.' (L. Frank Baum, *The Wizard of Oz*, 1900)

They take the circuits out of people's brains that make it possible for them to think for themselves. Their world is like the one that George Orwell depicted in his novel. I'm sure you realize that there are plenty of people who are looking for exactly that kind of brain death. It makes life a lot easier. You don't have to think about difficult things, just shut up and do what your superiors tell you to do. (Haruki Murakami, *1Q84*, 2011)

INTRODUCTION

Can we expect Post Keynesian economics to be embraced and taught in mainstream academia? If ever there were a compelling case for Post Keynesian economics in both theory and policy it would be now in light of the anemic recovery in the global recession of 2007–9 and the levels of high unemployment that have persisted long after that recession was to have ended officially. Interventionist policies during that recession were, however, too late and too little, hampered by an antipathy among policy makers toward such policies. At one level removed there was also a corresponding economic mainstream view based on closed system thinking

– predicated on the *impossibility* of economic fluctuations for the economy as a whole – that admitted to no theoretical basis for lending support to these policies. In the place of expansionary fiscal and monetary policies that were put into force we are now seeing a call for a return to economic growth by the traditional policies of fiscal austerity and monetary restraint. The persistently high and prolonged unemployment world-wide is deemed to be structural, not remediable by interventionist monetary or fiscal policies. Post Keynesian concerns about failures of effective demand in an open-system framework, involuntary unemployment (beyond the control of the atomistic *individual* of the mainstream), large and growing inequalities in income and wealth (abhorrent in their own right and a significant cause of the paucity of aggregate demand), and a preponderance of speculation and financial circulation over enterprise and industrial circulation are no longer taken seriously (if they ever were) (see Davidson, 2009).

Mainstream macroeconomics has redirected its attention toward fending off its interventionist critics, defaulting to the hydraulics of the quantity theory of money (the voices of the inflation hawks becoming louder by the day) with the rallying cry that the long-run consequences of myopic sustained low short-term interest rate targets and various forms of quantitative easing could portend inflationary disaster – with the appropriate lag, of course.[1] Budget deficits and sovereign debt crises are the current boogiemen held with great conviction to be crowding out more efficient private sector spending. Large deficits, it is believed, will encourage higher inflation expectations and therefore higher nominal and real interest rates or will invoke Ricardian Equivalence effects causing individuals to curtail current consumption in favor of increased current saving (out of what income?) so that they will be able to pay the higher taxes that will surely be imposed in the future to cover the higher deficits today (see Dow, 2012, pp. 80–81).

It is business as usual in the teaching of economics, beginning and ending with the relative market consequences of individual choices of products and productive processes framed in deductivist mathematical models (see Lawson, 2012a, p. 10). One should not be surprised that the call for a greater plurality in the teaching of economics, especially Post Keynesian economics, has fallen on deaf ears. There is neither an acknowledgment, let alone a comprehension of true Keynesian and Post Keynesian perspectives. What is understood to be 'Keynesian' economics by the mainstream focuses on imperfect information and other obstructions and intrusions into the conventional market model. Returns to full employment are seen as the result of stickiness of relative wages and prices and other structural mismatches in the labor and goods markets. Alleviate the frictions and imperfections in those markets, allow for appropriate time for readjustment, and all will be well in theory and policy. In that case, Keynesian economics (as J.R. Hicks asserted so persuasively 75 years ago [1937]) reduces to nothing more than a variant of the traditional mainstream perspective: 'Macroeconomics is redundant,' is how Chick voiced it so well (1998, p. 1863).

Genuine Post Keynesian economics is neither taken seriously nor given the slightest degree of legitimization in mainstream economics departments. Mainstream economics is the only standard by which economists are measured; it is the only body of work by which the discipline is defined and understood.[2] One is taught only mainstream economics in graduate school and the top journals contain only articles that require models formulated around mainstream reasoning. At a deeper level, the mainstream is articulated and disseminated in such a way that its language and its visual representations make imperceptible the types of fundamental frameworks on which a Keynes/Post Keynesian analysis are founded (see Kurtz, 2010, p. 12; Rotheim, 2006).

From the outside looking in one can ask all too easily how is it possible for economists to formulate their analyses on frameworks that are illogical, unreal and misleading. And yet, they do it with no idea that those analytical frameworks suffer from any of those defects. It is the dominant, the *only* game in town. Students planning to go into the discipline will not make it through graduate school unless they master the mainstream in all of its dimensions. The specific requirements of the discipline – a strong training in mathematics and a psychological predisposition toward thinking in such closed-system terms (see Rotheim, 2002) – not only allow such individuals to succeed but assures that they will embrace the mathematical modeling foundations of the discipline to be what 'economics' is all about.[3]

At the end of the day, the answer to the question posed to me whether we can expect Post Keynesian economics to be embraced and taught in mainstream academia is *no*: the perceptual lenses, the fixation with modeling, the psychology and perhaps even the ideology of mainstream economics is ingrained too deeply in the academy and in the political realm for heterodox, especially Post Keynesian, economics to be acknowledged or taken seriously. Post Keynesian economists will not be given a place at the table, let alone be allowed to have this pretense of a discipline put on the menu. The Great Depression of the 1930s could not get Keynes to be embraced by the mainstream (Hicks and Samuelson took care of that problem); and the Great Recession of 2007 to the present has not been any more successful with Keynes and Post Keynes in being accepted either in the academy, legislatures, executive offices, central banks or the media. I agree with Lawson that the primary culprit is the fixation in the discipline with deductive mathematical modeling (I use the term 'fixation' in the same way it is used by psychologists) (Lawson, 2012a). I would still hold, however, that there is lurking below the surface an important ideological component to that project, although it is in most cases unbeknownst to the majority of proponents and practitioners of the mainstream approach, because they are not trained to think about the social ontology of their 'scientific program' (Rotheim, 2006).

In this chapter I shall focus on a few of the points that address why mainstream economics has built an impenetrable wall around itself such that it cannot envision, let alone take seriously, any alternative economic perspective beyond its own. It is in this way that I affirm my assertion that the likelihood of Post Keynesian economics being accepted into the corpus of teaching in the academy is near impossible. In the next section I will address what I see as the fundamental deductivist element of the mainstream project: confusing metaphors in space with processes in time, to employ the picture painted by Joan Robinson (1953). The mainstream project perceives and operates in a metaphor of space, giving life (timeful conceptualizations) to points in space that are timeless and lifeless. Emerging from these timeless conceptualizations is a language of spatial metaphors that reflects what Herbert Marcuse called 'functionalized language.' These I will address in the section to follow. From there I shall give examples of how these timeless conceptualizations lead to perceptions and policies that reinforce the mainstream deductivist project, focusing on the question of unemployment as it is perceived by the mainstream.

CONFUSING METAPHORS IN SPACE WITH PROCESSES IN TIME

> It lulls rather than clarifies thought to reply that a law is a statement of tendency or that a theory is intended to explain. (Dobb, 1929, p. 506)

The *mode of theorizing* of the mainstream project, as Lawson calls it (1997, p. 91), is deductive mathematical modeling. Lawson identifies this mode as the ability 'to explain an actual event or state of affairs . . . to deduce a statement of it from a set of initial or boundary conditions plus universal "laws" (constant conjunctions of the form 'whenever event *x* then event *y*")' (Lawson, 1997, p. 91). I agree. What is especially telling is that this mode of theorizing is both a fiction and a delusion. Any deductive statement implies that there exists some *power* in the word 'whenever' as Lawson writes it. The mainstream view is a fiction because there is no *power* in a model whose components are mere descriptors without the ability to act or to have an effect on each other. The delusion is that proponents of the mainstream project believe that their descriptors under the deductivism of their models are elements with the power to describe, to effect and to act. Here one is reminded of the subject of Oliver Sachs' (1970) study who mistook his wife for a hat. The brain damage experienced by his subject caused that unfortunate delusion – what was there and what he believed was there were not the same thing. In like fashion, mainstream economists' obsession with closure creates a fictional delusion that the closures themselves are living entities that inform us of things that could only have meaning if the world were open, not closed. And yet the power of this mode of theorizing is so pervasive among the mainstream that those out of the mainstream who approach such modes with caution find themselves excluded from the core of the discipline.

Mainstream economics sees what is not there, gives life to what is not there, tests what it believes is there but is not there, and then predicts and makes prescriptions about what is not there but what is perceived to be there. What we have is an ontological question, as Burstein notes (1991, p. 49).[4] Mainstream economics has created a simulacrum of a reality that does not exist while finding comfort in its serving as a substitute for a reality which it cannot and may dare not broach. Confusing? Not really, if we understand the general context by which these statements are considered.

The key to creating coherence out of this apparent confusion was provided by the Cambridge economist Joan Robinson in a number of pieces focusing on the notion of *time* in economics. In an unpublished and now obscure piece written in 1953, Robinson asserts that economists in the mainstream (whom she calls 'neoclassical economists') confuse what she calls metaphors in space with processes in time. It is worth reproducing her argument verbatim:

> Think of a tutor explaining to a freshman the meaning of equilibrium. The tutor is a neoclassical economist. If the cap fits put it on, and if it does not, no one will be better pleased than I. The tutor might say to the freshman: 'E is the point of equilibrium of supply and demand,' and if the young man asks: 'What is the equilibrium of supply and demand?' he answers: 'It is the point E.' So he has holed out in one. He has given the freshman a short excerpt from an illustrated dictionary.

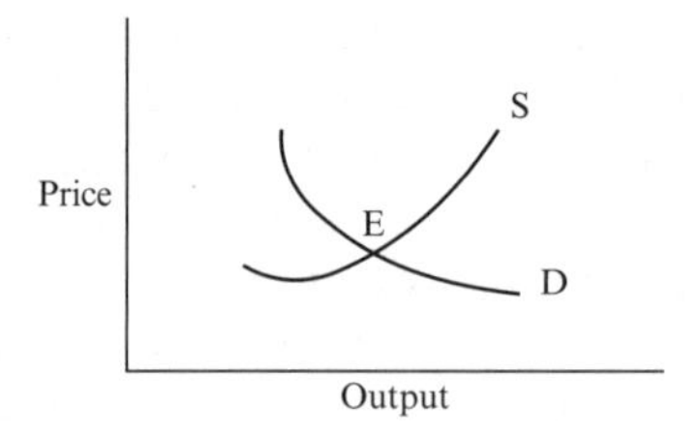

> Or he may say:
>
> When price is 0 P.1, supply exceeds demand and price tends to fall. When it is 0 P.2 demand exceeds supply and price tends to rise. Price may never actually be in equilibrium, but it is always tending towards equilibrium.
>
> 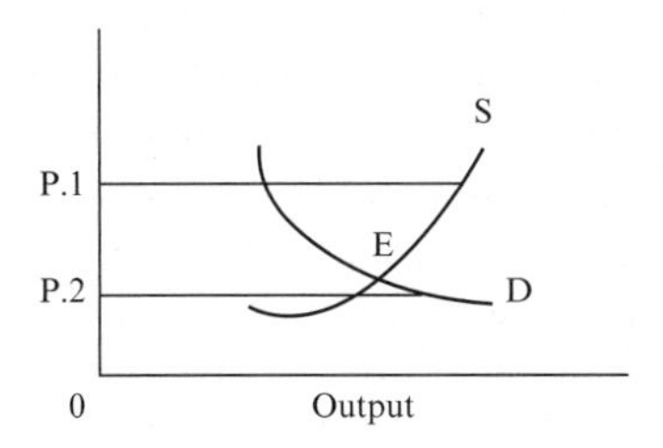
>
>
> Now he has gone clean off the rails. Why? He is using a metaphor based on space to explain a process which takes place in time.

Let me focus on her notion of a *metaphor based on space*. The point E exists in two-dimensional space: the quantity that is supplied is the same as the quantity that is demanded and there is some price that corresponds to that coincident point of supply and demand. We can identify other points *in space* where supply exceeds or falls short of demand, each coexisting in space with some price. There are an infinity of points in space at which supply and demand may not be the same at some price. These are all points in space. We may add dates, times, atmospheric conditions at each of those points in space, and so on. These descriptors are lifeless, timeless notions. None embodies an organic composition – it is just *there*, occupying a space defined by the person who chooses to define the typography of that space. Nothing can be said about how the points might interact because there is no dimension of *time* in that typography. 'Time,' Robinson wrote, 'may be conceived to lie at right angles to the page' (1962, p. 22).

The idea of *tending* toward equilibrium is a malapropism.[5] There is no *time* to be conceived of in such a representation in space. Things can *be* in space, but if they are not organic entities then there is no possibility for them to *move* let alone *interact* in a way that might affect them organically:

> The . . . point about space is that there is none of this stuff about tending (which the freshman, pour soul, finds extremely fishy). If you give your bodies time, they actually do get into equilibrium. Time will help you with space. But take as much space as you like – how is that going to help you with time? (Robinson, 1953, p. 256)

Mainstream mathematical modelers do not worry about these irritating issues. Components of a model are defined in name but not by any living matter that gives them their existence. And because there is nothing organic in their nature, one simply defines the axiomatic (mathematical) conditions by which all can approximate certain criteria (equilibrium) given certain explicitly stated preconditions. These states of coexisting components are not equilibria.[6] The delusion in this case occurs by interpreting equilibrium as a balance of forces despite the fact that no forces can be identified within the perceptual field of the investigator. Forces do not exist *in space*. There can be no balance of forces, therefore, in such a mathematical model. Change occurs in this model when one or more of the explicitly stated preconditions are respecified. They are referred to as exogenous *shocks* as if something actually *happens*, after which a new set of axiomatic conditions for coexisting components becomes identified.[7]

The source of the delusion, as I have described it, is that proponents of the mainstream project conduct their business as if these coexisting components can be viewed as living entities to the extent that they can be assigned causative and effectual powers within a functionalized mathematical model. The most egregious case of mistaken identity occurs when one of the coexisting components appears as a ratio, such as the real-wage, real-return to capital, real-rate of interest, and so on. These words (or perhaps *phrases* would be a better descriptor) emerge from the ratio of two things coexisting in space (money wages/money returns on capital/money rates of interest relative to some price measurement). These words give the impression of being compound phrases which coexist with other compound phrases (marginal product of labor, capital, and so on; whatever the word *marginal* might mean), which are then given an existence of relationality: at the point of equilibrium (remembering that this word is itself a simulacrum of reality – states being mistaken for balances of forces) the real-payment to a factor of production *equals* the extra contribution to the total output of that factor of production (with the deceptive belief that some change *in time* has occurred), all at some level of employment. And from there it is just a simple step to asking the axiomatic questions mistaken for *temporal* questions: what effect will a change in the *real-factor payment* have on the quantity of that factor *demanded* and *supplied*, or if supply were not equal to demand then how will the real factor prices change to reestablish that equilibrium?

It does not end there, however, because this faux temporal possibility (occurring in what Robinson called *logical* time) of supply, demand and price entities morphs into something called a *market*. In markets, the *forces* of tastes, income, relative prices, distribution, and so on, *cause* resources to *move* between and among industries as these forces move prices up and down. The words that sound like things we associate with demand, supply, price, factors of production, productivity of those factors, and so on, come to life, leading to what economists refer to as the object of their study – a market economy. Beginning with an axiomatic set of conditions the mainstream economics project has holed out in nil, not one, because something has emerged from nothing. Mainstream economists have mistaken a *mathematical model* for a *market*, and live in that world where the language of discourse emanates from the conditions of the model and what sounds just like reality.

Let us consider in greater detail the nature of these language structures that are the instruments and vehicles of the theoretical delusion of the mainstream which allows them to give life to something that has no life (an economic homunculus model). They appear to be real, they are assumed to exist, they receive names, and they have definite relational properties that allow them to engage with other specified components. I shall focus on these names that sound real and which are a part of the living discourse of the mainstream, what Herbert Marcuse refers to as *functionalized language*. In the section to follow I will give a few examples of how these mathematical models of the mainstream provide for a unified vision in terms of theory and policy with respect to unemployment, an area where the mainstream and Post Keynesian economists find one of their biggest sources of difference.

HYPNOTIC FORMULAS AND FUNCTIONALIZED LANGUAGE

> We never arrive at fundamental propositions in the course of our investigation; we get to the boundary of language which stops us from asking further questions. (Ludwig Wittgenstein, Lectures, 1930)

Among the many factors that reinforce the mainstream focus on closed-system mathematical models and which make it virtually impossible for proponents to let in other perspectives on the discipline, especially Post Keynesian economics, is the comfort level with the language of discourse that emanates from that confusion of mistaking models for markets. Here I address what Herbert Marcuse (1964) referred to as 'functionalized language structures', modes of discourse that are constructed so as to serve a particular limiting purpose or function in analytical reasoning. Marcuse argues that these language structures '[close] the meaning of the thing, excluding other manners of functioning':

> At the nodal points of the universe of public discourse, self-validating, analytical propositions appear which function like magic-ritual formulas. Hammered and re-hammered into the recipient's mind, they produce the effect of enclosing

> it within the circle of the conditions prescribed by the formula. (Marcuse, 1964, p. 89)

There emerges a universalization of language that is taken for granted by all and used in such a way as to reproduce the images and realities that the language presents.[8] Meaning becomes closed in the sense that there exists a universalized set of nouns, along with prescribed juxtapositions of specific adjectives and nouns that ring naturally to our ears. We express them freely as if they were true-to-life, functioning entities:

> The fact that a specific noun is almost always coupled with the same 'explicatory' adjectives and attributes makes the sentence into a hypnotic formula which, endlessly repeated, fixes the meaning in the recipient's mind. He does not think of essentially different (and possibly true) explications of the noun. (Marcuse, 1964, p. 91)

Functionalized language reinforces such logic and leads to interpretations of reality and policy that follow from that language. In Rotheim (2006, p. 10) I wrote:

> The language that we use in the discipline serves both as a screening device by which we take in sense data and as a limitation on the spectrum of possibilities that form our perception of those data. Not only do the questions we ask follow from the language we employ, but other questions are thereby ruled out; they are not excluded consciously, but rather they do not exist as the language itself purges those questions from our perceptual field.[9]

The functionalized language of discourse frames and allows us to enter prescribed domains of perception. It directs us to partition the world into what is perceived (and perceivable) and what is not perceived (and not perceivable). In that regard, we can imagine a circle (virtuous or vicious, depending upon who is considering it) in that we can see things only if we already believe them, while our belief in them is either created, enforced or reinforced by how we are persuaded to see them – Marcuse's 'hypnotic formulas.' We are trained to believe we see things to be there and then we formulate language structures that seduce us into knowing with assurance that they are there. Maurice Dobb expressed these same ideas 30 years before Marcuse when he wrote in an important essay that was to have a major impact on Keynes's own understanding of the methodological traps set by what he called 'classical economics' in his *General Theory* (1936):

> It can often lull us into thinking that we understand the words that we are using when we actually do not – into resting our thought on a number of assumptions which we have not explored and of which we may not even be aware. (Dobb, 1929, p. 506)

The mesmerizing nature of functionalized language emanating from closed mathematical models in space but not time can be illustrated well by what the mainstream calls the labor *market*. This notion of a labor market is consistent with the overall mainstream perspective on the causes and consequences of unemployment; it is the first line of attack when thinking about the problem because at its heart is the fundamental principle that all economic entities derive their meaning from some model cum market. Unemployment, then, is all about labor's adjusting to differing circumstances – the objective and subjective elements that go into these demand and supply decisions, the time it takes for such adjustments to occur, and the incentives and barriers to labor's making these adjustments. The evidence over the last few years, from those within the mainstream, that the preponderance of the persistent high levels of unemployment in the US and abroad are 'market driven' is weak, by all accounts, save for those few at the extreme ends of the mainstream for whom the evidence is ignored or pushed aside. The residual between the current high levels of unemployment and the level accounted for by 'market' phenomena is relegated to what they call 'demand or cyclical factors.' What they do not acknowledge is that their own framework, which is the first set of lenses through which they view the problem, is not suited to asking questions or coming to conclusions about changes in 'demand or cyclical factors.' Some may refer to these factors as 'Keynesian,' although Keynesian, for them, has something to do with a simplistic text-book ISLM model where the labor market is out of equilibrium. What they would never think of doing is to find out what Keynes or his Post Keynesian interpreters might have to say about the nature of unemployment within what Keynes called a *theory of effective demand*. Keynes exists only as a name associated with situations of deficiencies of *aggregate demand* in an AD–AS model, not *effective demand*. Post Keynesian economics does not exist at all. No wonder, then, that even when the mainstream has nothing to say about the current unemployment crisis, we still find that there is no room at the academic table for any analyses outside of the mainstream vista.

THE LABOR *MODEL AS MARKET*: THE CAUSES AND CONSEQUENCES OF UNEMPLOYMENT

No better example can be given of the confusion between models existing in space and processes occurring in time with the hypnotic formulas that help broaden that chasm than the mainstream notion of the labor market. Labor markets come in two forms, depending upon whether the noun is preceded by an indefinite or definite article – 'a' labor market or 'the' labor market. The roots of the first emerge at the same time as did writings on markets in general during the 18th Century. The second emerges in the late 1920s into the 1930s when mainstream economists reacted to the publication of Keynes's *General Theory* (1936). Keynes accused the first of serving as the basis for the mainstream understanding of unemployment, despite the fact that it could speak only of movements of labor between and among industries but had nothing to say about changes in the quantity of labor in the economy as a whole (see Preface and Chapter 19). There could also be nothing approximating *the* labor market because it was impossible for the supply of and demand for labor for the economy as a whole to be independent functions, each responsive in traditional fashion to changes in something called the real-wage (see especially Chapter 2). Mainstream economists are not aware of these criticisms, to no one's surprise. Thus they go along thinking either in terms of 'a' or 'the' labor market, both of which have spatial dimensions; neither of which has any meaning as a process in time.

The first labor market identifies the spectrum of the supply and demand for labor for each and every firm and industry in an economy. The axiomatic starting point, as always, occurs when the supply and demand for each and every worker is equal at some money wage and corresponding price index of the goods that labor purchases. What we have here is a moment in space whose solution contains the elements: supply (and the preferences of factor supply decisions), demand (and the output of factors of production and the number of factors employed), money-wages of labor, and price of wage goods for each and every firm and industry. The labor *market*, when thinking along these lines, is the identification of the adjustment processes that occurs when supply and demand for labor are posited not to be equal in all markets. The problem that we face, as Joan Robinson pointed out, is that we can identify something called equilibrium in space, but not in time for each and every labor market. To speak of adjustment processes where things *tend* in any such a fashion, however, is confusing metaphors in space with processes in time; once again a mathematical model is being mistaken for a market. Observing axiomatic conditions in closed conditions is possible, although nothing can be learned from such an observation. Proceeding to posit conditions when they are not equal is beyond the scope of what the model can do – *relationality* should not be elicited from axiomatic points.

The origins of this conceptualization can be found as far back as J.B. Say's *Treatise on Political Economy* (1803) and in his *Letters to Mr. Malthus* (1821), where he tried to explain the possibility, or more correctly *perception*, of overproduction of output (gluts) and unemployment for the economy as a whole within his model of the economy when such overproduction and unemployment for the economy as a whole are impossible in fact. Say envisioned the possibility of there being an overproduction of goods in *selected* markets equal in value to an underproduction of goods in other markets (see Kates, 1999; Rotheim, 1999a). One could envision, therefore, what appeared to be unemployment pervasive in the economy, easily misconstrued to reflect a *general* overproduction of goods for the economy as a whole. Resources would be redirected, in time, when relative prices adjust and owners of resources decide to make those shifts in product and direction. This view of a labor market comprising a multitude of occupations and firms stood at the heart of the work of William Beveridge in his landmark book *Unemployment: A Problem of Industry* (1909; revised 1930). Unemployment was described clearly by Beveridge as a phenomenon reflecting the challenges of labor in industries for which demand has fallen finding appropriate employment in industries for which demand has expanded.[10]

This impression of how this labor market functions, with adjustments in relative prices (output and factor) and movements of resources with the appropriate amount of adjustment time, taking into account frictions and impediments to those adjustments, has framed the functionalized language structure held by the mainstream for over 200 years. Nothing much has changed over that period, except for some details, elaborations and refinements.[11]

Actual market processes occur in open-system frameworks, in what Joan Robinson called *historical* time. Once things unfold, the organic interactions that might occur among the foundational elements of the system and the organic interdependencies that might follow make it impossible for us to speak of independent supply and demand functions mediated by the functionalized language which economists call *real-wages*.[12] In this economic-sounding configuration there are just labor markets in each of the many things that are produced. There is a labor market in the picking of oranges; another in apples, another in automobiles, another in financial securities, and so on. Each of these markets is preceded by the indefinite article, *a*. But they are not *markets* because nothing can happen, nothing can move, no directions can be identified – such markets do not exist in a closed system; they are indescribable in an open system.

Undeterred, as we would expect of the mainstream, most assessments of the current state of high unemployment in the US and Europe (broadly conceived) are seen through the initial lenses of what has come to be called the Structuralist position. In the tradition of J.B. Say, it is assumed that the demand and supply for labor in the economy as a whole remains unchanged; a critical assumption, indeed. There may occur exogenous shocks attributable to changes in tastes or technology upsetting the equilibrium states in each of the many labor markets in the economy (the *indefinite article* labor market).

Keynes, of course, was quite aware of this historical line of explanation for the perception of unemployment. He wrote in the Preface to the *General Theory* that what he called Classical economics could address the *direction* of employment, only, but not its quantity. They could describe movements between and among different occupations in different industries, but the total quantity of employment for the economy as a whole was given from the outset and not capable of changing. Nothing much has changed since Keynes made his keen observation on what the mainstream could and could not pretend to say about unemployment, as can be noted from recent statements from two Presidents of Federal Reserve Banks (and often voting members of the Federal Reserve's policy-making Open Market Committee):

> Firms have jobs, but can't find appropriate workers. The workers want to work, but can't find appropriate jobs. . . . *Most* of the existing unemployment represents mismatch that is not readily amenable to monetary policy.(Narayana Kocherlakota, President of the Federal Reserve Bank of Minneapolis, August 17, 2010; emphasis added)

> One impediment to more rapid employment growth is the extent of the mismatch between the skills of unemployed workers and the skills sought by firms seeking to hire. Recessions and recoveries always involve shifting resources from declining industries to expanding industries in response to emerging technologies and new patterns of demand; expansions are often not the mirror image of the preceding contraction. While many workers who lose jobs in a downturn will find jobs in newly expanding firms as the economy recovers, the search process that connects unemployed workers to new jobs can be lengthy and can require significant training. The costs and delays associated with reallocating workers to expanding industries can elevate unemployment and impede the rate of job growth. The extent of this type of skills mismatch is difficult to measure with any precision, but my reading, based on both statistical research and informal contacts with businesses in our District, is that mismatch is a *significant factor* in the labor market weakness we are seeing today. (Lacker, 2012, emphasis added)

Keynes was interested in developing a theoretical framework by which one could understand what determined the quantity of employment and changes in that quantity for the economy as a whole. The mainstream theory had no method of analysis for handling that problem, he observed (see 1936, p. 260). The only way that it could begin to broach such questions was to assume that changes in axiomatically specified variables (money-wages, especially) had no effect on either the conditions of supply or demand for labor for the economy as a whole. For all intents and purposes we are operating in the timeless realm of space. Opening the system to allow for changes in the objective and subjective circumstances that were identified in the axiomatically specified mathematical statements changed the circumstances under which individual firms could continue their operations, making impossible the smooth functional relations defined in space and all of the causal statements that presumably emerged from those axiomatic statements. The doors to understanding the determination of the level of employment for the economy as a whole and changes in that level have now been opened wide, but the functional tools that made up the arsenal of the mainstream had to be checked at the door – they were of no use to the economist who wanted to ask questions about changes in the level of employment for the economy as a whole.

Those in the mainstream have no knowledge of this fundamental objection lodged by Keynes, nor do they have any knowledge that Keynes's alternative framework, his *General Theory of Employment*, laid the basis for most of the work done to address these salient questions post Keynes. One should, therefore, not be surprised that most research done on the explanation of the current high levels of unemployment begins by looking through the windows of the Structuralist framework.[13] Each of these studies shows quite clearly that no matter how one measures it, the effects of skill-mismatch and other Structuralist interpretations have very little weight, occurring a bit at the beginning of the crisis and abating by the time the crises hit its trough.[14] They go on to admit that most of the observed unemployment must have occurred because of demand and cyclical factors. These results are of no surprise to anyone who is well grounded in Keynes's theory of effective demand; we would have *begun* our inquiries into looking into the conditions of demand and supply for the economy as a whole (including the impacts of different levels of income distribution). For us, our first line of attack would be to posit that most of the high levels of unemployment emanated from our well-specified analysis, where the organic interdependence of the conditions of demand and supply for output for the economy as a whole comprised a theory of effective demand. There would have been a theoretical framework, defined by underlying generative mechanisms depicting the theory of effective demand, from which those conclusions would have emanated. Such is not the case with those in the mainstream, however. They begin with an untenable axiomatic framework in space to understand unemployment as determined structurally, only to find that there is no evidence for those conclusions. The subsequent claim by them that the *residual* between the observed levels of unemployment and those levels predicted by the Structuralist vision as cyclically determined has no theoretical leg to stand on – they have no method for analyzing the problem of determining changes in the scale of employment for the economy as a whole, as Keynes stated so clearly 75 years ago.

The second way that mainstream economists use the phrase occurs when they identify something called *the* labor market. Here they imagine one composite good produced in the economy (GDP perhaps), where there is *the* aggregate supply and *the* aggregate demand for labor, each independent of the other, and where these independent aggregate relations are mediated by something called *the* real-wage. This labor market plays an important role in completing the ISLM model and continues to date in most macroeconomic textbooks under the heading *Keynesian* unemployment – where the real-wage is too high to clear *the* labor market. In this conceptualization of unemployment the market is *tending* toward equilibrium or there are a host of factors that prevent *the* real-wage from falling sufficiently to allow the *tending* process to reach completion, so-called *New Keynesian* economics (see Mankiw and Romer, 1992; Rotheim, 1998). Equilibrium in this labor market also can be identified axiomatically, in space, in lifeless fashion.

Talking about adjustments in *the* labor market when those axiomatic conditions in space are not met fall either into Mrs. Robinson's trap, the delusion of confusing metaphors in space with processes occurring in time, or they must admit to circumstances characterized by openness, in which case we are pushed all too uncomfortably into the framework of what Keynes called *the theory of effective demand.* In space it is possible to specify the demand for labor and the supply of labor for the economy as a whole and to attach some level of money-wages and the price of consumer goods at that point where the demand and supply of labor in the economy as a whole are equal. When considering processes occurring in time, Keynes made it eminently clear that there was no way that one could understand the idea of a labor market for the economy as a whole, modeled on the demand and supply of labor for an individual firm or industry. Unless, of course, it was assumed that output for the economy as a whole could not change (see Keynes, 1936, Chapters 3 and 19). When we move the analysis into the realm of time where organic interdependent processes are occurring then it is impossible to posit supply and demand relations for labor in the economy as a whole that are independent of one another. The mechanical modeling of the mainstream view where the real-wage serves as the independent variable and the levels of supply and demand for labor for the economy as a whole are seen as dependent variables is upset when each of the conditions underlying those categories, including the money-wage and price of consumer goods, is now capable of change and in directions that are unpredictable *a priori.*

All of this realism is a mystery to those in the mainstream because they have no sense of Keynes's theory of effective demand reflecting organically interdependent processes occurring in time or the research conducted post Keynes on this important topic. Instead, they continue to retreat to the most illogical of programs emanating from the mainstream model of their distorted view of Keynes either in terms of the ISLM or more recent AS/AD model (with downward sloping AD curve in price level/output space). The window through which they approach questions of unemployment is once again seen in terms of informational asymmetries or other forms of wage stickiness (real and nominal; see Mankiw and Romer, 1992) in *the* labor market, which, as we know, can only be posited if it is assumed that the quantity of labor employed does not change for the economy as a whole. And when thinking about policy within this timeless spatial model of the economy, current research focuses on the mainstream Phillips' Curve (as distinct from the relationality implied by the original work of Phillips, himself). Now that the unemployment rate for the economy as a whole has remained at historically higher than normal levels post trough, could it be that the Phillips' Curve has somehow shifted upward? Is 8 per cent the new natural rate of unemployment or has the Beveridge Curve shifted upwards?

The Friedman Phillips Curve posits the inflation rate on the ordinate and the unemployment rate on the abscissa. The argument underlying this incarnation of the relation considers the effect that monetary intervention would have on lowering the rate of unemployment. Increases in the inflation rate brought about by increases in monetary intervention will not reduce unemployment in the long-period because a well-specified labor supply function, especially one based on rational expectations, will anticipate fully any increase in the inflation rate, thereby allowing labor to build in cost of living adjustment clauses to their money-wage bargains assuring a constant real-wage and therefore no change in the demand for labor (for a given production function and therefore specification of the marginal product of labor). Expansionary monetary policies will only *cause* inflation to increase if it is assumed from the outset that output for the economy as a whole cannot change. Full employment, as the criticism goes, is assumed from the outset. So what, then, can it mean to say that expansionary monetary policy cannot affect the level of employment if the level of employment is assumed not to change from the start? Monetary policy should not be a policy tool to reduce the unemployment rate if the unemployment rate cannot be reduced. Metaphors in space masquerading as a process occurring in time. The mainstream has gone so far as to define the natural rate of unemployment as that rate of unemployment at which monetary policy is not an effective policy tool (see Orphanides, 2012).

In the first case we use the functionalized language of what we believe is a labor market to understand why the *real-wage* does or does not fall sufficiently to cause an equilibration of the independent aggregate supply and demand relations. And surely this configuration reflects the language of discourse among the mainstream of the discipline. Here the discourse is closed by the language, itself, where specified nouns (wage) are always preceded by prescribed adjectives (real) such that all that is acceptable to the mainstream falls within its perceptual field. Unemployment must be occurring because *real* wages are too high relative to labor productivity; those who supply labor must be asking for *real* wages higher than what the market (*the* market) values their services in *real* product, which is relative to the *real* contribution they make to the creation of the output produced, given the technological specification of production.

Effective Demand failure (or what they call 'cyclical unemployment') is the 800 lb. gorilla in the room. Yet economists are compelled to begin their discussions of unemployment with the structuralist position, even if they must admit that there is no credibility to that view, especially at this moment. They admit, therefore, to the preponderance of the current sustained unemployment to be 'cyclical' by nature, but their analyses end at that point. Theirs is a conclusion by default – cyclical unemployment as unexplained residual – without any theoretical framework to support it. As I have asserted in this chapter, there *is* no theoretical framework at their disposal in the axiomatically closed system in which they operative and by which they perceive reality.

CONCLUDING REMARKS

Economics, at least to me, is all about: 'who's eating; who's not; and why?' It perhaps explains why so much of my writing over the years has focused on how we think about questions of employment and unemployment. For most economists, economics is all about the allocation of scarce resources to satisfy unlimited individual wants. It's about markets and individuals functioning within markets. Unemployment, for them, is understood in terms of matters of labor supply and demand mediated by some wage (normally a real-wage) in something called a labor market. One should not be surprised that even amidst the most severe economic times, the first line of attack in perceiving unemployment comes, therefore, by considering the conditions that constitute matters of supply of labor, demand for labor and the real-wage. In this current economic crisis, those in the mainstream enter the investigative terrain through this perceptual framework. Most have rejected it, to their credit, but only because it has not manifested itself in fact. One should have rejected it at a deeper level because it was a metaphor in space (a model) that mistook itself for a process in time (a market). And as Keynes said in assessing the underlying logical nature of what those in the mainstream considered to be the labor market: 'they had no method of analysis for solving the problem'. They have no method of analysis for claiming that the current unemployment is 'cyclical' or 'demand driven', either, as that conclusion would need to have emanated from Keynes's theory of effective demand. They would not know that, however, because they have never read Keynes, nor have they allowed his modern interpreters to sit at their table in academia.

My intention in this rather dismal prognosis for the future of Post Keynesian economics in mainstream curricula was not meant to be disobliging, to use Joan Robinson's colorful word. But I cannot see how the obsession with closure that creates the fictional delusion such that matters in space take on a real-life in the minds of the mainstream will ever allow those who control all of the *means and sources of knowledge* in the academy to recognize, accept and legitimize approaches to the discipline that embrace truly open-system processes. The mainstream has imposed what it believes to be openness on strict closure, ruling out any economic theory that is founded on openness, itself. And that is the fundamental *psychological* – both individual and social – barrier to the possibility that the mainstream will ever embrace a Keynes/Post Keynes economic theory.

NOTES

* Thanks to Stephanie Blankenberg, Victoria Chick, Geoff Harcourt, Jesper Jespersen, Prue Kerr, Mogens Ove Madsen and Tony Lawson.

1. Both the Federal Reserve System and the European Central Bank have individuals sitting at their helms, Ben Bernanke and Mario Draghi, respectively, who are resisting this Anschluss of inflation hawk sentiment, although one always wonders how long that resistance can be sustained.
2. 'Formal techniques are powerful tools, but they can also be dangerous; the problem is to identify applications where they can be used safely. The debate on that issue has hardly been joined, because of the hegemony of the formalists. Their certainty that any other approach is inferior or downright wrong, and the view that those who do not embrace formal techniques are against their use, has stifled debate' (Chick, 1998, p. 1861).
3. With reference to the Nobel Memorial Prize in Economics, David Romer said he thought the selection committee did a good job of 'taking a stand,' given the breadth of viewpoints among economists. 'You have to decide what's good economics and what's not good economics,' said Romer, adding that the Academy 'has made a judgment that most of the important work in economics has been done by mainstream academic economists' (Wirtz, 1999).
4. Referring to Joan Robinson's use of the phrase logical time and disequilibrium he writes: 'the proper subject is not so much disequilibrium as the ontological impropriety of the idea of equilibrium' (Burstein, 1991, p. 50).

5. See Harcourt (1981) on the problem with *tending* in mainstream economics.
6. Marx wrote of the economic growth theories of James Mill and David Ricardo that embrace 'the "metaphysical equilibrium of purchases and sales,"... an equilibrium which sees *only* the unity, but not the separation in the process of purchase and sale' (1863, pp. 503–04).
7. We make an almost biblical analogy by beginning in equilibrium (Eden), having there be an exogenous policy shock (snake and fall from grace) and an individual struggle to get back to equilibrium (second coming; heaven).
8. 'Any system of ideas, religious, artistic, or logical, so far as it is articulated in meaningful language, attains a general connotation and necessarily claims to be true in a universal sense' (Horkheimer, 1972, p. 144). See Rotheim (2006, p. 10).
9. 'Functionalization of language helps to repel non-conformist elements from the structure and movement of speech' (Marcuse, 1964, p. 86).
10. In his revision of 1930, influenced heavily by the writing of A.C. Pigou in the late 1920s, Beveridge gives more weight to the intractability of displaced labor's unwillingness to accept lower wages in light of the fall in demand for their services.
11. The significance of this mainstream perspective on 'perceived' unemployment within a *market* framework was confirmed with the awarding of the 2012 Sveriges Riksbank Prize in Economics to Peter A. Diamond, Dale T. Mortensen and Christopher A. Pissarides '*for their analysis of markets with search frictions.*' See, for example, Pissarides (2009) and Petrongolo and Pissarides (2008).
12. That one could not speak of independent supply and demand curves for labor in anything resembling a labor *market* was a point made clearly by Dobb (1929) and incorporated in Keynes's criticism of what he called *Classical* economics (1936). Both Dobb and Keynes recognized that thinking along the lines of the mainstream when the system was open (when output for the economy as a whole was allowed to change) made impossible the method that the mainstream was using to analyze such problems.
13. See Barnichon and Figura (2010); Şahin, et al. (2011); Estevão and Tsounga (2011), Daly, et al.,(2011), Lindner and Tasci (2010), Bernanke (2012), Lazear and Spletzer (2012), and Orphanides (2012).
14. The most recent admission comes from one of the icons of the market approach to employment questions, Edwin Lazear, who writes: 'structural changes . . . are not the major factors causing the fall of employment or the rise in unemployment that occurred during the recent recession' (Lazear and Spletzer, 2012, p. 5).

BIBLIOGRAPHY

Barnichon, R and Figura, A. (2010). 'What Drives Movements in the Unemployment Rate? A Decomposition of the Beveridge Curve,' Finance and Economics Discussion Series 2010–48 (Washington: Board of Governors of the Federal Reserve System, August).

Bernanke, B. (2012). 'Recent Developments in the Labor Market,' Speech At the National Association for Business Economics Annual Conference, Washington, D.C. March 26.

Beveridge, W. (1909, revised 1930). *Unemployment: a Problem of Industry* (London: Longman, Green, and Co.).

Bharadwaj, K. (1991). 'History versus Equilibrium,' in I. Rima, ed., *The Joan Robinson Legacy* (Armonk, NY: M.E. Sharpe), pp. 80–103.

Burstein, M. (1991). 'History versus Equilibrium: Joan Robinson and Time in Economics,' in I. Rima, ed., *The Joan Robinson Legacy* (Armonk: M.E. Sharpe), pp. 49–61.

Chick, V. (1998). 'On Knowing One's Place: The Role of Formalism in Economics,' *Economic Journal*, November, pp. 1829–36.
Chick, V. and Dow, S. (2001). 'Formalism, Logic and Reality: A Keynesian Analysis,' *Cambridge Journal of Economics*, November, pp. 705–22.
Daly, Mary, Bart Hobijn, Ayşegül Sahin, and Robert Valletta (2011). 'A Rising Natural Rate of Unemployment: Transitory or Permanent?' Federal Reserve Bank of San Francisco Working Paper 2011–05.
Davidson, P. (2009). *John Maynard Keynes* (London: Palgrave).
Dobb, M. (1929). 'A Sceptical View on the Theory of Wages,' *Economic Journal*, December 506–19.
Dow, S. (2012). 'Different Approaches to the Financial Crisis,' *Economic Thought*, 1(1), pp. 80–93.
Estevão, M. and Tsounta, E. (2011). 'Has the Great Recession Raised U.S. Structural Unemployment?' IMF Working Paper, May.
Gibson, W., ed. (2005). *Joan Robinson's Economics: A Centennial Celebration* (Cheltenham: Edward Elgar Publishing).
Hahn, F. (1982). *Money and Inflation* (Oxford: Blackwell).
Harcourt, G.C. (1981). 'Marshall, Sraffa and Keynes: Incompatible Bedfellows?' *Eastern Economic Journal*, January, pp. 39–50.
Hicks, J.R. (1932). *Theory of Wages* (London: Macmillan).
Hicks, J.R. (1937). 'Mr Keynes and the Classics: a Suggested Interpretation,' *Econometrica*, April, pp. 147–59.
Horkheimer, M. (1972). *Critical Theory* (New York: Herder and Herder).
Kates, S. (1999). *Say's Law and the Keynesian Revolution: How Macroeconomic Theory Lost its Way* (Cheltenham: Edward Elgar Publishing).
Keynes, J.M. (1936). *The General Theory of Employment, Interest, and Money* (London: Harcourt, Brace, and World).
Kurtz, H. (2010). 'On the Dismal State of a Dismal Science?' *Homo Oeconomicus*, 27(3), pp. 1–21.
Lacker, Jeffrey (2012). 'Economic Outlook,' Speech to the Economics Club of Hampton Roads Economic Conference, Norfolk, VA., May 2.
Lawson, T. (1997). *Economics and Reality* (London: Routledge).
Lawson, T. (2002). 'Mathematical Formalism in Economics: What Really is the Problem?' in P. Arestis, M. Desai and S. Dow, eds., *Methodology, Microeconomics and Keynes: Essays in Honour of Victoria Chick*, vol. 2 (London: Routledge), pp. 73–83.
Lawson, T. (2003). *Reorienting Economics* (London: Routledge).
Lawson, T. (2012a). 'Mathematical Modelling and Ideology in the Economics Academy: Competing Explanations of the Failings of the Modern Discipline?' *Economic Thought*, 1(1), pp. 3–22.
Lawson, T. (2012b). 'Ontology and the Study of Social Reality: Emergence, Organisation, Community, Power, Social Relations, Corporations, Artifacts and Money,' *Cambridge Journal of Economics*, July, pp. 345–85.
Lazear, E. and Spletzer, J. (2012). 'The United States Labor Market: Status Quo or a New Normal?' Federal Reserve Bank of Kansas City Economic Symposium on *The Changing Policy Landscape*, Jackson Hole, WY, September.
Lindner, J. and Tasci, M. (2010). 'Has the Beveridge Curve Shifted?' Federal Reserve Bank of Cleveland, *Economic Trends*, August.
Mankiw, G. and Romer, D. (1992). *New Keynesian Economics*, 2 vols. (Cambridge, MA: MIT).

Marcuse, H. (1964). *One Dimensional-Man* (London: Routledge).
Marx, K. (1863). *Theories of Surplus Value*, vol. II, (Moscow: Progress Publishers), 1968.
Mearman, A. (2006). 'Critical Realism in Economics and Open-Systems Ontology: A Critique,' *Review of Social Economy*, vol. 64, no. 1, pp. 47–75.
Orphanides, A. (2012). Discussion of Lazear and Spletzer, 'The United States Labor Market: Status Quo or a New Normal?' Federal Reserve Bank of Kansas City Economic Symposium on *The Changing Policy Landscape*, Jackson Hole, WY, September.
Pigou, A.C. (1913). *Unemployment* (London: Williams and Norgate).
Pissarides, C. (2009). 'The Unemployment Volatility Puzzle: Is Wage Stickiness the Answer?' *Econometrica*, September, pp. 1339–69.
Pissarides, C. and Petrongolo, B. (2008). 'The Ins and Outs of European Unemployment,' *American Economic Review Papers and Proceedings*, May, pp. 256–62.
Robinson, J. (1953). 'A Lecture Delivered at Oxford by a Cambridge Economist,' manuscript, *Collected Economic Papers*, vol. 4, 1973 (Oxford: Blackwell).
Robinson, J. (1962). *Essays in the Theory of Economic Growth* (London: Macmillan).
Robinson, J. (1974). 'History versus Equilibrium', Thames Papers in Political Economy, Thames Polytechnic, London.
Robinson, J. (1980). 'Time in Economic Theory,' *Kyklos*, 33, pp. 219–29.
Rotheim, R. (1992). 'Interdependence and the Cambridge Economic Tradition,' in B. Gerrard and J. Hillard (eds.), *The Philosophy and Economics of J.M. Keynes*, (Aldershot: Edward Elgar Publishing).
Rotheim, R. (1998). 'On Closed Systems and the Language of Economic Discourse,' *Review of Social Economy*, Fall, pp. 324–34.
Rotheim, R. (1999a). 'Post Keynesian Economics and Critical Realist Philosophy,' *Journal of Post Keynesian Economics*, Fall, pp. 71–103.
Rotheim, R. (1999b). 'Review of S. Kates: *Say's Law and the Keynesian Revolution: How Macroeconomic Theory Lost its Way*,' *Journal of Economic Literature*, September, pp. 1178–79.
Rotheim, R. (2002). 'Timeful Theories, Timeful Theorists,' in P. Arestis, M. Desai and S. Dow, eds., *Methodology, Microeconomics and Keynes: Essays in Honour of Victoria Chick*, vol. 2 (London: Routledge), pp. 62–72.
Rotheim, R. (2006). 'Persuasive Devices,' *Cambridge Journal of Economics*, July.
Sachs, O. (1970). *The Man who Mistook his Wife for a Hat* (New York, NY: Touchstone).
Şahin, A., Song, J., Topa, G. and Violante, G. (2011), 'Measuring Mismatch in the US Labor Market,' FRB-NY, Working Paper, revised October.
Say, J.B. (1803). *A Treatise on Political Economy* (reprinted NY: A.M. Kelley), 1971.
Say, J.B. (1821). *Letters to Mr. Malthus, on Several Subjects of Political Economy, and on the Cause of the Stagnation of Commerce. To Which is added, A Catechism of Political Economy, or Familiar Conversations on the Manner in which Wealth is Produced, Distributed, and Consumed in Society*, trans. John Richter (London: Sherwood, Neely, and Jones).
Tasci, M. and Zaman, S. (2010). 'Unemployment after the Recession: a New Natural Rate?' *Economic Commentary*, FRB-Cleveland, September 8.
Walras, L. (1874). *Elements of Pure Economics* (Illinois: Irwin), 1954.

Wirtz, R. (1999). 'The Beauty (Pagent?) of Economics: The Nobel Prize in Economics,' *Fed Gazette*, FRB-Minneapolis, September.
Wittgenstein, L. (1930). *Wittgenstein's Lectures, Cambridge, 1930–32 From the Notes of John King and Desmond Lee* (Cambridge: CUP).

3. The future is open: on open-system theorising in economics

Victoria Chick*

INTRODUCTION

Open systems should form the core of economics teaching on the grounds of their superior relevance, but there are psychological difficulties attendant on this approach. Many students have expressed dissatisfaction with the content of economics teaching. The French PostAutistic network, the first group to complain about the economics curriculum in an organised and powerful way,[1] now has a sister organisation in Cambridge, the Cambridge Society for Economic Pluralism.[2] Students walked out in protest at Mankiw's lectures at Harvard,[3] and the number of students applying to study the subject is falling in most countries.

The name 'PostAutistic' reflected those students' perception that economics has lost its connection with the outside world, and that was the perception of the 'Mankiw rebels' too. There is a need to move beyond that and get back in touch with reality. All theory involves some departure from reality or it would not be theory, but open systems are superior to the closed systems that form the bulk of economics today, both because their abstractions tend more closely to reflect underlying reality and because they force a consciousness about the abstractions one is choosing (Dow 2002; Jespersen 2009; Lawson 1997, 2002; Rotheim 2002).

The autistic character of modern economics is often attributed to its formalism, particularly its reliance on mathematics, but the problem arises at a stage before mathematics is brought into play: the choice of closed, rather than open, frameworks of analysis. Mathematics encourages the closed-system approach to theory construction, but since it has been shown that mathematical methods are not incompatible with open-system theorising (e.g. Setterfield 2003; Skott 1989), the mathematisation of economics is neither a necessary nor a sufficient explanation of the isolation of economics from reality.

But if one is going to teach open-system theories, one must be prepared for even more student resistance than usual, for understanding open systems requires open minds and their attendant characteristics, which are in short supply for reasons I shall try to indicate. From the structure of that analysis I suggest, elaborating on the work of Peter Earl (2000), certain ways that we might try to help students reach a stage of development at which open systems can be appreciated. The open system I know best is Keynes's *General Theory*, and I shall use it as an example. The chapter opens with a discussion of the different dimensions of closed and open systems and their properties.

PROPERTIES OF CLOSED AND OPEN SYSTEMS

We have all been brought up on 'models': systems of just-identified simultaneous equations which are supposed to constitute theory. These models are closed; they conform to the conditions listed in Chick and Dow (2005, p. 367):

1. All relevant variables can be identified.
2. The boundaries of the system are definite and immutable; it follows that it is clear which variables are exogenous and which are endogenous; these categories are fixed.
3. Only the specified exogenous variables affect the system, and they do this in a known way.
4. Relations between the included variables are either knowable or random.
5. Economic agents (whether individuals or aggregates) are treated atomistically.
6. The nature of economic agents is treated as if constant.
7. The structure of the relationships between the components (variables, subsystems, agents) is treated as if it is either knowable or random.
8. The structural framework within which agents act is taken as given.

Lawson's (1997) extrinsic condition for closure, isolation from external forces, is similar to but less stringent than the combination of our criteria 1 and 3. The intrinsic closure conditions amount to our criteria 4–7, phrased in terms of event regularities. The question of boundary – where it is, how precisely it is specified – to me in many ways the most interesting matter – is not explicitly mentioned, though it is implicit in the distinction between included and omitted variables.

Models of this type are very comforting: they give definite, and demonstrable, results. These results can be very illuminating. But their applicability is severely restricted by the very closure conditions that made definite results possible.

In an open system, one or more of the criteria given above for a closed system is not met. The criteria for openness are not symmetrical with those for closure: there are as many ways for a system to be open as there are criteria for closure, and there can even be more than one alternative to a single criterion. These asymmetries save this definition from dualism: openness is a spectrum with closure at one end.

i. The system is not atomistic; therefore at least one of the following holds:
   a. outcomes of actions cannot be inferred from individual actions (because of interactions);
   b. agents and their interactions may change (e.g. agents may learn).
ii. Structure and agency are interdependent.
iii. Boundaries around and within the social or economic system are mutable; for at least one of the following reasons:
   a. social structures may evolve;
   b. connections between structures may change;
   c. the structure–agent relation may change.
iv. Identifiable social structures are embedded in larger structures; these may mutually interact, for the boundaries of a social system are in general partial or semi-permeable.

Open theoretical systems may have some or all of the following properties:

v. There may be important omitted variables or relations and/or their effects on the system may be uncertain.
vi. The classification into exogenous and endogenous variables may be neither fixed nor exhaustive.
vii. Connections and/or boundaries between structures may be imperfectly known and/or may change.
viii. There is imperfect knowledge of the relations between variables; relationships may not be stable (Lawson 1997, p. 366).

There can be many types of openness. Which criterion is emphasised is of great importance. In critical realism, because of the scepticism about event regularities, there is a focus on criterion iv, the possibility that the internal relations between variables may not be constant. If this means that events in open systems present a chaotic appearance, this is not a happy state of affairs, either to those who wish to infer underlying mechanisms from perceived event regularities or for those who perceive causal relations at the level of events themselves. On this criterion it could be said that open systems are inimical to theory; this is not at all what I am advocating. Open-system thinking has also been characterised as 'anything goes' (Davidson 2003–4); this is in my view, most definitely not the case (see Dow's 2005 rebuttal and Davidson's rejoinder, 2005).

Among those who assume that some behaviour is sufficiently stable to allow analysis, Setterfield (1993, 1999) built path-dependent models[4] in which agents make crucial decisions that change the future. (Such decisions are unique and irreversible. Shackle (1970, pp. 109–10) called them 'crucial experiments', to which probability theory does not apply, because they are unique decisions.) By contrast, in *The General Theory* investment is a crucial decision, but it is only allowed to affect the future (the productive structure) in the long period (Chapter 17). While Kregel (1976), Chick (1983, Chapter 2), Chick and Dow (2001), Dow (2002) and Loasby (2003) fully acknowledge the importance of closed systems in deriving results, they stress the importance of partial and provisional closures to create these systems within an open system.[5] No system can be completely open, of course; boundaries must exist, however ill-defined. Theory needs a structure, just as we need structures in life.

DIMENSIONS OF OPENNESS

Not only are there many ways in which a system may be open, but also there are many dimensions of openness. I have identified four: subject matter, the object of study, the level of study (micro and macro) and time.

Subject Matter

The boundaries of the economy are necessarily fuzzy, as the economy is a part of, and embedded in, social life. Yet social life is studied from many points of view: economics, sociology, politics, philosophy, history, and so on, each of which emphasises a particular aspect. One might expect the borders of economics as a subject, like the borders of the economy, to be fuzzy, but never completely open. Rather, the position of the boundary may be vague and the boundary itself semi-permeable. At the other end of an open–closed continuum, the subject can be defined – has been defined – in very narrow and closed ways. Robbins (1932) famously defined economics as the study of the allocation of scarce resources. The early Joan Robinson (whom the later Joan repudiated) considered economics to be coterminous with its technique (1932). As a modern manifestation of that idea, today many in the mainstream take the view that anything which falls outside the formalist method is somehow 'not economics'. This view would insulate economics from other social and historical disciplines. In practice some theorists respected few borders between economics and other disciplines (consider the work in the 1980s and 1990s illuminating the relationship between Keynes's epistemological, political and ethical philosophies and his economics, the combination of economics and sociology (e.g. Ingham 2004) or economics and psychology (e.g. Tuckett 2011)). While mainstream economists reject the influence of other disciplines on economics, they have not hesitated to apply their techniques to such matters as crime, marriage or discrimination. The extent of interpenetration of the disciplines is variable. The borders of economics are not clear; economics as a thought-system is open, in spite of many attempts to close it.

Objects of Study

Within economics, the borders of the objects of study are also ill-defined and movable. Is this chapter about economic method, or the teaching of economics, or Keynes's *General Theory*? Anyone who has tried to select just one JEL classification for his/her work knows what a straightjacket those classifications can be – yet of course they are immensely helpful as approximate categories, as partial and provisional closures of a larger thought-system. Macroeconomics may encompass consumption theory, investment theory, wage bargaining/industrial relations, a theory of money and finance, and international trade. The problem is particularly important when it comes to money, which can only be separated from the rest of macroeconomics if the Classical Dichotomy is accepted. As Hayek put it,

> [T]he task of monetary theory is a much wider one than is commonly assumed; . . . its task is nothing less than to cover a second time the whole field which is treated by pure theory under the assumption of barter. (Hayek 1931, quoted by Keynes 1931, p. 234)

Level of Study

The question of the level of study is particularly tricky. The charge that macroeconomics has no microfoundations is wearily familiar, and unresolved (see, for example, Denis and Toporowski, eds, forthcoming; King 2012). When applied to Keynes's *General Theory* there is a sense in which this charge is absurd, but there is some truth in it, too. It is absurd in the sense that *The General Theory* discusses motivation and decisions – to consume, to produce, how liquid to be, how much labour to hire, what wage to offer and to accept – which can only be taken by individuals acting on their own account or as representatives of organisations. But there is truth in the allegation that the link between these micro elements and the macro theory is incomplete and imperfect. There are good reasons for this. The economy, and this theory of it, is a complex system, where the interaction of plans produces surprising results, unintended consequences of individual actions. The paradox of thrift; the possibly adverse effect on employment of a fall in money wages; the dual role of money, 'lulling our disquietude' while causing a signalling problem for producers; the ability of securities markets to provide liquidity to the individual while not being able to do so for the system as a whole – these are all examples of the impossibility of generalising from micro decisions to macro outcomes: the fallacy of composition.

From the fallacy of composition it follows that, short of specifying every transaction and the precise time that it takes place, the link between micro and macro not only is not tight but cannot be tight. It is bound to be ambiguous. Neoclassical economics has its own ways of dealing with this problem. One way or another it relies on the representative agent. Either the macroeconomic relations are worked out and then each individual is assumed to replicate $1/n^{th}$ of the aggregate, as it were, or individual behaviour is postulated and, on the assumption of atomism, aggregated to form the macro story. The fit is perfect and the system as a whole is closed. Rational expectations allow individuals to be ignorant of 'the correct model' for a time but gradually to correct their understanding of the system so that they replicate it.

Keynes's system, however, is open, potentially in both directions. Micro agents act, but their interaction (the 'system') may confound their intentions. If we knew the timing of each economic transaction, and had rules for deciding what the outcome would be in case of conflict, we might be able to deduce the macro outcome from micro decisions. But this is to require the kind of information attributed to the Walrasian auctioneer. Under more acceptable assumptions, the move between the micro and macro levels necessarily involves compromise (Chick 2002).

Time

A system may also be open in time. Time plays havoc with closure, and the uncertainty or imperfect knowledge that comes with it is inimical to 'rationality' in the mainstream sense, so closed systems must abolish it – and Hicks hints at the feeling of greater safety that that brings:

> [The ISLM diagram] is now much less popular with me than I think it still is with many other people. It reduces the *General Theory* to equilibrium

> economics; it is not really *in* time. That, of course, is why it has done so well. (Hicks 1976, pp. 289–90)

There are well-established ways of abolishing time in economics: static analysis, which is truly timeless; analysis in terms of rates of change, as in much of growth or inflation theory; and convergence to an asymptote, which is the end-point of the analysis, often equated with a long-run result. In conventional dynamics, too, time is abolished, for despite having dated variables, everything necessary to define the whole trajectory of the variable in question is known at the beginning. The trick in general equilibrium analysis of defining state-contingent choices is also a device for bringing the future back to the present. As is necessary in closed systems, all future states are assumed to have been identified; this is a world without surprises, which exists independently of its agents. Agents can at best apprehend it, where by contrast in Shackle (1979), for instance, they create it.

How do open-system theories cope with time? There are different timescales, even in this question. Let us take first the sweep of history. We know that only part of history can be taken into account; the question is, which part? History manifests itself in economic systems as changing networks and institutions, conventions, social systems and behaviour. Open systems can allow for the influence of history by means of the same device that was explored above: the partial and provisional closure – choosing a period for analysis that exhibits sufficient regularity to allow analysis and changing theory when that regularity breaks down. A good example of new circumstances requiring new theory is found in Keynes's theory of liquidity preference: with the development of active and substantial trading in the stock of existing financial assets (which began in earnest though on a small scale with the trading of gilts after the foundation of the Bank of England), loanable funds theory, based as it is on new lending and borrowing with no trade in existing assets, was hopelessly misleading. Similarly, the evolution of the banks into a system which could lend without any corresponding prior saving was responsible for reversing the causality between saving and investment of the classical economists (Chick 1986). History can make a theory which was right for its time become wrong as the economy evolves and the theory ceases to capture the salient relationships. It is for the theorist to judge whether a period of time has sufficient uniformity or coherence to make it a suitable subject for theory.

History also plays a narrower role in *The General Theory*, as explained so succinctly by Joan Robinson (1978, p. ix): the theory starts, as the economy starts every new day, with a stock of capital inherited from the past. This capital defines possibilities, in particular for production. Even when planning an expansion of capacity, one has to produce with the capital one has already. Thus the use of the Marshallian short period when output and employment are the dependent variables makes sense. It is realistic. The short period is a temporary closure, which creates a sub-system in which time is in some sense suspended. Changes in the capital stock are 'let out of the pound of *ceteris paribus*' in Chapter 17.

Many have complained that the analysis of *The General Theory* is static and therefore timeless (Gilbert 1982, even Shackle (!) 1967, p. 182). There is a tension in *The General Theory* between timefulness and timelessness: Hicks (1976, p. 288) describes it as having 'one leg which is in time, but another which is not'; I used the phrase 'a static theory of a dynamic process' (Chick 1983). It is the technique of partial and provisional closure which creates this tension but also allows theory to proceed. There is the prospect of path dependency in *The General Theory*: when short-period expectations are not fulfilled, producers may change those expectations. If they do, it will be difficult to say where the system will end up. Since both price and output change at every point on both the aggregate supply curve and the expected demand curve, when one curve changes the other will also. Only money wages are constant along these curves, and the expected profit which will motivate producers' new strategy depends not only on wage costs but also on output and prices. So the system is path-dependent, but there are many paths the system might take. Keynes cut through these limitless possibilities by the use of short-period equilibrium: a configuration which would replicate unless disturbed. Thus he extracts from an open system one pattern about which a good deal can be said, without foreclosing the path dependency (Chick 1998). The full range of other possibilities remains; the equilibrium solution, though fruitful to analyse, would, he warned us, in practice be achieved only by accident.

What I hope can be seen in the above account is that the open system constructed by Keynes bears a closer relation to reality than most closed-system models (Jespersen 2009). This is in large part due to the wise choice of temporary and partial closures. It is, in fact, a theory which encompasses several closed-system models. I assert that the system, or theory, is also sufficiently flexible to accommodate a range of modifications – technological change, an analysis of bank credit, and so on. It can do this because its boundaries, both between components inside the theory and between it and other theories, are not rigid.

EDUCATIONAL PROBLEMS WITH OPEN SYSTEMS

Teaching open systems will give rise to problems beyond the usual ones of doing something which is not mainstream. One will confront some psychological barriers. Chief among these is an adverse reaction to the lack of definiteness or certainty. The boundary of the model is not always clear. The categories of exogenous and endogenous variables may shift from one sub-system to another. It can even appear that something is true and not true at the same time, if the contingency of *ceteris paribus* is not understood. The partial and temporary closures are constructed using judgement about what is appropriate and/or useful, and judgement tends to be underdeveloped in the young and inexperienced (at least they have an excuse). There are no demonstrable proofs. Internal consistency may also be (will be in the case of macroeconomics) lacking, because of the need to make compromises. On what criteria are students supposed to judge the results? Finally, they are expected to sustain various ambiguities, to work somewhere between perfect knowledge and total ignorance, to accept apparent contradictions, to think in terms of both/and instead of either/or (what determines investment: cold calculation or animal spirits? – both (Dow and Dow 1985)). All this goes against the Cartesian mode of thought which has dominated Western thinking for a very long time (Dow 1996) and is bound to create anxiety (Gordon 2003).[6]

There are some explanations of the resistance to open systems in the psychological and education literature, of which I single out four: Rokeach's (1960) study of the structure of the belief systems held by open and closed minds; Rotheim (2002) on the question of time; Perry's work on the levels of maturity of students, as reported in Earl (2000); and Maslow's work on the structure of needs and the self-actualising personality (many works, but here mainly 1968).

Open systems are created by open minds and require open minds to understand them. I take the following characterisation from Rokeach (1960). What follows sounds like a sharp dichotomy but is in fact a matter of degree. As a 'primitive' (primary?) belief, the closed mind perceives the outside world as hostile, threatening, the open mind as friendly. Although we all rely on external authority to tell us more about the world than we can experience directly, the belief that the world is threatening is responsible for the closed mind's conflation of the source of information and the information itself. Authority for them, in the learning context as elsewhere, depends on the ability to mete out reward and punishment. Knowledge thus imparted by the subject's authority figures is taken as a 'package' that the subject cannot dismantle into its components, making it difficult, if not impossible, to evaluate particular ideas on their merits. New ideas that do not conform to her/his belief structure are either rejected or modified to fit in to that structure. The border between her/his belief system and the rejected contents (what might be called the disbelief system) is strong, impermeable. The closed mind will choose to learn about her/his disbelief system from representatives of her/his belief system. (Rokeach gives the example of a Baptist learning about Roman Catholicism from fellow Baptists rather than consulting Roman Catholic sources; it is easy to think of the economics equivalent, in particular the preference among students for secondary rather than primary sources.)

Openness can be characterised by the degree to which a person can react to relevant information from outside her/his belief system on its own intrinsic merits, without contamination. The extent of rejection of the disbelief system is less for the open minded, so new information, if considered valuable, is assimilated not by distorting the information to fit but by altering the belief system. The borders of the belief system are permeable.

The attitude to time is perhaps the most striking of Rokeach's conclusions. Closed minds have a narrow, future-orientated time perspective, while in open minds the past, present and future are all represented and seen as related. He reasons:

> To evaluate information on its own merits is necessarily to be oriented with both feet in the here and now. . . . [Evaluation] implies a disciplined concern with the immediate, foreseeable future. . . . [A] restraint is placed upon knowing the distant future, since it cannot, by its very nature, be known. . . . [This restraint] is lifted if a person cannot or will not evaluate information on its own merits. Thus, in closed [belief] systems, the main cognitive basis is missing from the distinction between the immediate and remote future. Knowledge about the remote future is impossible to refute and, hence, one can be safely preoccupied with it. (1960, pp. 63–4)

One is strikingly reminded of the different treatment of long- and short-term expectations in *The General Theory*, and of the complete lack of coherence between the short and long 'runs' of much neoclassical theory.

Rotheim (2002) develops this theme. He puts together the escape from the present and the perception of a threatening world – a connection which Rokeach did not exploit. The person with a closed mind wants to get out of the present as quickly as possible. 'Not being able to focus on the present moment causes one to lose the ability for generating knowledge from the inside. . . . With an internally generated sense of self . . . [one can] safely experience ambiguity, uncertainty and openness' (p. 69).

Rokeach's and Rotheim's characterisations seem static, reflecting the importance of childhood experience in the formation of personality. If character were so fixed, about all the teacher could do is identify the students to whom open systems will make sense and those to whom it will not. But hope is at hand: Rokeach speaks of learners becoming 'more and more open in their belief systems' (1960, p. 65).

A description of progression from closed to more open forms of learning is found in Perry's stages of student maturation, here summarised from Earl (2000):

- Stage 1: Dualism. Students see everything in dualistic terms: black/white, right/wrong, true/false. The teacher imparts Truth. Their concept of learning is to memorise facts. They see no value in student discussions, as students have no authority. Teachers who do not give clear answers are either incompetent in their subject or bad teachers.
- Stage 2: Dualism questioned. Students have been exposed to different points of view but they assume that one view is right and the other wrong. They might compare two views but cannot analyse why they differ.
- Stage 3: Multiplicity, for the moment. They observe that there are many views but believe that the experts will eventually sort out the confusion. If experts can disagree for so long, are they really experts?
- Stage 4: Anything goes? If teachers don't know the Truth, then perhaps students' views are as good as theirs. As they become more challenging, they may begin to see the value placed on supporting views with reasons.
- Stage 5: Relativism. Begin to see the importance of other points of view. Teachers are viewed as guides to critical thinking. They begin to value feedback.
- Stage 6: Commitments to personal viewpoints. Knowledge is relative, but what should students believe? They begin to argue their corner yet they are open to change.

Stages 1–3 are concerned with the closed thinker; the later stages show the emergence of greater openness. Earl was concerned in his article to prevent a mis-match between teaching methods and student maturity and to make concrete suggestions for pushing students up the Perry stages a little faster than they might go unaided. It is an enormously valuable article. Perhaps it can be deepened just a little by capitalising on the work of Maslow.

Maslow's most famous contribution is to describe a hierarchy of needs that emerges from the earliest stages of life – physiological and safety needs, social needs and the need for self-esteem arise successively. These are urgent, but once life is organised to provide for these needs, the process of 'self-actualisation' or 'self-realisation' can proceed. It is evident that part of the explanation for the reliance on authority which characterises the closed mind can arise in childhood, while the first two sets of needs are being met by parents and other authority figures. Social and esteem needs are probably still very high on most university students' agenda. If only good academic performance were seen as contributing to the student's sense of self-esteem!

University and the work-place are usually the first places where 'finding oneself' becomes an issue. They may even be the first places where self-actualisation becomes feasible, as the student is out of the orbit of parents and other early authorities, but they may transfer their need for authority onto us, their lecturers and tutors. In terms of Perry's scheme, they do not shed their reliance on authority until Stage 5. Indeed within the terms of the scheme, Earl's main pedagogic suggestion, to offer copious feedback on essays and past examination questions, while very desirable, will only really work on Stage 4+ students.

Let us look at the dynamic problem as seen by Maslow. A person is always poised between the potential for growth and the desire for safety. Growth, by definition, involves moving away from safety, reaching into the unknown. The impetus for growth is curiosity, and satisfying curiosity requires work. It is rewarded by delight (I cannot believe that a student who has felt the penny drop when something has been truly understood would not like to revisit the experience), the discovery of new connections, and mastery of new actions or ideas. The student develops confidence, judgement and self-esteem. But curiosity, the driving force, is self-motivated; it is not something teachers can demand or instil. All we can do is demand that they work, whether motivated by curiosity or the threat of examinations.

There are powerful forces inhibiting personal growth. The other attractor is safety, to which people are drawn by fear. Growth involves change of an unknown sort. To choose growth therefore requires courage, which can be inhibited by feelings of inadequacy, or even the sense that one is venturing into forbidden territory (Maslow here invokes the story of the forbidden Tree of Knowledge).[7] Better to leave well alone, stay where we feel certain. For the closed personality, s/he may fear losing the approval of her/his authority figures. S/he is orientated towards pleasing them, not her/himself, following their instructions, not her/his own wishes or instincts. Increased knowledge may also be a threat to one's (childhood) authority/safety figures; we all know parents who fear their children growing up and overtaking them, a phenomenon sometimes replicated in relations between older and younger academics. Finally there is the levelling influence of peer pressure not to work, not to be teacher's pet, to be one of the crowd, and so on.

Without sufficient safety, embarking on growth is impossible. We cannot do anything about students' backgrounds; we have to start with material which is formed already, whether well or badly. The trick is to give a feeling of safety sufficient to allow growth without reinforcing the dualistic approach, while giving positive encouragement to growth. Of course to Stage 1–2 students 'sufficient safety' means spoon-feeding, and I am not suggesting that. And if one's students have already been indoctrinated with closed-system approaches – the usual situation in most economics departments – safety may mean starting from there, so the project is half-sunk before it starts.

I don't know how to turn the trick, but I offer some observations. Obviously, the safety of certainty is reinforced by teaching closed models and mathematical proofs. The tendency to appeal to authority is reinforced by problem-solving assignments: there is only one right answer and the setter knows what it is. Multiple choice tests and short-answer questions have the same fault. Coursework which counts towards the final mark encourages the flight to safety and discourages experiment and originality. The semester system, with its frequent examinations, leaves no time for understanding to develop and connections to be made. All these reinforcements are currently popular, some of them for resource reasons. Strained resources also dictate using graduate student teaching assistants, who are more likely to be at earlier stages of development themselves.

The crucial matter, probably, is getting students to see that they are responsible for their own learning. The Oxbridge system is quite good at that, but my lack of deep knowledge of the system means my remarks are directed elsewhere. A factor reinforcing the role of authority is that we set up the hoops we expect students to jump through. Why not ask students to formulate their own questions for essays? Are we afraid they would set something too easy? (There are logistical problems of course; the essays would have to come towards the end of the course.)

Trying to get students to listen to each other and ask each other questions, I have put a student in charge of running 'tutorials' (classes of about ten students) and tried to play the observer role from the back of the room. This was only moderately successful: they didn't have enough practice with it to break the mould. I have had students mark each others' papers, which they found embarrassing[8] but was somewhat useful. And I have insisted that students use at least one source not given in the reading list and material from at least three authors. (When I first came to UCL we didn't give reading lists; students were expected to find their own way round the library!) The Stage 1–3 students chose textbooks, which was rather dispiriting, but some of the others stumbled on great books and enjoyed them. Almost none chose the sensible route of following up references. (Why? What element is missing from their understanding about how knowledge is built up?)

The most important elements, however, must be the strategy adopted by Earl, of giving frequent feedback (coupled, I should say, by the student re-writing and re-submitting the work) and having long enough between examinations to allow understanding to mature.

CONCLUSION

The person who wishes to teach open-system theory faces an uphill battle. There are three groups of forces ranged against the enterprise: the hegemony of closed systems, current views on education and the resource situation in universities, leaving aside the vital matter of early personality-formation. But there is one pressure in our favour: the disaffection with economics as shown in applications and, in some places, admissions. If economics is to regain respect, it must, in my view, re-engage with the world, which means, broadly speaking, rejecting closed-system theorising in favour of open systems. As Rotheim (2002) has pointed out on the matter of openness to time, open-system thinking is not widely available. A pessimist would say that the odds are overwhelmingly against success, and after writing this chapter I am tempted to agree. But to give up and teach what is in the text-books is, I argue, to court failure in another way: the further loss of interest in the subject. It is difficult to predict what will happen to economics as an academic subject if it continues along its present path: its future is open. All we can do is to try, against the odds, to teach open systems in an open-minded way, and hope to open the minds of our students.

NOTES

* Acknowledgements: I am grateful for comments from Sheila Dow and Mogens Ove Madsen. I owe a general debt to Mearman (2002).

1. www.paecon.net/HistoryPAE.htm. Accessed 1 March 2013.
2. Read their open letter here: http://hpronline.org/harvard/an-open-letter-to-greg-mankiw/. Accessed 1 March 2013.
3. www.societies.cam.ac.uk/csep/. Accessed 1 March 2013.
4. By path dependency I do not just mean lock-in but the broader concept of systems in which the initial conditions of each period are determined by what happened in the previous period. It includes hysteresis and cumulative causation, for example.
5. Setterfield (2003) calls this the Open System *Ceteris Paribus* (OSCP) method.
6. I am indebted to Sheila Dow for this reference.
7. A student came to see me, saying she thought economics was not for her – this in her final year. A long, meandering exploration followed, from which eventually I thought I sensed what was really at issue: 'Are you telling me that for the first time you have understood that you're being asked to think for yourself, and you feel inadequate to the task?' She thought a long time and said, 'Yes, I suppose that is what I'm saying.' I replied that, though my response might seem odd to her, if that was what was bothering her it was the best news I'd had for months. I could then reassure her: of course she felt inadequate; this was new territory for her, but it would become familiar with practice.

8. It seems they didn't mind submitting shoddy work to me but were upset that fellow students would see it.

REFERENCES

Chick, V. (1983) *Macroeconomics After Keynes: A Reconsideration of the General Theory*, Cambridge, MA: MIT Press.

Chick, V. (1986) 'The evolution of the banking system and the theory of saving, investment and interest', *Economies et societes*, Cahiers de l'ISMEA, Serie 'Monnaie et Production', no. 3, 111–26.

Chick, V. (1998) 'A struggle to escape: equilibrium in *The General Theory*', in S. Sharma, ed., *John Maynard Keynes: Keynesianism into the Twenty-First Century*, Aldershot: Edward Elgar Publishing, pp. 40–50.

Chick, V. (2002) 'Keynes's theory of investment and necessary compromise', in S.C. Dow and J. Hillard, eds, *Beyond Keynes*, Vol. 2: *Keynes, Uncertainty and the Global Economy*, Cheltenham: Edward Elgar Publishing, pp. 55–67.

Chick, V. and S.C. Dow (2001) 'Formalism, logic and reality: a Keynesian analysis', *Cambridge Journal of Economics*, 25 (6), November, pp. 705–22. Reprinted in G.M. Hodgson, ed., *Mathematics and Modern Economics*, Cheltenham: Edward Elgar Publishing, 2012, and under its original title, 'The non-neutrality of formalism', in S.C. Dow, *Foundations for New Economic Thinking*, Basingstoke: Palgrave Macmillan, 2012.

Chick, V. and S.C. Dow (2005) 'The meaning of open systems', *Journal of Economic Methodology*, 12 (3), September, pp. 363–81. Reprinted as Chapter 11 in S.C. Dow, *Foundations for New Economic Thinking*, Basingstoke: Palgrave Macmillan, 2012. Page quoted in text refers to original.

Davidson, P. (2003–4) 'Setting the record straight on a history of Post Keynesian economics', *Journal of Post Keynesian Economics*, 26 (2), 245–72.

Davidson, P. (2005) 'Responses to Lavoie, King, and Dow', *Journal of Post Keynesian Economics*, 26 (3), 393–408.

Denis, A. and J. Toporowski, eds, 'Symposium on microfoundations', *Journal of Economic Methodology*, forthcoming.

Dow, S.C. (1996) *The Methodology of Macroeconomic Thought*, Cheltenham: Edward Elgar Publishing.

Dow, S.C. (2002) *Economic Methodology: An Inquiry*, Oxford: Oxford University Press.

Dow, S.C. (2005) 'Axioms and Babylonian thought: a reply', *Journal of Post Keynesian Economics*, 27 (3), 383–9.

Dow, A. and S.C. Dow (1985) 'Animal spirits and rationality', in T. Lawson and H. Pesaran, eds, *Keynes' Economics: Methodological Issues*, Armonk, NY: M. E. Sharpe.

Earl, P.E. (2000) 'Indeterminacy in the economics classroom', in P.E. Earl and S.F. Frowen, eds, *Economics as an Art of Thought: Essays in Memory of G. L. S. Shackle*, London: Routledge, pp. 25–50. Revised version in E. Fullbrook (ed.), *Pluralist Economics*, London: Zed Books, 2008, pp. 193–214.

Gilbert, J.C. (1982) *Keynes's Impact on Monetary Economics*, London: Butterworth.

Gordon, K. (2003) 'The impermanence of being: toward a psychology of uncertainty', *Journal of Humanistic Psychology*, 43 (3), 96–117.

Hayek, F.A. (1931) 'Reflections on the pure theory of money of Mr J.M. Keynes', *Economica*, 34 (August), 270–95.
Hicks, J.R. (1976) 'Some questions of time in economics', in A.M. Tang, F.M. Westfield and J.S. Worley (eds), *Evolution, Welfare and Time in Economics*, Lexington, MA: Lexington Books. Reprinted in Hicks, *Money, Interest and Wages: Collected Essays on Economic Theory*, Vol. II, Oxford: Blackwell, 1982, pp. 282–300.
Ingham, G. (2004) *The Nature of Money*, Cambridge: Polity Press.
Jespersen, J. (2009) *Macroeconomic Methodology: A Post-Keynesian Perspective*, Cheltenham: Edward Elgar Publishing.
Keynes, J.M. (1931) 'The pure theory of money: a reply to Dr Hayek', *Economica*, 34 (November), 387–97. Reprinted in *The Collected Writings of J.M. Keynes*, Vol. XIII, London: Macmillan, pp. 243–56. Page quoted in text refers to reprint.
Keynes, J.M. (1936) *The General Theory of Employment, Interest and Money*, London: Macmillan.
King, J.E. (2012) *The Microfoundations Delusion: Metaphor and Dogma in the History of Macroeconomics*, Cheltenham: Edward Elgar Publishing.
Kregel, J.A. (1976) 'Economic methodology in the face of uncertainty: the modelling methods of Keynes and the Post-Keynesians', *Economic Journal*, 86 (June), 209–25.
Lawson, T. (1997) *Economics and Reality*, London: Routledge.
Lawson, T. (2002) 'Mathematical formalism in economics: what really is the problem?', in P. Arestis, M. Desai and S.C. Dow, eds, *Methodology, Microeconomics and Keynes*, London: Routledge, pp.73–83.
Loasby, B.J. (2003) 'Closed models and open systems', *Journal of Economic Methodology*, 10 (3), 285–306.
Maslow, A.H. (1968) *Toward a Psychology of Being*, 2nd edition, New York: van Nostrand Reinholt.
Mearman, A. (2002) 'A Contribution to the Methodology of Post Keynesian Economics', PhD thesis, University of Leeds.
Robbins, L.C. (1932) *An Essay on the Nature and Significance of Economic Science*, London: Macmillan.
Robinson, J. (1932) *Economics is a Serious Subject*, Cambridge: Heffer and Son.
Robinson, J. (1978) 'Introduction – 1978'. in *The Generalisation of the General Theory and other Essays*, London: Macmillan, 1979.
Rokeach, M. (1960) *The Open and Closed Mind*, New York: Basic Books.
Rotheim, R. (2002) 'Timeful theories, timeful economists', in P. Arestis, M. Desai and S.C. Dow, eds, *Methodology, Microeconomics and Keynes*, London: Routledge, pp. 62–72.
Setterfield, M. (1993) 'Toward a long-run theory of effective demand', *Journal of Post Keynesian Economics*, 15 (3), 347–54.
Setterfield, M. (1999) 'Expectations, path dependency and effective demand', *Journal of Post Keynesian Economics*, 21 (3), 479–501.
Setterfield, M. (2003) 'Critical realism and formal modelling: incompatible bedfellows?', in P. Downward, ed., *Applied Economics and the Critical Realist Critique*, London: Routledge, pp. 71–88.
Shackle, G.L.S. (1967) *The Years of High Theory*, Cambridge: Cambridge University Press.
Shackle, G.L.S. (1970) *Expectations, Enterprise and Profit*, New York, NY: George Allen and Unwin.

Shackle, G.L.S. (1979) *Imagination and the Nature of Choice*, Edinburgh: Edinburgh University Press.
Skott, P. (1989) *Conflict and Effective Demand in Economic Growth*, Cambridge: Cambridge University Press.
Tuckett, D. (2011) *Minding the Markets*, Basingstoke: Palgrave Macmillan.

4. Teaching open-system economics[1]

Sheila Dow

INTRODUCTION

The urgency of the need to address the financial and economic crisis which began in 2007 has encouraged public discussion of Keynesian theory and policy. The focus has almost exclusively been on Keynes's views on the role of fiscal policy in addressing deficient aggregate demand. Given the inattention in the mainstream literature in recent decades to fiscal policy, and even more to Keynes, this is a remarkable development. It is to be hoped that the economics curriculum adapts in order to introduce students to Keynes and Keynesian policy.

But this renewed interest in Keynes is very selective, being confined to what Coddington (1976) characterised as 'hydraulic Keynesianism'. This approach was contrasted with what he called 'fundamentalist Keynesianism', which drew much more extensively on Keynes's work and particularly on his views on uncertainty, within his theory of knowledge. Many Keynesians in the 'fundamentalist' mould have drawn attention to the wider importance of Keynes's theory of knowledge, not only in order to explain the crisis, but also to suggest policy solutions (for example, Skidelsky 2009). But this wider focus on Keynes has not penetrated the mainstream discourse, with the notable exception of Stiglitz (2010), who addressed it only to dismiss it.

The limited understanding of Keynes among mainstream economists can be understood in terms of what makes sense and what does not within their approach to economics. The distinction between hydraulic Keynesianism and fundamentalist Keynesianism corresponds roughly to the distinction between closed-system thinking and open-system thinking, respectively.[2] Hydraulic Keynesianism made sense from the perspective of the neo-classical synthesis, such that debate between Keynesians and monetarists could be conducted within a common IS–LM framework. So a discussion of fiscal policy now in terms of macroeconomic relations which are treated as known (within probability distributions) and stable makes sense within the mainstream closed-system approach. To take on board the wider, 'fundamentalist' understanding of Keynes requires a different, open-system framework.

This requirement to consider frameworks poses challenges, not only for communicating with economists trained in the closed-system approach, but also for teaching students. The purpose of this chapter is to consider the challenges particularly for teaching, but these are closely related to the challenges for the profession as a whole. The discussion starts by reviewing the nature and implications of a closed-system approach and an open-system approach to economics. We then focus in on the ways in which society copes with being an open system and how economists address the resulting uncertainty. This provides the basis for considering how students react to different ways of teaching about the economy. The chapter concludes with a consideration of teaching according to an open-system approach, drawing on my own experience.

CLOSED AND OPEN SYSTEMS

Following Adam Smith, it is conventional to understand the economy as some kind of system; without some systemic features, it would be impossible to make any theoretical statements about the economy. Following Smith, too, knowledge about the economy in turn is also generally understood as a system (Loasby 2003). It has become conventional to understand mainstream economics as taking a closed-system approach to knowledge while heterodox economics takes an open-system approach (see further Jespersen 2009: ch. 5). A closed-system approach has been shown to require that the subject matter is so systematic as to yield law-like generalisations, while an open-system approach aims rather for conclusions as to tendencies which may vary (in potentiality and in actuality) between contexts (Lawson 2003).

Chick and Dow (2005: 367) set out the conditions which must all be satisfied in a closed-system theoretical approach, as shown in Table 4.1.

An open system is not the dual of a closed system since there are many possibilities for open systems. A system is open if *any one* of the conditions for a closed theoretical system is not met. Thus within non-mainstream economics there is a range of schools of thought according to how the (open) social system is understood. Chick and Dow (2005: 366) list the possibilities for openness of the social system itself, as shown in Table 4.2.

Recognising openness in the economic system has profound implications for theoretical systems, listed by Chick and Dow (2005: 366) as shown in Table 4.3.

Table 4.1 Conditions for closed theoretical systems

1. All relevant variables can be identified.
2. The boundaries of the system are definite and immutable; it follows that it is clear which variables are exogenous and which are endogenous; these categories are fixed.
3. Only the specified exogenous variables affect the system, and they do this in a known way.
4. Relations between the included variables are either knowable or random.
5. Economic agents (whether individuals or aggregates) are treated atomistically.
6. The nature of economic agents is treated as if constant.
7. The structure of the relationships between the components (variables, subsystems, agents) is treated as if it is either knowable or random.
8. The structural framework within which agents act is taken as given.

Table 4.2 The conditions, any one being satisfied means that a system is open

1. The system is not atomistic; therefore at least one of the following holds:
   a. outcomes of actions cannot be inferred from individual actions (because of interactions);
   b. agents and their interactions may change (for example, agents may learn).
2. Structure and agency are interdependent.
3. Boundaries around and within the social or economic system are mutable; for at least one of the following reasons:
   a. social structures may evolve;
   b. connections between structures may change;
   c. the structure–agent relation may change.
4. Identifiable social structures are embedded in larger structures; these may mutually interact, for the boundaries of a social system are in general partial or semi-permeable.

Table 4.3 The consequences of economic openness for theoretical systems

1. There may be important omitted variables or relations and/or their effects on the system may be uncertain.
2. The classification into exogenous and endogenous variables may be neither fixed nor exhaustive.
3. Connections and/or boundaries between structures may be imperfectly known and/or may change.
4. There is imperfect knowledge of the relations between variables; relationships may not be stable.

Thus open systems of knowledge, like the subject matter, evolve and are therefore provisional. Being permeable, they are open to inputs from other disciplines. Perhaps of greatest importance, however, is that they are subject to uncertainty and require the exercise of judgement.

Closed-system economics is based on classical logic, which deduces propositions on the basis of a chain of reasoning starting from premises which are taken to be true. It is based on deductivist mathematics, with propositions tested against what are taken to be independent facts. The result is a system which is aesthetically appealing in its simple logic and its certain conclusions. The focus is on the quality of the logical reasoning and the robustness of empirical testing. There is a requirement that all argument be expressed in terms of formal deductivist mathematical logic, such that internal consistency of reasoning can be ensured. Further mathematisation in this way renders all arguments commensurate; mathematics is regarded as a neutral language which allows all arguments to be considered together within the overall logical system.

But if the economy is an open system then any representation in terms of deductivist mathematics severely limits what can be addressed; mathematical expression is not neutral (Chick and Dow 2001). An open system calls for a different kind of logic: human or ordinary logic. This is better suited to material where the premises themselves are subject to uncertainty and where different chains of reasoning may be applied to different premises, depending on the problem at hand. This is the logic which Keynes (1921) analysed as the general case for philosophers (economists) and society alike. It involves drawing on a range of sources and types of knowledge, including conventional understandings, in order to build up a picture. The more these different stands of argument support a particular conclusion, the greater is the weight of argument. This is a pluralist approach to argument. The starting point for Keynes's exploration of how we form grounds for belief as a basis for action was that the scope for certain knowledge (that is, closed-system knowledge based on classical logic) is very limited. Nevertheless we can function by means of human logic, although the conclusions are not demonstrably definitive.

A closed-system approach poses tremendous challenges in its application to an open-system economy. Experience shows however that, within mainstream economics, internal consistency is given higher methodological priority than applicability to the real world. Empirical testing has not proved to be definitive as a criterion for applicability, for good reasons (including the Duhem–Quine thesis[3]). The challenges of open-system thinking however are internal to the methodology and therefore cannot be avoided.

THE CHALLENGE OF OPEN-SYSTEM THINKING

Closed-system thinking has an aesthetic appeal, but also a psychological appeal because of the certainty (or certainty-equivalence) attached to conclusions. The uncertainty of open-system thinking prevents the building up of an aesthetically appealing closed system. The different strands of argument and types of evidence are inevitably incommensurate, since otherwise they could be reformulated into a closed system. But the consideration of these different arguments and evidence together in order to form a view requires the exercise of judgement. Inevitably any view will still be partial, starting from some understanding of the economy or another and employing some range of methods or another. There is no basis for a single best conclusion, but we can argue for the merits of the conclusions which follow from our own approach relative to alternative approaches. The decision as to how best to establish a policy proposal, for example, must be based on persuasion.

By comparison with closed-system thinking, an open-system approach is conditioned by uncertainty and this is uncomfortable. While, therefore, a closed-system approach poses technical challenges, an open-system approach poses much more complex challenges. But, whereas closed-system thinking faces the potential challenge of addressing an open-system subject matter, open-system thinking is specifically designed for such a purpose. While mainstream economics is presented as being rigorous, this refers to its internal logic; open-system theory is rigorous in the different sense of its logical relations with the subject matter.

Since uncertainty is the norm in an open system, society has evolved mechanisms and structures to deal with it. The formation of institutions of various kinds can be understood as addressing the need for reducing uncertainty – as to property rights and their enforcement, for example. Money evolves through the development of banking systems in order to provide an asset of relatively certain value to hold in times of particular uncertainty about the value of other assets. Central banks develop mechanisms to promote more confidence in the banking system and thus in money. Production is organised in firms and commerce in organised markets. Work, borrowing and lending are all organised according to contracts. Within these forms of organisation, practices such as price stickiness and habitual behaviour are constraints in a closed-system model. But in an open-system world they put limits on outcomes and thus on uncertainty, facilitating action.

Within these structures, and given these practices, knowledge is also organised in such a way as to address uncertainty. Keynes (1937) argues that, given the limits to which reason and evidence can provide grounds for belief in an open system, they are supplemented by conventional beliefs born of long experience, expert judgement and extrapolation from the past. In everyday life, therefore, we employ a pluralist strategy with respect to building knowledge under uncertainty.

For the discussion to follow below about the teaching of economics, what is particularly important is the question of how expert opinion – the opinion of academic economists – is formed. Here the general approach is the same, that beliefs are formed by means of a pluralist strategy. McCloskey (1983) has shown that even those professing a closed-system approach in their 'official discourse' will employ a range of arguments in their 'unofficial discourse' (including the less formal aspects of teaching). But the official discourse within mainstream economics is centred on formal deductivist mathematics. Deductivist models are taken to encapsulate the essence of theory. When the results of these models are contradicted by evidence, the response is to try to develop a better model. Of course in practice it is normally very difficult to be definitive as to contradictory evidence. But a crisis situation which was not predicted by a model, for whatever reason, is hard to ignore. Nevertheless it is remarkable how tenacious is the continuing hold of mainstream methodology in spite of the current crisis, such that the closed-system approach has not been supplanted.

The closed-system approach itself sets the framework by which the experience of crisis is addressed. Being dualistic, the framework specifies what is known (or knowable) with certainty. Everything else is outside the system, classified equally as uncertainty or ignorance or irrationality. This goes beyond the category of random shocks, since the knowledge of randomness is held with certainty. There have been many analyses of the basis for the mainstream approach, such as physics envy. But the fact that fundamental uncertainty continues to be absent from the mainstream approach, in spite of the palpable uncertainty spawned by crisis conditions, implies that there may also be some psychological aversion to contemplating uncertainty. In contrast, the importance of uncertainty to much of heterodox economics, and especially to Post Keynesian economics, indicates a willingness to engage with it. Indeed the plurality of open-system approaches within heterodox economics may be understood partly in terms of varying attitudes to uncertainty. Those that focus on creativity for example will see particularly the positive side of uncertainty arising from the unforeseen possibilities resulting from creativity. Others prefer their knowledge of the economy to focus more on structure and thus on minimising uncertainty.

Each open-system approach has developed a methodology on the basis of a particular understanding of the economy, so that each methodology draws on a particular range of methods. Part of a pluralist strategy which seeks some structure may thus include formal models, which are small closed systems. But this closure within an open theoretical system is very different from the fixed, universal closure of mainstream economics. It is the provisional, partial closure involved in segmenting the subject matter for purposes of analysis. The process of segmentation and then of application of its results by unwinding segmentation was best put by Keynes (1936: 297–8):

> The object of our analysis is, not to provide a machine, or method of blind manipulation, which will furnish an infallible answer, but to provide ourselves with an organised and orderly method of thinking out particular problems; and, after we have reached a provisional conclusion by isolating the complicating factors one by one, we then have to go back on ourselves and allow, as well as we can, for the probable interactions of the factors amongst themselves. This is the nature of economic thinking. Any other way of applying our formal principles of thought (without which we would be lost in the wood) will lead us into error. It is a great fault of symbolic pseudo-mathematical methods of formalising a system of economic analysis . . . that they expressly assume strict independence between the factors involved and lose all their cogency and authority if this hypothesis is disallowed; whereas, in ordinary discourse, where we are not blindly manipulating but know all the time what we are doing and what the words mean, we can keep 'at the back of our heads' the necessary reserves and qualifications and the adjustments which we shall have to make later on, in a way in which we cannot keep complicated partial differentials 'at the back' of several pages of algebra which assume they all vanish.

We have touched on structures and mechanisms employed to address uncertainty, but they cannot eliminate uncertainty. Crisis periods in particular challenge conventional judgements, expert opinion and the past as a guide to the future. Confidence in institutions and practices may be eroded. The outcome is a marked increase in uncertainty. But the response of non-mainstream economists differs from that of mainstream economists. Rather than the mainstream duality of certainty–uncertainty/ignorance, uncertainty is understood to be a matter of degree. Theory of stable periods will already have incorporated uncertainty, particularly if, as in Minsky's (1986) theory of financial instability, instability is the product of stability. While existing theories may be challenged, the expectation is that new circumstances will require theory adaptation. While these changed circumstances might include new institutional arrangements and practices, there will already have been an understanding of the institutions and practices which predated the crisis. This kind of understanding is precluded by the deductivist mathematical approach (such that mainstream money-macro theory before the crisis did not include banks or, in some cases, money). A new situation could call forth a range of competing explanations and theories on which to base policy solutions, drawing on different approaches. Recognising this as the norm, pluralist non-mainstream economists have enough understanding of different approaches to engage in constructive debate.

In order to pursue this open-system approach, economists require a range of skills, background knowledge, methodological awareness and the capacity for judgement to put together a plurality of analyses in order to formulate opinions and policy recommendations. Keynes (1924: 173–4) put it as follows, in his essay on Marshall:

> [T]he master-economist must possess a rare *combination* of gifts. He must reach a high standard in several different directions and must combine talents not often found together. He must be mathematician, historian, statesman, philosopher – in some degree. He must understand symbols and speak in words. He must contemplate the particular in terms of the general, and touch abstract and concrete in the same flight of thought. He must study the present in the light of the past for the purposes of the future. No part of man's nature or his institutions must lie entirely outside his regard.

The challenge of meeting Keynes's requirements, compared to the requirements of a deductivist mathematical system, were spelled out in his report of a conversation with Planck (Keynes 1924: 186n):

> Professor Planck, of Berlin, the famous originator of the Quantum Theory, once remarked to me that in early life he had thought of studying economics, but had found it too difficult! Professor Planck could easily master the whole corpus of mathematical economics in a few days. He did not mean that! But the amalgam of logic and intuition and the wide knowledge of facts, most of which are not precise, which is required for economic interpretation in its highest form is, quite truly, overwhelmingly difficult for those whose gift mainly consists in the power to imagine and pursue to their furthest points the implications and prior conditions of comparatively simple facts which are known with a high degree of precision.

It is a challenge for practising economists to meet Keynes's requirements. But acquiring such skills should be the focus of economics teaching. In many ways the challenges for the practising open-system economist in a discipline dominated by closed-system thinking carry forward into teaching, since they relate specifically to issues of communication and persuasion. But the challenges take on a particular form when considering how to design an open-system economics programme. We turn to consider these challenges for teaching in the next section.

THE CHALLENGE FOR TEACHING

How we approach the challenges of teaching economics depends on our approach to economics. Teaching conveys knowledge not just about models and theories but also about understandings of the real world and about ways of building knowledge. Education was something which Kuhn (1962) discussed, focusing on the role of exemplars in propagating a particular paradigm. A closed-system approach conveys knowledge about a bounded set of models, built deductively from axioms taken to be true, yielding propositions which can be demonstrated with certainty to be true. There may be competing models and theories, but the expectation is that it is feasible to arrive at a conclusion as to which is best. Econometrics courses teach students how to reach such conclusions by empirical testing. Applied courses apply the chosen models to policy questions, again with the expectation that one policy solution can be demonstrated to be best. This approach to teaching puts bounds on what students need to know and puts the emphasis on the acquisition of technical skills which for many students pose the greatest challenge.

An open-system approach in contrast leaves the subject matter open-ended, not least since it is expected to evolve over time but also because it includes contextual detail and does not raise the prospect of demonstrable proof with respect either to theory or policy. The challenge for students, then, is to learn not only a large body of material but also the art of judgement. Open-system learning thus develops different skills from closed-system learning. Students perceived to be weaker (in technical capacities) tend to be recommended to take non-technical courses as being easier for them. But generally, in my experience, they have found such courses much more difficult.

Which is the more challenging depends on the interests of the students, as well as on their prior training and psychological make-up. Both approaches purport to address real-world problems and offer some guidance as to how to address them. But, in practice, closed-system economics prioritises teaching technical skills over applicability, something which has been found to cause concern among US graduate students (Colander and Klamer 1987). If students are interested in real-world applicability of theory then they will be more motivated to take on the challenges of open-system thinking than the technical challenges of the closed-system approach. Further, just like practising economists, some students come to the subject with prior psychological leanings towards closed-system thinking or open-system thinking. Chick (2003) applies Rokeach's (1960) notion of open minds and closed minds to economics and economics education.

But the education process itself influences students' capacities for open-system thinking. Chick draws on Earl's (2000) application to economics education of the framework developed by the psychologist Perry (1970). Perry argued that disposition evolves with education through a series of levels, ranging from the dualism of closed systems up to the level at which students are able and willing to commit to one of the many approaches on offer. To this framework Chick adds Maslow's (1968) hierarchy of needs, with the first need being the need for security; closed-system thinking, with its clear bounds and demonstrable conclusions, provides just such security. We would therefore expect a progression of increasing capabilities for open-system thinking as education proceeds.

There are particular difficulties however in effectively starting with a closed-system view of the world and a methodology to match if the goal is to educate within an open-system approach. To this is added the complication of some members of teaching staff continuing with a closed-system approach as students progress through the programme. Earl (2000) and Chick (2003) offer a range of useful ideas as to how to address these difficulties. In what follows, I will draw some provisional conclusions from my own experience of teaching economics.

First I would argue for consistency in the broad approach taken to economics. The need for security in the early stages of economics education, combined with the need to take things one step at a time, means that it is useful to employ simple models. This is controversial among open-systems economists who embrace higher degrees of openness. Models do entail some closure (even if the closure is permeable and provisional), by abstracting from other factors. But their use is a compatible method within some open-system, pluralist methodologies (Chick and Dow 2005). But in any case economists have to be able to operate within a discipline which most economists identify exclusively with models and therefore they have to be able to engage on the subject of models, even if to argue against their use. What is important is that it be made clear to students that all models are only partial contributors to any discussion and assume away a lot of important factors which will be discussed elsewhere. It is in my view damaging to students' confidence in their education to present models at the start as if they produce demonstrably true conclusions, only later on to reject them as false, replacing them with more complex models as those which are really the best, again to be replaced at the graduate level.

In my view, therefore, the teaching of any models should be embedded in a broader discussion of the factors left out by the model in order to teach how models can be useful, but also to demonstrate their limitations. While models should not be the centrepiece of economics education, inevitably safety-seeking early learners will tend to concentrate on them.

Further, early teaching limits how much can be addressed. The simplest way to conduct pluralist analysis at a basic level is to address a topical issue which inevitably applies to a particular context, thus limiting the extent of relevant detail. Since students will be aware (or can be encouraged to become aware) of different views on topical questions, they can learn how to go about assessing the relative merits of different views.

This type of discussion also gradually introduces students to the fact of differing perspectives within economics and to the skills required to address them. A closed-system approach involves teaching theories or models as 'correct' or 'best', even if alternatives are taught first in order then to be rejected.[4] This dualistic practice of rejection is one which has invaded much of the general economics discourse. But it is not the only option: Chick (1995) explains three other possible reactions to difference: containment, paradox and synthesis. Closed-system thinking leads to the familiar 'I'm right – you're wrong' way of handling difference, such that argument is confused with hostility. It turns out that 'argument' is yet another word whose meaning depends on whether a closed-system approach is being taken or an open-system approach. Within an open-system approach critical argument is simply the normal way for social scientists to proceed in debate over different approaches which draws on reason and evidence. There is no need for it to be hostile. Rather, argument is how constructive exchange proceeds, including the exchange between researcher and journal referee just as between teacher and student (Earl 2000). Indeed the post-autistic movement made an early contribution by advocating teaching by means of debates (see further Dow 2003).

What is being advocated here is an open-system approach to teaching which incorporates methodological material in an integrated way. While there is certainly room for specialist courses in methodology, and indeed in history of economic thought, simple methodology and reference to some history of thought should be embedded in teaching of theory from an early stage (Dow 2007, 2009). Otherwise there is a risk of incoherence between courses taught from different perspectives without these differences being addressed within each course. The same argument could be made for embedding material from history particularly, but also from sociology and psychology, in economics teaching. But this proposal poses the further challenge for economics educators whose earlier training was of the mainstream, closed-system variety, without embedded input from other disciplines. Separate specialist courses, in economic history for example, might be advocated on pragmatic grounds.

It was the Scottish tradition in higher education for all students to start with philosophy as a grounding for all subjects, and for all subjects to be taught with reference to their history. Further economics was understood as political economy, with scope for input from sociology and psychology. This educational approach was grounded in the Scottish enlightenment approach to epistemology which we would now classify as an open-system approach. This was the tradition in which I was educated, so it comes naturally to me to teach in this way, though taking account of the fact that most students have not had any prior philosophical training.

In order to tie down this general discussion, let me explain how I approached teaching in money and banking. Most students, both Honours undergraduates and Master's students on a Money and Banking programme, were motivated to take the relevant courses by their wish to pursue a career in the financial sector. A closed-system mainstream course would not do, not least because mainstream monetary theory neither explained money nor included banks. Instead I included historical material, history of thought and material on modern institutional developments. I also included material on the mainstream approach because it is an important influence on policy. But more importantly mainstream theory lies behind the design of institutions within which policy must be framed, notably independent central banks with inflation targets and the architecture of the euro zone. In any case students understood better both the meaning and significance of the Post Keynesian theory I was teaching them by counterposing it with mainstream theory and by being encouraged to form their own opinions about the different approaches.

I used a range of methods, including some formal methods, to convey ideas. For example a useful tool to convey difference of approach was one I picked up from Brian Loasby; this illustrates the power, particularly of diagrams, to convey particular ideas. The students were encouraged to watch carefully as I drew what, *ex post*, were two identical diagrams with time and the rate of growth of output on the axes, and say which was mainstream and which Post Keynesian. It all depended on which of two lines was drawn first: the trend rate of growth with (incidental) fluctuations round it (the mainstream presumption of stability as the norm) or the fluctuations with a trend superimposed upon them (the Post Keynesian presumption of instability as the norm).

Of course a financial and economic crisis has the silver lining of being a wonderful case study for teaching Post Keynesian economics. At other times it can be difficult for students to engage with the nature and causes of instability. But even in relatively stable times, the Post Keynesian theory of money and banking and monetary policy all provide wonderful material by which to convey methodological and theoretical issues as being of topical importance.

As a realist approach, Post Keynesian economics can more easily engage in real issues than approaches which assume the economy to be a closed system. Students who are motivated to better understand real processes respond favourably if open-system economics is exposed to them carefully so as not to be psychologically uncomfortable.

CONCLUSION

Here we have explored what is involved in open-system thinking in economics, relative to the dominant closed-system approach. The first point to emphasise is that there is a range of possibilities for open-system approaches. But all hold in common the idea that a range of approaches is not only possible but also both inevitable and desirable; the idea that theories and, in particular, models are partial and provisional; and that ideas from other disciplines should be embedded in economics (rather than tacked on *ex post*). Open-system thinking can be uncomfortable in its uncertainty but satisfying in its efforts to engage with real-world problems.

Many of the challenges facing open-system economists in a predominantly closed-system discipline carry over into economics teaching. From an open-system perspective, communication and persuasion are critical. So is argument as a constructive exercise rather than an exercise in hostile rejection. Economists need to develop skills in the judgement required to navigate a pluralist analysis of a complex open economic system. Just as open-system economists have to function among closed-system economists, so they must also devise effective means of communicating ideas to students who are also taking closed-system economics courses.

But in an ideal world of teaching, where economics programmes are designed along open-system lines, the emphasis on technical skills would be substantially reduced in order to make way for the philosophical, historical and institutional material required to equip students for building up their capacity for judgement. Even where such a programme included some closed-system economics, the students would become equipped to form their own views about it. But, given the psychological appeal for many of closed systems, particularly in the early stages of learning, great care must be taken in building up to open-systems thinking. Here I have argued, however, for consistency in explaining the provisionality of a starting point which might include some simple models.

NOTES

1. The chapter has benefited from helpful comments from Victoria Chick and Jesper Jespersen.

2. Coddington's other category of reconstituted reductionists is more clearly a closed-system approach; hydraulic Keynesians might more accurately be seen as occupying a position close to the 'closed system' end of a spectrum of system openness and closure.
3. The Duhem–Quine thesis explains the difficulties of definitive empirical testing which arise from the complexity of tests and what is being tested; if the results appear to contradict the predictions of a theory it is in practice difficult to identify exactly what has been falsified.
4. This is a rhetorical technique used more generally in academic discourse (Klamer 1995).

REFERENCES

Chick, V. (1995) '"Order out of Chaos" in Economics?', in S.C. Dow and J. Hillard (eds), *Keynes, Knowledge and Uncertainty*. Aldershot: Edward Elgar Publishing, pp. 25–42.

Chick, V. (2003) 'The Future is Open: On Open-System Theorising in Economics', paper presented to the Economics for the Future Conference, Cambridge, September.

Chick, V. and Dow, S.C. ([2001] 2012) 'Formalism, Logic and Reality: A Keynesian Analysis', *Cambridge Journal of Economics*, 25 (6): 705–22, reprinted in G.M. Hodgson (ed.), *Mathematics and Modern Economics*. Cheltenham: Edward Elgar Publishing.

Chick, V. and Dow, S.C. (2005) 'The Meaning of Open Systems', *Journal of Economic Methodology*, 12 (3): 363–81.

Coddington, A. (1976) 'Keynesian Economics: The Search for First Principles', *Journal of Economic Literature*, 14 (4): 1258–73.

Colander, D. and Klamer, A. (1987) 'The Making of an Economist', *Journal of Economic Perspectives*, 1 (2): 95–112.

Dow, S.C. (2003) 'The Relevance of Controversies for Practice as well as Teaching', in E. Fullbrook (ed.), *The Crisis in Economics: The Post-Autistic Economics Movement: The First 600 Days*. London: Routledge, pp. 132–4.

Dow, S.C. (2007) 'Pluralism in Economics', in J. Groenewegen (ed.), *Teaching Pluralism in Economics*. Cheltenham: Edward Elgar Publishing, pp. 22–39.

Dow, S.C. (2009) 'History of Thought and Methodology in Pluralist Economics Education', *International Review of Economics Education*, 8 (2): 41–57.

Earl, P.E. ([2000] 2008) 'Indeterminacy in the Economics Classroom', in P.E. Earl and S.F. Frowen (eds), *Economics as an Art of Thought: Essays in Memory of G.L.S. Shackle*. London: Routledge, pp. 25–50. Reissued in revised form in E. Fullbrook (ed.), *Pluralist Economics*. London: Zed Books, pp. 193–214.

Jespersen, J. (2009) *Macroeconomic Methodology: A Post-Keynesian Perspective*. Cheltenham: Edward Elgar Publishing.

Keynes, J.M. ([1921] 1973) *A Treatise on Probability. Collected Writings*, vol. VIII. London: Macmillan, for the Royal Economic Society.

Keynes, J.M. ([1924] 1972) 'Alfred Marshall', reprinted in *Essays in Biography. Collected Writings of John Maynard Keynes*, vol. X. London: Macmillan, for the Royal Economic Society.

Keynes, J.M. ([1936] 1973) *The General Theory of Employment, Interest and Money. Collected Writings*, vol. VII. London: Macmillan, for the Royal Economic Society.

Keynes, J.M. ([1937] 1973) 'The General Theory of Employment', *Quarterly*

Journal of Economics, February. Reprinted in *The General Theory and After: Defence and Development. Collected Writings*, vol. XIV. London: Macmillan, for the Royal Economic Society.

Klamer, A. (1995) 'The conception of modernism in economics: Samuelson, Keynes and Harrod', in S.C. Dow and J. Hillard (eds), *Keynes, Knowledge and Uncertainty*. Aldershot: Edward Elgar Publishing, pp. 318–33.

Kuhn, T.S. ([1962] 1970) *The Structure of Scientific Revolutions*. Chicago, IL: Chicago University Press.

Lawson, T. (2003) *Economics and Reality*. London: Routledge.

Loasby, B.J. (2003) 'Closed Models and Open Systems', *Journal of Economic Methodology*, 10 (3): 285–306.

Maslow, A.H. (1968) *Toward a Psychology of Being*, 2nd edition. New York: van Nostrand Reinholt.

McCloskey, D.N. (1983) 'The Rhetoric of Economics', *Journal of Economic Literature*, 21 (June): 481–517.

Minsky, H.P. (1986) *Stabilizing an Unstable Economy*. New Haven, CT: Yale University Press.

Perry, W.G., Jr (1970) *Forms of Intellectual and Ethical Development in the College Years: A Scheme*. New York: Holt, Rinchart and Winston.

Rokeach, M. (1960) *The Open and Closed Mind*. New York: Basic Books.

Skidelsky, R. (2009) *Keynes: The Return of the Master*. London: Allen Lane.

Stiglitz, J. (2010) 'The Non-existent Hand', *London Review of Books*, 32 (8), 22 April.

5. Pluralism in economics education*

Andy Denis

INTRODUCTION

This paper, originally the introduction to a special issue of the *International Review of Economics Education* (IREE, Volume 8, Issue 2), attempts to establish a framework for the discussion of the topic of the special issue, "pluralism in economics undergraduate education". The first section identifies economics as a plural discipline taught monistically: there are many economics, but, by and large, the teaching of economics reflects the dominant paradigm and identifies that with economics *per se*. The suggestion that economics pedagogy should reflect the plural character of the discipline immediately raises the issue of quality; it is argued that this has to be confronted. The paper then turns to a definition of two grades of pluralism – *permissive pluralism*, involving a recognition of academic freedom, and a more student-centred *assertive pluralism*. Subsequent sections address why and how we might move towards pluralism in economics education. It is argued that pluralist education enjoys a natural advantage over current pedagogy in underpinning citizenship, equipping students to become productive employees, preparing students for further study in the area, and in having fun. It is argued that the key to founding a pluralist curriculum is *history* – both *the history of economic thought* and *the history of the economy*. A final substantive section addresses the important issue of *subject benchmarking*, specifically in relation to the subject benchmark statement for economics established in the UK by the Quality Assurance Agency for Higher Education (QAA).

A PLURAL DISCIPLINE TAUGHT MONISTICALLY

We start with two salient facts about the world. The first fact is that there are, not one, but *many*, sciences of economics. To illustrate: as well as the neoclassical family of schools of thought – including neoclassical Keynesians, monetarists, new Keynesians, new classical and real business cycle theorists, new institutionalists, new economic geographers and analytical Marxists – there is a constellation of heterodox schools, including Post Keynesians, Marxians, Austrians, institutionalists, Georgists, Associative economists, feminists and critical realists, as well as Muslim, Christian and Buddhist economists, in so far as they regard their religion as informing their economics. My suggested system of classification may (in fact certainly does) lack consensus, but the basic fact of interest here is indisputable. There are many economics: many sciences, many practices, many visions and paradigms of economics – that is simply a fact that we have to recognise and to deal with.

The second salient fact is that the teaching of undergraduate economics, both in the UK and elsewhere, is – given this heterogeneity within the discipline – remarkably homogeneous. Typically, undergraduates are taught a core of mainstream textbook microeconomics and macroeconomics in their first two years, alongside courses in mathematics and statistics, and then a range of optional applications of that core to specific topics in such specialisms as financial economics, industrial economics, labour economics, health economics and monetary economics, in their final year. Economics is typically seen within the discipline as analogous to engineering – there is thought to be little valid or interesting controversy on fundamentals, and what controversy there is can only be addressed on the basis of a common technical apparatus: the mastery of this technical basis is therefore the principal or sole preoccupation of undergraduate, and indeed postgraduate, tuition. The degree to which we are systematically failing to expose our undergraduates to alternative paradigms should not be underestimated. In my third-year, second-term, optional module in history of economic thought, I discovered a year or so ago, in the first lecture of that year's series, that none of the dozen students present had ever even heard of Hayek – and that's the group of students who, presumably, were least averse to learning about the past of their discipline.

The contrast between the heterogeneity of the discipline and the homogeneity of our undergraduate pedagogy is striking, and worth dwelling on.

Every science is rhetorical, but social science is rhetorical in a double sense. Every science consists of a *body of knowledge* and an *image of knowledge*: the first is the substance of the science, the knowledge of the world which the science claims to offer; the second concerns what the discipline thinks it is and should be, how it presents and justifies itself to itself and to the world (Giocoli, 2003). The body of knowledge comprises the accumulated theoretical and empirical knowledge of the science, the methods it has adopted, and the open questions and features of the world the science should address. The image of knowledge comprises the identity of the science: how it thinks of itself and presents itself – both to itself and to the world, the identification of the open questions deserving most urgent attention, the grounds and criteria upon which these open questions are to be resolved, what constitutes an authoritative statement of the science, and how novices are inducted and socialised. Economics is no exception and this is the first sense in which we can identify a rhetoric of economics: it has a self-image.

Amongst the sciences, however, the social sciences present a special case, in that their content addresses *interests*: their almost every pronouncement leads or tends towards one policy prescription or another, including the prescription to do nothing. We are all fallible beings, but, mostly, we are not stupid. We can often see where a line of thought is going to take us, and the temptation to choose the line of thought in the light of its expected terminus may frequently be overwhelming. Given the variety of interests in the world, which may be served or frustrated by the pronouncements of economists, it is not then surprising that there is also a variety of economic lines of thought. And of course, the notion of interest need not be interpreted in any crude or mechanical way: it is well known that we perceive it to be in our interest to adopt new ideas when they are consistent with what we already think we know. Science is blighted by confirmation bias. Empirically we see every day that people do indeed believe what they want to believe, and that that is frequently what they perceive it to be in their interest to believe. It would be odd if economists were immune. The image of knowledge thus feeds back into the body of knowledge and a variety of *images* can be expected to give rise to a variety of *bodies*, a range of sciences of economics. This is the second sense in which the social sciences, and in particular economics, is rhetorical. Its outputs, its insights, its theories, its prescriptions, serve and frustrate interests. So much the more pressing, then, that these outputs be presented, to the economists themselves as much as to the end-users of their outputs, as the product of pure, dispassionate science. To the extent that a social science must, in serving knowledge, serve also interests, its image of knowledge has a doubly rhetorical function: each economics must find a way not only to justify itself, to present itself as scientific, but also to justify its specific content, its particular body of knowledge.

While this is true of social science in general, it is particularly true of economics because of its proximity to the policy-making, and in particular the economic policy-making, process (Freeman, 2009: 36). Interests within society, the potential winners and losers from the implementation of this or that policy, often stand to win or lose more as a consequence of economic policy decisions than of any other, and indeed almost every policy issue has an economic dimension. Such interests do not hesitate to attempt to influence the kind of economics which is performed in the hope of influencing its outputs in their favour. The hope that cold fusion does or does not work does not give those hoping for one or the other outcome much incentive to support this or that kind of physics. Few believe that the outcome can be influenced in this way: at best discoveries can be hastened or delayed. But with, say, minimum wages, the case is quite different: every organised interest with a stake in the matter is free to commission its own research, in-house or bought in from private and public sector research organisations, in the same way as it might employ legal staff to defend its interests at law. The purpose here is less the discovery of truth, than the generation of effective rhetoric. Those hoping for cold fusion would generally accept that there is a truth, and they're probably better off knowing it sooner rather than later. Those whose interests will be promoted or damaged by this or that policy on minimum wages, or some change to the tax system, are principally interested in ensuring that their interest is represented as the interest of society, and hence acquiring social acceptance for their desired outcome. As long as interests within society are various, therefore, we can expect economics itself to be various.

So the discipline is inevitably and intrinsically plural, and our transmission of it to the next generation is overwhelmingly singular. Perhaps needless to say, this monism extends well beyond the particular issue of undergraduate pedagogy that we are considering here – research and postgraduate education are similarly dominated by a single standpoint. Undergraduate education is merely a particularly salient and egregious instance. Progress towards pluralism in undergraduate education, should we decide that this is what we want, is most unlikely to be achieved in that domain in isolation, but presupposes parallel shifts from monism towards pluralism in postgraduate education and in research. Later I will say more about the desirability or otherwise of this contrast between a plural science and a singular representation of it. Here I want to address an important 'knee-jerk' response to the idea of pluralism in economics education.

Given that economics is inevitably plural, there can be no neutral ground on which to stand, outside of the many competing paradigms, from which we can pronounce upon the legitimacy of these schools of thought, or the quality of what representatives of those schools say. The alternative, then, is either *pluralism* – a tolerant, critical conversation (McCloskey, 1998), or *monism* – what we have today: the hegemony of a particular approach. Other social sciences, by contrast, take a multiplicity of positions and methodological discussion for granted.

The suggestion of relaxing the monism of the discipline immediately raises a concern: does open-mindedness mean empty-headedness? This is addressed in almost every defence of pluralism today: pluralism, it is said, does not mean that 'anything goes' (Dow, 2009: 41; Freeman, 2009: 27). A Google search for the key words *pluralism*, *economics* and '*anything goes*' yields nearly 12,000 hits. Pluralism, that is, raises the spectre of legitimising cranks and cults, unproductive and damaging hangers-on that are parasitic on the discipline. Parallels in medicine and in other sciences immediately spring to mind. But the difference is this: in general, we *know* what is wrong with previous, exploded theories such as those of phlogiston, the luminiferous ether and the inheritance of acquired characteristics, on the one hand, and current heterodox notions such as intelligent design, homœopathy and astrology, on the other, because they have been theoretically and empirically *comprehensively refuted*. Moreover, the knowledge of these past and heterodox notions remains – to a greater or lesser degree – at the disposal of the current generations of these disciplinary practitioners and theoreticians, available to them to draw on, should new phenomena challenge the accepted view. In medicine and the natural sciences we continually see the heterodox becoming the orthodox (and vice versa). The Wilson and Sarich finding in 1967 that humans and apes diverged 4 to 5 million years ago, an order of magnitude below the contemporary consensus, was discounted for decades before being accepted. Likewise with Julian Huxley's notion of clades. Elaine Morgan's aquatic ape hypothesis has never been accepted by the majority of palaeontologists, but the idea is well known and new facts, and new interpretations of the facts, are often compared with its predictions.

The situation is quite otherwise in economics, however. The past, and the periphery, are not overcome in theory but simply forgotten, and excluded. There is, in my opinion, no cogent neoclassical critique of – for example – Marx's labour theory of value, Keynes's theory of aggregate demand or Hayek's theory of social evolution. These contributions have not been refuted; they are simply ignored. And that ignoring, that ignorance, is not a passive failing, but an active process: the long drawn-out process of squeezing the history and methodology of the subject out of the curriculum is part of an organic process of quarantining and sequestering heterodox thought in the discipline. Heterodox economic thought today embraces a great variety of standpoints within it – and they cannot *all* be right. But whatever its flaws, it cannot be compared to the eccentric attachment to astrological and homœopathic notions rightly dismissed by astronomy and medicine. Until the process of intellectual settling of accounts has taken place, we cannot know who are the cranks, which are the cults. No doubt we all have our suspicions.

WHAT IS PLURALISM?

I believe that we can identify a lower and a higher grade of pluralism in economics undergraduate education, which I shall refer to respectively as *permissive* and *assertive* pluralism.

The lower grade of pluralism simply involves permission: allowing or advocating permission for many schools of thought and modes of teaching to exist. In this view, intellectual diversity is advocated, or at least tolerated. It can be regarded as teacher-centred, since it permits teaching which fits with the inclinations of the teacher. What is taught is not necessarily particularly pluralist; the pluralism lies rather at the aggregate level, simply in the fact that more than one approach is taught, or may be taught. This minimal pluralism is required to satisfy the principle of academic freedom.

The higher grade of pluralism presupposes permissive pluralism but goes further: permissive pluralism is necessary but not sufficient. Assertive pluralism requires the mutual engagement of different schools of thought. In this approach, it is recognised as a necessary part of undergraduate education in economics that students be exposed to competing paradigms. It can be regarded as student-centred, as aiming to give students an adequate induction into the discipline, one which educates them about the plurality of their discipline and inculcates the skills required to deal with that plurality. This grade of pluralism is pluralistic in practice, as what each student gets is tuition in the range of economic approaches, past and present, and assistance in acquiring the knowledge, understanding and skills required to discriminate between them. This is the kind of pluralism for which the Association for Heterodox Economics (AHE) is committed to strive (Freeman, 2009: 24). It is the difference between tolerating diversity and embracing diversity.

Nevertheless, it is very important to underline that pluralism in economics education cannot be identified with heterodoxy, and monism with orthodoxy. Pluralism is not about replacing one approach or family of approaches (the current orthodoxy) with another (one or other current heterodoxy) – which thereby becomes the new orthodoxy. Pluralism is categorically *not* about combating the mainstream – there are many pluralist individual economists, institutional units and processes within the mainstream. Indeed, pluralism requires a debate with heterodox as much as orthodox currents since it is perfectly possible for heterodox economists to be quite convinced in the correctness of *their* particular heterodoxy and to wish to see it become the new orthodoxy. Salerno (2009), for example, wishes to see the Austrian school become 'THE new neoclassical mainstream'. Rather, assertive pluralism breaks with the notion that progress means replacing one orthodoxy with another, or even that it means the renewal from within of an existing orthodoxy. It rejects the idea that where we are – now or at any other time – can be reduced to a single doctrine or canon. Pluralism is a challenge to the heterodox and orthodox alike. Indeed, those paradigmatically attached to the current mainstream have a strong incentive to support pluralist pedagogy since, as was argued in the papers in the special issue of IREE on pluralism in economics education (Denis, 2009), it promotes deeper learning of orthodox theories, by contrasting them at every point with their rivals.

For assertive pluralism, the starting point in constructing the undergraduate curriculum has to be that economics is plural, that is, that there is more than one approach, theory and proposed solution to every problem. Pluralism, Freeman argues, *is* the tradition of controversy (Freeman, 2009). All major economic doctrines are born and sustained in controversy. This is the nature of the discipline, which, if we are honest, we have to communicate to our new students from the outset of their studies. It is significant that the 'post-autistic' movement of French students explicitly demanded the teaching of economics via controversy. Controversy, according to this understanding or pluralism, is not something for the footnotes or closing chapters in the textbooks, nor something to be focused on in optional modules towards the end of the students' undergraduate studies. Rather, controversy is the method, the tool, the means of instruction from the very beginning of that instruction.

Pluralist undergraduate education in economics is a process of teaching and learning focused on the coexistence of multiple approaches – all of which are presumed to be valid, until theoretically and empirically refuted. It uses controversy between these schools of thought as the means towards developing pluralist students, that is, students with the capacity not simply to reproduce and apply one particular theory, but who are knowledgeable about, and have insight into, the main intellectual trends within the discipline, and the ability to discriminate between their pronouncements on the basis of logical cogency and empirical relevance. The aim of pluralist teaching is to equip students to exercise their own professional judgement as economists. To this end, pluralism cannot be reduced to synthesis or inclusion, but has to be based on systematic deployment of controversy as means of understanding and educating. It means introducing students to controversy and debate from day one of their programme.

WHY PLURALISM?

The first answer one can give to the question, 'Why pluralism?', is a very simple one – it is the truth: the discipline is plural; we have to tell the students that. Failure to inform the students of the plurality of their discipline is just dishonest.

The bigger answer is that by failing to expose our students to plurality, by failing to use controversy as a pedagogical instrument, we make it much more difficult for ourselves to do our job as teachers. The pedagogical advantages of pluralism, the papers in the special issue of IREE (Denis, 2009) concluded, are overwhelming. The process of contention and discussion between differing standpoints is an essential component of progress towards an adequate understanding of the world.

Economics undergraduate education has four broad purposes – to underpin citizenship, to equip students to be productive employees, to lay the basis for further professional education and training in economics, and to have fun. For those few unconvinced by the fourth goal suggested here, an instrumental approach can be adopted: if teachers are enjoying themselves, they're probably going to do a better job; and students who enjoy their courses are more likely to be learning effectively. All of these goals are supported by pluralist pedagogy, though the consequences for the enjoyability of economics education will be left implicit on this occasion. The claim made in the papers published in the special issue of IREE (Denis, 2009) is that pluralism supports vocational goals both by teaching the standard content of economics degrees more effectively, and by setting that in a far-reaching social context. Student understanding is deeper, and they are better able to learn and integrate new material. All four goals are supported by enabling students to become life-long learners. The central claim is that basing pedagogy on controversy leads to the development of critical independence, which itself leads to better citizenship and employability, and better mastery of the discipline.

The subject matter of economics is marked by diversity, openness, fragmentation and complexity. In these circumstances it is possible that the application of a range of approaches will lead more reliably to valuable insights than reliance on any one method, however good. This is related to the well-known idea, in domains from meteorology to finance, that averaging a range of forecasts, impounding different forecasting approaches, will lead to greater accuracy. The various paradigms within economics may thus be complementary. No paradigm is complete, none has the last word: all have lacunae and blind-spots; it is possible for diverse approaches to contribute to our understanding of the world, even though they may appear to be mutually inconsistent. In other words, there can be a cross-fertilisation between paradigms. This leads to the idea of a pragmatic, heuristic pluralism, a horses-for-courses approach potentially valid both in research and teaching. It might be judged desirable to teach our students to practise heuristic pluralism and to seek insights from a range of standpoints. Teaching via controversy is more likely to lead to good economics.

It is well known that people display greatly varying abilities to do the same task, depending on how the task is presented. An example is the Wason test. A number of cards is displayed and subjects are asked to turn over the minimum set required to prove or disprove some hypothesis about the obverse and reverse of the cards. People are in general surprisingly bad at it, but research has shown that they do much better when it is presented – for example – as detecting violations of an implicit social contract (Ridley, 1994). Similarly, a blue-collar worker with limited mathematical schooling can often quickly execute complex arithmetical calculations in the bookmaker's shop. By presenting economic questions in terms of controversy about important issues with which students can engage, it may be that they can learn faster by recruiting brain modules not normally employed for the task.

Teaching economics by using the controversy between a range of economic paradigms allows students to see themselves and the issues they care about as part of the discussion, encourages student engagement with the interests of the agents involved, and underlines that economic choices have moral, social, cultural and civic dimensions. Students are enabled to identify with agents, to take sides, to care about outcomes, and to identify the human significance and moral status of economic interpretation and policy prescription (Peterson and McGoldrick, 2009). We all respond better to a story, and students are no exception.

Pluralism leads to deep learning, partly because it speaks to matters which students care about, and hence recruits brain modules not otherwise engaged, and partly because the use of controversy itself requires students to take sides and hence to find reasons for the views they adopt. By viewing the phenomena in question from multiple perspectives, pluralism raises the issues of uncertainty, complexity and context. This requires students to develop strategies for coping with all three. Different paradigms dispute the evidence and its interpretation, dispute the logical and theoretical framework within which the evidence is to be understood, and dispute the normative, policy-orientated consequences to be drawn from theoretical consideration of the evidence. At each level the student is challenged to understand, to diagnose and to judge. The competing points of view interpret differently the borders between economics and contiguous subjects, leading students to a deeper understanding of context, the definition of economics and how it relates to its cognates.

Whatever stance a student takes with respect to a specific issue, exposure to controversy will help the student to cope with uncertainty about the truth of, and challenges to the correctness of, his own arguments. We are likely to do less damage when we are aware of our ignorance, and of the existence of alternatives, than when we think we have the answers. What is needed is reflective judgement, the ability to make judgements in the context of uncertainty, and a commitment to questioning one's own purposes, evidence, implications, assumptions and standpoint, as much as those one opposes.

Pluralist teaching leads to better citizenship. It teaches the student to be participatory, critical and informed, and emphasises powers of judgement. The Enlightenment goal of student intellectual independence lies at the heart of the pluralist pedagogical project. Presenting the alternative theories for every phenomenon requires students to make up their own minds, and requires the instructor to help the student to do so. Students learn to think for themselves and to negotiate their way through difficult issues on which there are many perspectives. What is prized above all in this perspective is the student's ability to think critically, independently and objectively.

Pluralism helps students learn to become life-long learners. They are encouraged to engage with the learning process itself: understanding why the content is being taught via controversy leads to conscious reflection on learning and the promotion of active learning. Ever-deeper understanding of the roots of controversy between economic paradigms underpins the capacity to change one's mind, both to correct erroneous premises and to respond to changed circumstances. It encourages students to become conscious about their own learning and to learn about the learning process. Pluralist learners become active, self-directed learners.

Pluralist education is vocationally useful. Employers want oral and written communication and presentation skills, social and team-working skills and debating skills. They also want problem-solving skills with the ability to cope with complexity and interconnectedness. They want employees who are able to weigh up the sides of an argument. Some of this has already been mentioned above. Pluralism develops students' rhetorical powers in two ways. First, they must understand the rhetoric of the schools of thought whose pronouncements they are studying – how do these writers and thinkers attempt to gain support for their standpoint? But it also encourages students to become articulate communicators by getting them to engage with this issue and that, to put forward a case, orally or in writing, for this theory or that, that policy prescription or an alternative. All this makes students better, more attractive employees. Learning in a pluralist environment, students become more creative, better judges, better problem-solvers, more effective organisers.

Pluralism is associated with a more open and varied approach to pedagogy, that is, a greater variety of modes of instruction, with greater stress on student-centredness. This is to be contrasted both with 'Monecon' – the standard, single-paradigm, single-delivery approach – and with artificial attempts to graft a more open and varied pedagogy onto the mainstream approach, that is, in abstraction from any attempt to remedy the deficiencies of a monist pedagogy. It is through a hypostatisation of content and curriculum – a wilful narrowing of content and standardisation of the canon, not through failure to adopt the best teaching practices, that Monecon has become boring, divorced from reality and difficult to teach. As Wilson and Dixon (2009) elaborate, the attempt to isolate the *technique* of teaching as at fault, and to introduce innovative methods of teaching and learning without addressing the problems of a monist curriculum, generates counter-productive and perverse effects. Such methods can be hands on without being minds on. Pedagogically innovative techniques, combined with the interest of learning about and through controversy, by contrast, can lead to learning activities which are engaging, comprehensible, interesting and satisfying. They can capture student interest, question the underlying assumptions of the approaches considered, and illuminate different approaches. This is a world away from both the monolithic, inefficient rote learning and memorisation, or, rather, learning and forgetting, still associated with so much of the mainstream, and – Wilson and Dixon claim – with the attempt to paste 'teaching and learning', in particular via new technology, onto the monist mainstream curriculum without addressing the content.

HOW TO MOVE TOWARDS PLURALISM?

The question, whether a pluralist broadening of the curriculum is desirable, leads immediately into the question of how its proponents would envisage its implementation. Broadly there are two paths, which are not mutually exclusive but rather support each other, and which relate to the two grades of pluralism considered above. In the case of the lower grade of pluralism, permissive pluralism, the appropriate mode of procedure is for individual lecturers and departments to add heterodox material to the mainstream material, to infiltrate pluralism within existing modules and programmes. For the higher grade of pluralism, assertive pluralism, one approach worth considering is benchmarking for pluralism. I will address this in the next section.

It is not generally possible to start a pluralist or heterodox module or programme from scratch. There are exceptions, such as the recently launched master's and doctoral programme in Austrian economics at King Juan Carlos University, Madrid, and such opportunities are of course to be seized with both hands.[1] Nevertheless, at present they are the exception, not the rule. So the question is, how are we to infiltrate pluralism into predominantly mainstream modules and programmes? There will of course be random opportunities where specific members of staff have both the interest and expertise, and the confidence of their colleagues, to introduce alternative material. In many ways, the mainstream has become more internally pluralist than it has been in the past (Coyle, 2007; Dow, 2009): opportunities to exploit this internal pluralism do exist. On these occasions, instead of standard mainstream textbooks, the instructor may choose to deploy an alternative textbook, to read two textbooks in parallel, to compile a set of selected readings, or to use his or her own specially created notes and teaching materials. A project which ran from 2009–11, partly funded by the Higher Education Funding Council for England (*hefce*), via the Economics Network, and partly by City University London, attempted to collect heterodox teaching materials and make them publicly available on the Economics Network website (Economics Network, n.d.). The intention was to help teachers to introduce heterodox material alongside the standard, mainstream material, injecting an element of local pluralism into the students' education. A significant quantity of heterodox teaching materials was collected, but it is difficult to know how much of it was then used to inspire and inform the teaching of heterodox economics.

A more systematic approach to the problem of introducing heterodox material into existing modules and programmes is indicated in Dow (2009), namely via *history*, in particular via the history and methodology of economics, and via economic history and the history of economic policy. A strong case can be made that students need the historical background to the doctrines we are now teaching them, and which are now accepted by many practising economists, in order for them to fully understand what they are being taught. Equally, a strong argument can be made for introducing students to the history of the economic system, of which ostensibly they are embarking on a study, and the history of government policy and *laissez-faire*. But the history of economic thought cannot be taught without introducing students to controversy. The history of the emergence and development of even just the current mainstream ideas implies exploring the controversies giving rise to and sustaining those ideas. Likewise, the methodology of the subject cannot be taught without introducing students to a range of possible methodologies, and investigating the reasoning and motives behind the adoption of this or that methodology in the social and natural sciences. Finally, the history of the economy and of economic policy cannot be undertaken without examining the motivation and reasoning of the policy-makers and the evidence on the efficacy of their interventions in the history of the economy. All of these approaches, to the extent that they are taught effectively, teach students via the deployment of controversy and therefore not only tend towards the goals outlined above, but form a transition to a more assertive and systematic grade of pluralist pedagogy.

BENCHMARKING FOR PLURALISM

Undergraduate tuition in economics in the UK is benchmarked in the subject benchmark statement for economics (SBSE), established by the QAA (QAA, 2007). Subject benchmark statements 'describe what gives a discipline its coherence and identity, and define what can be expected of a graduate in terms of the abilities and skills needed to develop understanding or competence in the subject' (QAA, n.d.). The SBSE cannot be ignored. A recent Royal Economic Society–Economics Network study reported that 'the Benchmark Statement has been found to be robust and relevant to current employers' (O'Doherty *et al.*, 2007: 15). A number of reactions to the SBSE are possible. On the one hand, a casual inspection might lead to the impression that the SBSE is so anodyne that it is compatible with almost any interpretation and unlikely to obstruct the advancement of pluralism within economics education. The opposite extreme sees it as inevitable that a benchmark statement will dictate adherence to the orthodoxy, whatever the orthodoxy happens to be. The only possible response in this view is that the benchmarking system should be rejected, or, if we must suffer the imposition of benchmarking, then we should engineer the benchmark statement for economics to be as vacuous as possible.

The line taken by the AHE is different from both of these. It takes seriously the current statement and regards it as damaging to the profession, but at the same time argues (Freeman, 2009) that reforms to the SBSE can convert it into an important instrument for the pluralist reform of undergraduate education in economics in the UK.

The SBSE consists of seven sections – a very brief introduction, a definition of the nature and context of economics, the aims of degree programmes in economics, a summary of subject knowledge and understanding, a list of subject-specific and other skills, a section on teaching, learning and assessment, and, finally, a set of threshold and modal benchmark standards. Garnett (2009) notes that the SBSE already has some pluralist elements, and argues that rather than completely re-writing the SBSE from scratch, we need to 'beef up' these sections. For example, the very last modal benchmark standard says that the typical graduate should 'display familiarity with' – 'awareness of' in the threshold benchmark standard – 'the possibility that many economic problems may admit of more than one approach and may have more than one solution' (QAA, 2007: 8). However, this is the last of seven modal and threshold attainments and appears to have the status of a footnote. Moreover, it is highly ambiguous what 'more than one approach' actually means: it is quite possible to teach a range of neoclassical approaches to a single problem without ever drawing on a heterodox idea. And pluralists would claim that the threshold benchmark – indeed, the *very first* threshold benchmark – should require the graduate to display a profound familiarity with the *necessity*, not merely the possibility, that economic problems admit of many approaches and solutions.

Again, one of the possible attainments of an economics student is listed as 'Appreciation of the history and development of economic ideas and the differing methods of analysis that have been and are used by economists'. It is indeed laudable that the history and methodology of the subject are thus mentioned. But this comes in a list of possible 'indicative' attainments immediately after a disclaimer stating that which elements on the list are actually selected is a matter of individual institutional choice (QAA, 2007: 3).

Finally, under 'Subject knowledge and understanding', we read that 'students . . . should appreciate the existence of different methodological approaches' (QAA, 2007: 2), which, while welcome, is, to say the least, ambiguous – after all, even two standard econometric techniques, not to mention indifference curve analysis and ISLM models, could easily be interpreted as 'different methodological approaches'. This is exactly the same point as has already been made above about the references to possible plurality of approach mentioned in the seventh and final threshold and modal benchmark standards.

These elements, as Garnett (2009) implies, are features that a pluralist SBSE would incorporate, develop and build on. The AHE would certainly agree that *all* students should be familiar with the history of their subject, and of the different ways economists have conceived of their discipline, and that they should assume that *every* economic problem will admit of a plurality of approaches and solutions. But that is not enough.

It is worth stating exactly what it is which is objectionable about the current SBSE. The three lengthy paragraphs constituting the definition of the subject do not give the merest hint that there may be a number of schools of thought with very different views of the subject. The SBSE describes the mainstream view and calls it 'economics'. The extensive list under 'The transferable concept' in Section 5 (QAA, 2007: 4–5) comprises eight concepts, including incentives, the margin, equilibrium, gains from trade and expectations. Indeed, a very strong argument can be made for every one of these concepts. But that is not the point. The fact is that nearly every one of them is disputed – either rejected completely or interpreted in a quite different way – by one school of thought or another. But they are presented here as wholly uncontroversial. The assumption is that when we speak of 'economics', it is just the mainstream version of economics that we're talking about. Apart from the two ambiguous references, noted above, to a possible plurality of approach, and the reference to the history and methodology of economics as an optional target attainment, there is simply no mention or acknowledgement of controversy. That, for the AHE, is the core.

The starting point for the construction of a satisfactory SBSE must be that economics is plural: there is more than one approach, more than one theory, more than one proposed solution to every economic problem. The discipline is plural in the sense that a large number of competing schools of thought strive to make sense of the economic world we inhabit. Our education in economics simply has to reflect that fact. As argued above, in the section on assertive pluralism, this means that pedagogy has to be based on controversy. The SBSE has to prioritise controversy, criticism and the nurturing of dissent. The goal has to be the inculcation of critical independence, the ability to challenge received wisdom of whatever kind, and the production of students who are in a position to be able to make up their own minds. This is far from being a novel way of conceiving the role and structure of a benchmark statement: as the AHE submission to the review of the SBSE (Freeman, 2007) documents, other benchmark statements in the social sciences and beyond, from theology to accountancy, find ways to reflect the pluralism of their disciplines in ways that the SBSE signally fails to do.

It should not be thought that the pluralism being advocated here effectively displaces standards of quality. Pluralism itself constitutes a demanding standard of quality. Benchmarking for pluralism sets up pluralism itself as the expected standard throughout the discipline. A pluralist SBSE would set out benchmark standards for pluralism, establishing threshold and modal criteria for students' capacity for critical and pluralistic reasoning; knowledge of the variety of theories and standpoints, past and present, in the discipline as a whole and the specific field in which they are working; understanding of the presuppositions of these theories and ability to discriminate between their pronouncements on the basis both of the empirical evidence for their assumptions and predictions, and of their logical cogency; and the rhetorical skills both to understand the use of rhetoric which they will encounter, and the ability to present a powerful and cogent argument of their own.

In this approach, pluralism is regarded as both an output and an input. It is not just that the students' education is pluralist, but that the students produced by a programme meeting the standard of pluralism will themselves be pluralist – in the sense that they will accept, entertain and encourage difference, dissent and controversy. The goal is to teach pluralist courses which will produce pluralist students.

The pluralist SBSE, without dictating anything, would describe the discipline's expectations of what undergraduate degree courses in economics would consist of and what sort of graduates it would lead to. Each department and institution would be able to choose its own way forward. We should expect a very diverse range of courses and ideas, introducing students to the diversity of approach within the discipline and providing them with the intellectual tools to make sense of this diversity. It seems likely, however, that the historical approach mentioned above, and spelled out in detail in the paper by Sheila Dow (2009), would play a major role. The history of economic thought is a prerequisite for understanding the controversy between the schools of thought extant within the discipline today. A study of economic methodology of the subject is essential in order to gain a deep understanding of the differences between the approaches and the rhetorics deployed by those schools of thought. And, finally, a study of the history of the economy and of economic policy-making is essential in order to be able to appraise the various policy prescriptions of these schools of thought.

CONCLUSION

In this chapter I have tried to draw out the consequences for undergraduate education of the manifest contradiction between the plurality of the discipline and the singularity of the induction into it that our undergraduate students receive. I have argued that this contradiction cries out for resolution by giving our students a pluralistic education in economics, an education based on controversy. Further, education based in controversy is capable of delivering benefits for staff, students, employers and the polity of which they are citizens, via the development, in a manner closed to the current monist curriculum, of the students' intellectual independence and critical judgemental skills. A widespread concern is that allowing pluralism will be tantamount to diluting standards. I have argued that this concern is misplaced and that pluralism itself constitutes a demanding standard. Finally, I have outlined the view of the AHE that, while the current subject benchmark statement for economics is seriously deficient when viewed through the lens of pluralism, it would be possible to draft a benchmark statement which would establish pluralism as the standard by which undergraduate education in economics should be measured.

NOTES

* This paper is a revised version of the Editorial introducing the *International Review of Economics Education* (IREE) special issue on "Pluralism in Economics Education" (Volume 8, Issue 2, 2009). We are grateful to the publishers, the Economics Network, for permission to republish. I am particularly grateful to Victoria Chick. The usual disclaimer applies.

1. As pointed out above, there is nothing particularly pluralist itself in generating a heterodox programme such as this; the pluralism lies rather at the aggregate level, in the fact that the teaching of a plurality of approaches has been permitted.

REFERENCES

Coyle, C. (2007) 'Are Economists Conquering the World?', *Royal Economic Society Newsletter* 137, April, pp. 7–9.

Denis, A. (ed.) (2009) 'Pluralism in Economics Education', special issue of the *International Review of Economics Education*, Volume 8, Issue 2.

Dow, S. (2009) 'History of Thought and Methodology in Pluralist Economics Education', *International Review of Economics Education* Volume 8, Issue 2, pp. 41–57. Retrieved March 2013 from www.economicsnetwork.ac.uk/iree/v8n2/dow.pdf.

Economics Network (n.d.) 'Call for Economics Subject Leaders in Specialist Areas'. Retrieved March 2013 from www.economicsnetwork.ac.uk/projects/oer.htm.

Freeman, A. (2007) 'Catechism versus Pluralism: The Heterodox Response to the National Undergraduate Curriculum Proposed by the UK Quality Assurance Authority', Munich Personal RePEc Archive. Retrieved March 2013 from http://mpra.ub.uni-muenchen.de/6832/.

Freeman, A. (2009) 'The Economists of Tomorrow: The Case for a Pluralist Subject Benchmark Statement for Economics', *International Review of Economics Education* Volume 8, Issue 2, pp. 23–40. Retrieved March 2013 from www.economicsnetwork.ac.uk/iree/v8n2/freeman.pdf.

Garnett, Jr., R.F. (2009) 'Rethinking the Pluralist Agenda in Economics Education', *International Review of Economics Education* Volume 8, Issue 2, pp. 5871. Retrieved March 2013 from www.economicsnetwork.ac.uk/iree/v8n2/garnett.pdf.

Giocoli, N. (2003) *Modelling Rational Agents: From Interwar Economics to Early Modern Game Theory*. Cheltenham: Edward Elgar Publishing.

McCloskey, D.N. (1998) *The Rhetoric of Economics*. Madison, WI: University of Wisconsin Press.

O'Doherty, R., Street, D. and Webber, C. (2007) 'The Skills and Knowledge of the Graduate Economist. Findings of a survey conducted on behalf of the Royal Economic Society and the Economics Network', Economics

Network. Retrieved March 2013 from www.economicsnetwork.ac.uk/projects/employability2007full.pdf.

Peterson, J. and McGoldrick, K.M. (2009) 'Pluralism and Economic Education: A Learning Theory Approach', *International Review of Economics Education* Volume 8, Issue 2, pp. 72–90. Retrieved March 2013 from www.economicsnetwork.ac.uk/iree/v8n2/peterson.pdf.

QAA (n.d.) 'Subject Benchmark Statements', The Quality Assurance Agency for Higher Education. Retrieved March 2013 from www.qaa.ac.uk/ASSURINGSTANDARDSANDQUALITY/SUBJECT-GUIDANCE/Pages/Subject-benchmark-statements.aspx.

QAA (2007) 'Economics', The Quality Assurance Agency for Higher Education. Retrieved March 2013 from: www.qaa.ac.uk/Publications/InformationAndGuidance/Documents/Economics.pdf.

Ridley, M. (1994) *The Red Queen: Sex and the Evolution of Human Nature*. London: Penguin.

Salerno, J.T. (2009) 'Salerno Comments on the Mainstream', Mises Economics Blog. RetrievedMarch 2013 from http://blog.mises.org/archives/010164.asp.

Wilson, D. and Dixon, W. (2009) 'Performing Economics: A Critique of "Teaching and Learning"', *International Review of Economics Education* Volume 8, Issue 2, pp. 91–105. Retrieved March 2013 from www.economicsnetwork.ac.uk/iree/v8n2/wilson.pdf.

6. Truth and beauty in macroeconomics

Allin Cottrell

INTRODUCTION

'Beauty is truth, truth beauty.' So wrote John Keats. Paul Krugman thinks this doesn't apply in macroeconomics: beauty lies with neoclassical macroeconomics, which is untrue and useless as a guide to policy, while Keynesian economics – the nearest thing we have to truth – is ugly. In his popular article, 'How did economists get it so wrong?' (2009), Krugman disparages neoclassical macro as seriously misleading – a 'romanticized and sanitized vision of the economy'– and associates it with a 'Dark Age of macroeconomics in which hard-won knowledge has been forgotten.' Yet he also describes it as 'intellectually elegant' and talks of the 'clarity, completeness and sheer beauty that characterizes the full neoclassical approach.' And while he praises Keynes and says that 'Keynesian economics remains the best framework for making sense of recessions and depressions,' he holds that its realism is founded on recognition of messy 'flaws and frictions.' The revamped Keynesianism towards which he hopes the economics profession will evolve 'may not be all that clear' and 'certainly won't be neat.'

In the following I will defend Keats's view, arguing that truth and beauty in macroeconomics are more closely aligned than Krugman allows. Specifically, my claim will be that Keynes's theory, rightly interpreted, exhibits an elegance and coherence that Krugman somehow misses. Before launching that argument, however, I'd like to register substantive agreement with Krugman on the macro issues of the day. Paul Krugman is one of the few public intellectuals in the US, or anywhere else, who has consistently upheld a Keynesian perspective on the Great Recession; he has tirelessly argued that reduction of unemployment should be the number one priority and has patiently rebutted the fashionable but incoherent arguments of the 'inflationistas', 'Very Serious Persons' and 'deficit peacocks' who would have us return to the pre-Keynesian darkness. Nonetheless, his emphasis on the supposedly messy and inelegant nature of the theory he advocates is uncalled-for and unhelpful.

In the next section I briefly argue that the supposed 'beauty' of neoclassical macro is overstated. The third section supports at greater length the idea that Keynesian theory is not only right but also elegant, and the fourth attempts to fend off some predictable counter-arguments.

NEOCLASSICAL MACRO NOT SO BEAUTIFUL

First, a point of terminology. It is not so clear these days what to call the modern variant of what Keynes called 'classical theory.' In the 1980s one used the label 'new classical' for the theory espoused by Lucas, Sargent and others, but the topography of macroeconomics has changed since then. Before the financial crisis of 2008 we heard a lot about a 'new consensus' view that involved convergence on Dynamic Stochastic General Equilibrium (DSGE) modeling; with 'New Keynesians' jumping aboard this bandwagon the classical/Keynesian dichotomy was supposedly out of date. For my purposes here I shall go with the term used by Krugman, 'neoclassical macroeconomics.' It should be noted that this does *not* refer to what we used to call the 'neoclassical synthesis' (à la Samuelson), which combined IS–LM Keynesianism with neoclassical microeconomics. Rather, we are talking about DSGE and the representative agent approach.

At some level, one can understand why Krugman is tempted to call neoclassical macro theory 'beautiful' even as he rejects it as false. There is some inherent intellectual attraction in a theory that claims to unify economics on the basis of the paradigm of constrained optimization. But at the same time there is something ugly about a theory that is so violently maladapted to the analysis of its supposed object. This point is well made in Robert Solow's testimony to the House Committee on Science and Technology (2010). The proponents of DSGE, Solow says,

> take it for granted that the whole economy can be thought about as if it were a single, consistent person or dynasty carrying out a rationally designed, long-term plan, occasionally disturbed by unexpected shocks, but adapting to them in a rational, consistent way. . . . The protagonists of this idea make a claim to respectability by asserting that it is founded on what we know about microeconomic behavior, but I think that this claim is generally phony. . . . [T]he basic story always treats the whole economy as if it were like a person, trying consciously and rationally to do the best it can on behalf of the representative agent, given its circumstances. This can not be an adequate description of a national economy, which is pretty conspicuously *not* pursuing a consistent goal. (p. 2)

Neoclassical macro may be *internally* consistent, but there is a gross inconsistency between the nature of the theory and nature of the domain it claims to theorize. This is not just a matter of the theory 'not fitting the facts,' although non-fitting of specific facts emerges as a consequence.

One anecdotal illustration: some colleagues and I interviewed a candidate for a teaching position in macroeconomics, a person about to complete his PhD at a high-powered 'freshwater' US university. His thesis topic was the 'paradoxical' co-movement of investment and consumption across the business cycle. According to theory, one would expect investment and consumption to be negatively related: if a technology shock raises the expected return on investment then the representative agent will invest more and consume less today; and if a shock reduces the expected return he will invest less and consume more. So why do we see investment and consumption moving in the same direction? Our candidate proposed to unravel this paradox by means of some very subtle optimization-based reasoning, backed of course by elaborate mathematics. Apparently he hadn't heard of the multiplier, or had been led to believe that this was a theoretical fossil of no relevance to modern macro. Start with a basic mismatch of theory and object, and the simplest macroeconomic facts will become puzzles, requiring epicycles worthy of Ptolemy for their resolution. This is not intellectual beauty.

Of course, the most important fact that is turned into a puzzle by the neoclassical approach is unemployment. Blanchard (2008) candidly admits as much in relation to the New Keynesian (NK) variant of this approach when he says, 'One striking (and unpleasant) characteristic of the basic NK model is that there is no unemployment!' And talking of unemployment naturally brings us to Keynes.

KEYNES'S THEORY UNDER-APPRECIATED

The supposed 'messiness' of Keynesian economics is associated with the idea that Keynes's theory rests on the brute empirical fact of wage and/or price stickiness, and hence on market 'imperfections' – an idea that was part and parcel of the neoclassical synthesis, in the US in particular. We shall come back to this point, but first let me state the positive case for the elegance of Keynes's theory as set out in the *General Theory* (Keynes, 1936).

The elegance of the *General Theory* lies in the way Keynes is able to build a powerful engine of analysis, capable of illuminating a wide range of macroeconomic phenomena, on the parsimonious basis of a few, very general facts about the macroeconomy. These facts do not speak for themselves but Keynes is able to make them speak, via a process of careful and subtle (but not overly subtle) logical development. His theory leads to conclusions that at first seem counter-intuitive, but once understood they are compelling: this in itself is one hallmark of scientific elegance.

What very general facts do I have in mind? Perhaps the most general are those regarding the income–expenditure and saving–investment relationships: accounting identities when considered *ex post* but equilibrium conditions (or rather, one way of looking at the same equilibrium condition) if considered in terms of planned or intended magnitudes.

The most general fact here is that income and expenditure are necessarily equal. When money changes hands in exchange for goods and services, that flow of money is expenditure from the point of view of the buyer but income from the point of view of the seller. This is true of every transaction and therefore true of all transactions taken in the aggregate, and it follows that aggregate income and aggregate expenditure are numerically identical, being two ways of looking at the same thing.

Leaving aside government and foreign trade, there is a similar (in fact, derivative) necessary equality between aggregate saving and investment: saving is income minus consumption, and investment is expenditure minus consumption. The definition of saving as income minus consumption was not self-evident, and was resisted by some of Keynes's contemporaries, but it was part of Keynes's genius to see that this was the most theoretically illuminating definition.

What follows? Keynes emphasized the obvious fact that in a modern economy, decisions regarding how much to save and how much to invest are typically taken by different people (or more generally, agents) and it cannot be a *necessary* fact that the sum of the amounts people intend to save equals the sum of the amounts they intend or plan to invest. But if the intended aggregates differ – while the actual aggregates cannot – there are consequences: in general, one or both of the actual aggregates will differ from its intended value. For example, if saving exceeds intended investment, the most likely symptom is that firms find they are investing more than they intended, in the form of a run-up of inventory of unsold consumer goods. The further consequence of such unintended investment is that production will be curtailed – either in direct response to the 'quantity signal' or via the mechanism of a fall in prices and profitability – and a reduction in output means a reduction in income.

The next logical step in Keynes's argument rests on another very general fact, namely that households tend to alter their consumption in the same direction as changes in their incomes but by a lesser amount – the famous fractional marginal propensity to consume. On this basis Keynes is able to set up an equilibrating mechanism: when intended saving and investment diverge, income will adjust to bring these two quantities into line.

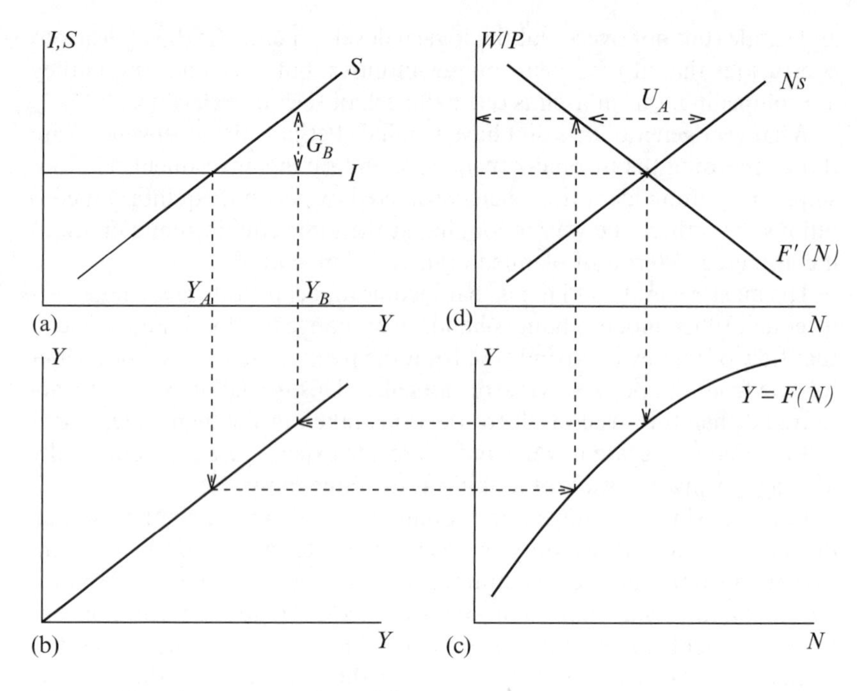

Figure 6.1 A representation of Keynes's system

Since my object here is to justify the claim that Keynes's theory should be considered elegant, not to explain the entire theory, perhaps I can fast-forward to the overall structure. As Keynes states in chapter 18 of the *General Theory*, he takes his 'independent variables' to be 'the propensity to consume, the schedule of the marginal efficiency of capital and the rate of interest.' He notes that each of these factors is 'capable of further analysis', but this 'further analysis' does not consist in reducing the variables in question to endogenous terms in a global optimization problem. The *relative* independence that Keynes accords to the schedule of the Marginal Efficiency of Capital and the rate of interest – which jointly govern the level of intended investment – licenses the idea that the burden of adjustment towards income–expenditure (or saving–investment) equilibrium is mostly borne by saving, as a function of income, rather than investment.

From this perspective, let's examine the idea that Keynes's conclusions rest on 'nominal rigidities' of questionable theoretical status. Here I draw upon the graphical presentation in Figure 6.1. I do not claim any great originality for this figure, but I think it helps to explicate the logic of Keynes's theory.

Start in panel (a), where aggregate saving, S, is shown as an increasing function of income, Y; and investment, I, is shown as an independently determined quantity, producing the so-called 'Keynesian cross.' This determines an equilibrium level of output and income, Y_A, at which saving equals intended investment. This level of output is then reflected via the 'mirror' in panel (b) into the space of a standard neoclassical production function (with fixed capital stock and diminishing returns to labor), in panel (c). Inverting the production function gives some definite level of employment, N, which is then sent into the labor market in panel (d). If – as Keynes assumes in the *General Theory* – the real wage somehow conforms itself to the marginal product of labor,[1] then we get a real wage (W/P) that stands above the level that would correspond to labor-market clearing, and we have unemployment equal to the horizontal gap between the labor supply and labor demand schedules, denoted by U_A.

Some caveats are in order in relation to the above but I shall hold them back until the main exposition is complete, so let's proceed. We shall now suppose that, given the unemployment U_A, wages start falling. Another basic factual point made by Keynes is that it is the *nominal* wage that is negotiated between workers and employers, but let's take the price level as 'given' (initially) so that any nominal wage reduction is also a real wage reduction; and for the sake of argument let's suppose that the real wage falls all the way to the level at which the labor market would appear to be in supply–demand equilibrium, as shown in Figure 6.1.

We then trace the resulting level of (full) employment back through the production function, and through the mirror, to panel (a). But here we find a problem. The corresponding income level is Y_B, at which the level of saving is higher than before while the level of intended investment remains unchanged. We therefore have a gap, denoted by G_B, between saving and intended investment, or in other words between income and intended expenditure. If this induces a fall in prices, the assumed fall in the real wage is at least partly undone. But in fact we can see that if income–expenditure equilibrium is to be regained, without a change in planned investment, the fall in the real wage must be *wholly* undone.

That is to say, 'flexibility' in the labor market is powerless to restore full employment so long as planned investment falls short of the volume of saving that would emerge out of full-employment income. Or in other words, downward flexibility of the nominal wage is helpful only if it is somehow conducive to an expansion of planned investment.

Those of us who have taught macroeconomics for a while know (sigh) of the mechanisms that might help: the so-called 'Keynes effect' whereby a fall in nominal income reduces the demand for money and hence lowers the interest rate, or the ultimate back-stop whereby the increase in the real value of a (presumably fixed) stock of 'outside' or fiat money eventually induces a sufficient positive wealth effect on consumption to remove the need for an increase in investment (the 'Pigou effect').

But hold it, on two grounds. First, if we're considering such arcane alleged benefits of deflation we had better consider the less arcane arguments for the perils of deflation: Irving Fisher's debt-deflation (highly relevant in an age of widespread deleveraging), as well as Keynes's arguments in chapter 19 of the *General Theory* (notably, that if current deflation induces an expectation of further deflation, it will lead to the postponement of expenditures) and Tobin's (1980) addendum to Fisher, namely that deflation redistributes wealth from borrowers, who presumably have a relatively high propensity to spend, to lenders, who presumably have a relatively low propensity.

Secondly, regardless of the virtues of these old arguments, it is now standard to represent monetary policy not in the shape of a fixed nominal stock of fiat money but in the shape of a 'Taylor rule.' In that context deflation is unambiguously unhelpful. *Disinflation* can be helpful, in that it permits a Taylor rule to recommend low interest rates, but deflation simply makes a low real rate of interest unattainable due to the Zero Lower Bound on the nominal rate (a point which Paul Krugman rightly emphasizes).

Now for the postponed caveats relating to Figure 6.1. First, some might quarrel with the use of the primitive 'Keynesian cross' in panel (a). If you prefer to put an IS–LM diagram in this panel you may do so, but in my view this represents a lossy compression of Keynes's ideas.[2] Recall that Keynes takes the rate of interest as one his independent variables, while admitting that it may be 'capable of further analysis.' The IS–LM system bossily takes charge of this 'further analysis,' installing a quasi-reduced form in which the interest rate is an increasing function of income and a decreasing function of the nominal money stock. This may be reasonable under some conditions but it is a restriction on the generality of Keynes's analysis, which allows for the possibility that the interest rate may be governed by 'convention' on the financial markets . . . or for that matter by a Taylor rule. An amendment more in line with Keynes's ideas might be to add an apparatus that explicitly references the MEC schedule and the rate of interest (see Figure 6.2) but I am not sure this is necessary to my argument.

Others might object to the inclusion of a standard production function with diminishing returns to labor in panel (c) of Figure 6.1, and the representation of its first derivative as a standard 'labor demand' schedule in panel (d), but here I am simply following Keynes in accepting the 'first classical postulate' for the sake of argument (see chapter 2 of the *General Theory*).

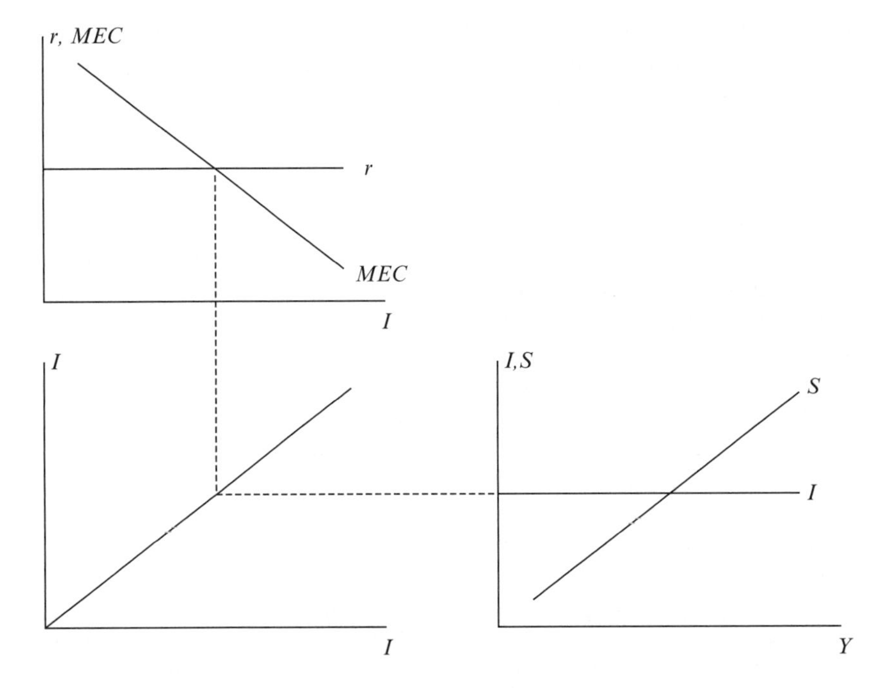

Figure 6.2 Optional extension of the first figure

SOME OBJECTIONS CONSIDERED

Some objections to the account of Keynes's theory given above are quite predictable, and it may be helpful to address them here.

First, I claimed that Keynes's theory represents a logical development from certain 'very general facts' about the macroeconomy. If these facts represent outcomes of calculations made by agents under a specific 'regime' then they could be subject to change if the regime were to change, as per the famous Lucas critique, hence undermining Keynes's conclusions. But a little reflection reveals that the facts in question are not really vulnerable in this way.

This is most obvious for the income–expenditure and saving–investment relationships. These are not outcomes of individual optimization but rather constitute an inexorable structure within which individual optimization takes place. The fractional marginal propensity to consume does not have that status, but it can easily be shown to be consistent with a wide range of optimizing behavior by households (notably smoothing of consumption over the life-cycle) and it is hard to see how a policy regime change could undermine that conclusion. The same goes for Keynes's downward-sloping MEC schedule. In fact, justification of the key behavioral relationships taken as facts by Keynes via robust optimizing arguments was a stock in trade of traditional macroeconomics textbooks. And note that the Phillips curve – the principal target of the Lucas critique – was not a relationship upon which Keynes relied.

Secondly, let's consider the question of unexploited potential gains from trade. If the trajectory of the macroeconomy is considered to be the solution to a unitary optimization problem, the idea that unexploited gains from trade should exist is inconceivable. Or at least, unexploited mutual gains could only be the result of externally imposed constraints such as minimum wage laws; they could not arise endogenously, provided agents are fully rational. And yet Keynes's 'involuntary unemployment' represents, it would seem, unexploited gains on a grand scale – so there must be something amiss in Keynesian theory.

Despite his skeptical take on neoclassical macro, it seems that Krugman is influenced by this idea. In a blog posting (Krugman, 2011) he writes:

> What economists have known since Bagehot (with regard to financial markets) and since Keynes (with regard to goods and labor markets) is that under some circumstances seemingly reasonable individual behavior adds up to very unreasonable macro outcomes. Bagehot wrote of panics in which the collective desire to shed risky assets and debt produced a downward spiral; Keynes of situations in which the collective desire to save but not invest led to mass unemployment. And in both cases these arguments suggested a case for government intervention to undo or limit the bad macro consequences of reasonable individual behaviour.

Fine – I have no quarrel with that statement – but Krugman then asks the reader to notice 'that I've framed this in terms of "reasonable" behavior; it's a lot harder to tell these stories in terms of perfectly rational, maximizing behavior.' Krugman doesn't actually say it is impossible to generate Keynesian results if agents are all assumed to be perfectly rational, but neither does he say it is possible.

Notice what is happening here. Krugman certainly does not think that people are all perfectly rational all the time. His recommendations to the profession in his 2009 article include, for example, a plea that macroeconomists should take behavioral finance seriously. Yet he is sufficiently influenced by classical views to suspect that *if* perfect rationality reigned it would be very hard to defend Keynes.

Let's back up for a moment: I started on this topic by stating that if the trajectory of the macroeconomy is seen as the solution to a unitary optimization problem, unexploited gains from trade become inconceivable.

Here's my point: saying that all agents are rational is not the same thing as saying that the state of the macroeconomy is the solution to an optimization problem. The latter claim is much stronger, and not defensible. Each agent may be optimizing and yet the macro outcome fails to maximize anything. I take this as one way of stating Keynes's key point.

We can make sense of this claim by taking another look at (and thinking a bit more broadly about) the graphical representation of Keynes's system given earlier (Figure 6.1). Start once again from the income–expenditure equilibrium at Y_A. A rational worker, currently unemployed, is willing to work for less than the going real wage. A rational price-taking employer is willing to hire this worker, on the assumption that the output price will remain unchanged. This is repeated over a large number of workers and employers. The result is that aggregate income increases and a saving–investment gap opens up, causing a fall in the price of output and undoing the initial fall in the real wage. The system can proceed to full employment only if the sum of the investment plans of the rational employers equals full-employment saving. But there is nothing in the bare idea that employers are optimizing that guarantees this outcome.

We can gain additional perspective by considering what it *would* take to eliminate the macroeconomic problem that Keynes diagnoses. A sufficient condition would be that we are in what Keynes called a 'cooperative economy' (in an early draft introduction to the *General Theory*). That is, workers are paid their marginal product in kind, not in money. In that case there is no problem of demand, and workers remain unemployed only if they choose to – that is, if the marginal disutility of work exceeds the real wage. Alternatively, the workers have a marginal propensity to consume of unity. This would rule out the specifically macro problem noted above, since an increase in income as employment rises would no longer generate a saving–investment gap. (A *microeconomic* problem might remain, if the composition of output fails to match the composition of consumer demand at the margin, but that's a different matter.) But if we live (a) in a monetary economy where (b) households want to save at the margin, Keynes's problem stands, no matter how rational people are.

CONCLUSION

I have argued that Keynes's macroeconomic theory has a coherence and elegance of its own: it is not just a matter of taking a basically classical system and throwing in a few 'frictions' and 'imperfections' (although this is a defensible description of New Keynesian economics). Rather, Keynes's theory is based on a careful tracing out of the logical consequences of some very general – one might almost say self-evident – facts about the object of analysis: a money-using, capitalist economy.

I am not saying that frictions, imperfections and bounded rationality are irrelevant to macroeconomics. If we want greater realism in our macro theory then – as Krugman says – we need to incorporate such things. But it is a commonplace observation that there is a trade-off between detail and conceptual clarity, and the desirable point on that trade-off depends on the particular question we are trying to address. What I am saying is that Keynes offers a clear 'high-level' conceptual account of the problem of demand-deficient unemployment in capitalist economies, and for some (not all) purposes that is enough.

NOTES

1. Keynes called this the 'first classical postulate,' and he accepted it; what he rejected was the 'second classical postulate,' namely that the real wage equals the marginal disutility of labor, or in other words that we are always on the labor supply curve.
2. In image processing and the digital music world, a 'lossy' compression method is one that irretrievably loses some features of the original signal, for example the MP3 format. This can be contrasted with 'lossless' compression, as with zip files containing documents that can be reconstituted exactly as they were before compression.

REFERENCES

Blanchard, O. (2008) 'The state of macro'. Massachusetts Institute of Technology, Department of Economics, Working Paper 08-17.

Keynes, J.M. (1936) *The General Theory of Employment, Interest and Money*, London: Macmillan.

Krugman, P. (2009) 'How did economists get it so wrong?', *The New York Times Magazine* (September 2).

Krugman, P. (2011) 'Golden oldies (wonkish)'. Blog posting. Available at http://krugman.blogs.nytimes.com/2011/04/11/. Last accessed 1 March 2013.

Solow, R.M. (2010) 'Building a science of economics for the real world'. Prepared testimony, House Committee on Science and Technology, Subcommittee on Investigations and Oversight. Available at http://www.econ.iastate.edu/classes/econ502/tesfatsion/Solow.StateOfMacro.CongressionalTestimony.July2010.pdf. Last accessed 1 March 2013.

Tobin, J. (1980) *Asset Accumulation and Economic Activity*, Oxford: Basil Blackwell.

7. Rhetoric in the spirit of Keynes: metaphors to persuade economists, students and the public about fiscal policy

Bruce Littleboy

A slogan is often more effective than a treatise.
Dagobert D. Runes (1966, p. 131)

INTRODUCTION

This chapter goes beyond reciting the letter of Keynes. It is about selling policies. Keynes had his mind on framing a valid theory so that its suitable application would enhance human wellbeing. Some of his policies were intended as short-period responses and others formed part of a strategy of social transformation. Keynes had personal and practical views about fiscal policy and about fiscal financing, but this chapter takes a different, less exegetical, direction. It veers unashamedly into rhetoric.

In each context some specific aspect of the truth may be revealed or concealed by the method used to convey it. This chapter explores how our metaphors reveal our assumptions, some of which are tacit and perhaps even unknown to the unreflective debater. Roger Garrison (1995) put it splendidly: 'the lens becomes more like a mirror'.

The global financial crisis has lent a pragmatic respectability to interventionism, but it has not revived interest by the profession at large in the deeper conceptual foundations of Keynes's macroeconomics. We may be missing a chance to make progress in widening the understanding of how Keynes strived to transform economics. Our rhetoric is not good enough; we are persuading neither our colleagues nor the public that fiscal intervention is based on prudence rather than espoused in desperation. By being too cerebral and remote, academics may be missing a rare historical opportunity to advance Keynes's ideas. Letters signed by hundreds of economists will not sway the public if the policy that is advocated conflicts with common sense.

Those who appreciate the economics of Keynes are frustrated by the superficial and limited way that policy makers and leading policy advocates are drawing some supposed inspiration from him. After the crisis passes, the trajectory of economics may return to normal. Neither Keynes himself nor his followers have conveyed their key ideas with sufficient persuasive power. But if our army is smaller, we will need to have superior rhetorical weapons. Having models with more realistic assumptions has not sufficed.

We can no longer take delight in the counter-intuitive and assert that governments enhance prosperity even by wasteful spending. Either we sell waste better or we try a new angle and sell fiscal policy as enhancing efficiency. This chapter explores both options.

The economics of Keynes has been too aggregated for too long. What used to be simplified has become simplistic. Our practised and our recommended fiscal and monetary policies look crude and ill-conceived, and governments and their electorates lose confidence when massive amounts are involved and the results appear so modest. Better targeting of policy may be much of the answer, and, if only to convince enough academics, there needs to be a corresponding re-formulation of simple theoretical and conceptual issues. By improving the marketability of Keynes, some of the market share captured by Austrian economics may also be reclaimed.

This chapter looks again at long-established ways to convey metaphorically the intuition of some of the arguments for and against demand stimulus during slumps. Robert Lucas (in Klamer, 1984) has derided the *General Theory (GT)* as poorly written, over-rated and out of date. If academic economics proceeded efficiently, the best available science would be embodied in the latest working paper written at the University of Chicago. (Generations ago there was a similar belief that it happened at Cambridge, of course.) Others may instead take a more Lakatosian view. While money on a pavement is soon picked up, good ideas are often left lost in the library. Science can backtrack and recover its lost treasures.

ON ANALOGIES – AND THINGS THAT ARE LIKE THEM

When it comes to metaphors, macroeconomics is well endowed. Our textbooks explain the circular flow of income, with its leakages and injections rendered concretely in the famous Phillips machine. Fortunately we have policy levers, and there are instruments that we can tighten and loosen.

Occasional pump priming may be needed in slumps. A rising tide indeed raises all boats. Funds are stored in government coffers from the surpluses we accumulate in good times. And premature fiscal and monetary easing may use up our ammunition too soon. Money has its own metaphors too: it serves both as a lubricant and a veil, but beware of the liquidity trap. Watch out for bulls and bears too.

It is now commonplace to say that economics has its rhetoric, and metaphor is part of rhetoric. Here I shall loosely slide between metaphor, analogy, simile, slogan and parable. All aim to distil difficult or unfamiliar interrelationships into a form that is more readily assimilable. Macroeconomic reasoning is not itself directly part of ordinary experience. Metaphor reduces complexity to something expressible. Familiar things need not be simple; we may strive to understand an unfamiliar complex system by finding similar patterns in complex systems that we know better. While formal mathematics can camouflage implausible combinations of assumptions,[1] plausible metaphors contain a cluster of recognisably context-consistent assumptions. Isn't a test of a good metaphor whether it is self-explanatory in its context? Debating the merits of a metaphor helps us probe what we are really talking about. Often what is contested is what may reasonably be held constant during some process, and differences emerge when rival metaphors collide.

Doubtless there is a learned literature (I am not familiar with much of it[2]) that maps the meaning and significance of analogy and metaphor in art, poetry, pedagogy and science.[3] A metaphor has three clear uses: it inspires new hypotheses, it is a means of education and spreading ideas, and (more ambitiously) it tests causal reasoning by permitting critical thought-experiments. Just swallowing one metaphor permits the absorption of a simplified model or a chain of reasoning. Simplified, heuristic models lie between vision (Schumpeter) and a formal analytical model, as Vercelli notes (1991, p. 8). A metaphor opens the mind to the heuristic by encapsulating key causal or conceptual linkages. The mind becomes more receptive to the basic model.

A metaphor can convey a bundle of subversive ideas directly, without the provocative labels and the off-putting jargon. There may be an alternative to a head-on assault on the citadel of orthodoxy. Post-Keynesian economics (if it exists as an entity) rightly or wrongly views itself as facing an effectively monolithic enemy. We often label it 'neoclassicism' as if the act of naming confers a reality. In Lakatosian terms, we face a mighty 'protective belt' that shields a potentially fragile core. It is as though we confront the Maginot Line and are wondering what to do next. This chapter asks a question of any reader it finds: 'Excuse me, which way is Belgium?'[4]

Even the most secluded of academics has likely noticed that recent fiscal stimulus packages initiated in several countries have been extensively criticised. Old debates and their modern corollaries are being re-argued spiritedly; see for example the web debate in *The Economist* (2009). Discussion among academics has been in the public arena, so the deep differences in the approaches of Keynesian and classical economics have been stated in plain and accessible terms. Analogies have been used to show the intuition underlying the case of each side. This has been a rare opportunity to get into the minds of the rivals who are major figures in the discipline. For decades technical economics has masked these deeper differences that have been long and deeply debated in the history of economic thought and never properly resolved. Neither side seems to be much aware of the exaggerations underpinning their confident claims and counter-claims. We are not just playing academic games now; ideas matter again. Keynesians have opportunities to make a positive case for fiscal policy, and there are counter-attacks on fiscal policy against which Keynesians can prepare defences.

DEFENSIVE STRATAGEMS

Most orthodox economists were taught Keynesian economics of a kind in their early training; the pragmatists among them may be swayable even if our paradigms may be incommensurable on some dimensions. But our early shared training may itself be a problem.

Conceptualising macroeconomic causality using the framework of the circular flow of income both permits and limits understanding. As well as encouraging the idea that macroeconomics is an engineering exercise in hydraulics, the famous Phillips machine evokes some dubious loanable-funds metaphors which pose potential difficulties. There is a reservoir containing a flow of saving that may or may not be re-injected. One needs to be careful to remember the game one is playing and the conceptual adjustments one is making. If one removes the world of deposit-creation and finance by credit, and if one wants to explain income-equilibration in such a highly stylised context, then it may become necessary to cast aside things a purist may regard as right thinking. It is awkward when introductory models actually place obstacles on the pathway towards more detailed and realistic ones.

Worse still, sometimes saving disappears from the circular into a wormhole. In these renditions investment spending is injected without the source of the finance being evident. Money appears or disappears as required. The size and structure of the financial sector seem a matter of indifference. There is a silent *ceteris paribus*. Investment and saving are disconnected but without explanation.

Many depictions of financing are instead based on the treasure-chest analogy. We refer to government coffers and bank reserves as though they had physical reality. And there is an uninvited connotation of loanable funds, a pool which can be built up and run down, and which is auctioned by banks according to willingness and ability to pay interest. If the government is added, the fate of fiscal surpluses and the source of deficits remain a mystery. (In one course, I was boldly Keynesian and represented government financing as a box on the circular-flow diagram with a printing press and an incinerator inside.)

UNPERSUASIVELY DEFENDING FISCAL POLICY

There are several themes that recur in criticisms made of Keynesian economics and its theoretical justification for demand stimulus in slumps. Modern revivals of the notorious Treasury View are commonplace. Money borrowed to fund fiscal deficits diverts funds from alternative, more productive, uses. Keynesians are prepared to spend wastefully. Besides, fiscal stimulus is small to non-existent. Keynesians do not understand the complexities of structural adjustments in a market economy and are crass aggregators. Keynesian reasoning is not merely flawed: it is absurd. A Keynesian is unlikely to convert hardline critics, but there may be a less committed middle ground that is open to persuasion. What follows are some counter-arguments and some suggestions intended as means to improve our arguments in support of fiscal activism.

DEBT IS GOOD!?

Many still suffer from deficit attention disorder. 'Deficit' is a word, not a sentence. It triggers moral panic (and even the 'yuk' response) in many circles, but Keynesians are almost blasé about it. We sound strange. Doing whatever needed to be done, and accepting whatever fiscal deficit resulted (i.e. functional finance), was once publicly acceptable; perhaps it still is with the contemporary proviso that over the cycle the budget should be balanced. (Building reserves in good times to run down in bad times should make tolerable sense to any conservative, even though Keynesians wince at the loanable-funds connotation.) According to Allan Meltzer (2009): 'When Keynes read Abba Lerner's paper on functional finance, he accepted Lerner's argument for large deficits, then he added: "but heaven help anyone that tries to put it across.'"

Followers of Keynes need to be able to argue plausibly that debt is warranted, even if expenditures incurred are wasteful in some sense.

WASTE IS GOOD!?

Government spending, especially when conceived and implemented in haste, is likely to prove wasteful. While Keynes preferred socially useful government spending to wasteful forms, a Keynes-style argument is that the latter would be much better than doing nothing. Spending for its own sake sounds very like a breach of trust though, and the idea is hard to sell: debts are incurred without assets to back them up and people are 'employed' doing essentially nothing.

There is the old, but influential, illustration from Bastiat about striving to stimulate trade by smashing windows so that glaziers will be busy repairing them. But for every metaphor there is a rejoinder. Keynesians need to be ready with them. For example, no Keynesian is advocating the policy-equivalent of breaking windows, but, if they are already broken by vandals, it makes sense to repair them. But this reply evades the issue: where are followers of Keynes prepared to stand, in theory and in practice, on the merits of 'wasteful' government spending as a means of providing fiscal stimulus?

Keynes took the most provocative line: demand stimulus is demand stimulus whatever its source. We can bury banknotes and dig them up, build cathedrals or (something normatively preferable) build houses and art galleries. To alleviate a slump, efficient spending is better than wasteful spending, but buying something is better than buying nothing.

Keynes's attitude and his reasoning are revealed in his example concerning towels.

In one case though, Keynes's rhetorical flair got the better of him:

> During a 1934 dinner in the U.S., after one economist carefully removed a towel from a stack to dry his hands, Mr. Keynes swept the whole pile of towels on the floor and crumpled them up, explaining that his way of using towels did more to stimulate employment among restaurant workers. (See Reddy (2009).)

Even on his own terms, this only makes sense if Maynard is sent the bill and pays it. Raising the private costs of doing business without raising demand (revenue) by at least as much does no good. (To risk a distracting digression, Keynes's likely error here may reflect his highly debatable suggestion that money-wage rises may boost total demand and jobs. If so, then thinking about the metaphor has exposed the fault in the analysis that inspired it.)

This case shows that wastefulness is not sufficient for providing a demand stimulus. It makes better rhetorical sense to focus on how markets can waste resources through idleness than to advocate wasteful activity by government.

Keynesians need some rhetoric that defends spending that appears to be wasteful but is not. Here is an example, but it is not a powerful one. During an emergency, it may be valid to tear sheets into bandages. (The metaphor does its job, but it needs a squad of more muscular helpers.) It is true that the cloth involved in the form of bandages may actually be more valuable than in the form of sheets, but my point here is that it is hard to sell such a seeming riches-to-rags story. And a possible rhetorical drawback of the sheets-to-bandages metaphor is that it points to the negligence of those involved: shouldn't there have been a supply of bandages ready for such emergencies? Indeed there ought to have been, which is embarrassing. We are trying to legitimise government activism and do not really want arguments that allude *en route* to the apparent prevalence of government incompetence.

EXPOSING THE COUNTERFACTUALS TO JUSTIFY FISCAL DEBT

We may regard the global financial crisis as akin to the system having a sudden heart attack. The emergency surgery appears to have little effect as the patient remains feeble, and we have yet to return to our former trend. And it has been financially costly: what have we to show for it except a debt scar?

A reply goes like this. It would be foolish to conclude that the triple bypass (fiscal stimulus) did little good and may have made things worse. The 'health recession' would have been rather worse without it. The counterfactual is not some presumed automatic recovery; death is the relevant counterfactual. The relevant benchmark is not the trend before the heart attack. So it is invalid to say that the scar (the government debt) was a needless cost.

There are related econometric issues. Keynesians will also need rhetoric to guard their kill from scavengers. If stimulus policies succeed, others will try to claim the credit for the resilience of markets. Econometricians may attribute recovery to a restoration of exports, and then trade, market forces and flexible exchange rates would be credited. But if higher government spending in one country draws in exports from others, it is important to realise that global fiscal expansion may be the true cause of the global rise in exports. A one-country analysis will discover a stronger relationship between GDP and exports than between GDP and its own structural fiscal deficit. There will be free-riders who did not provide stimulus but exported to those who did.

Also note that, for a global fiscal stimulus to meet a global downturn, net imports equal zero. We do not trade with the Martians. The global marginal propensity to import is zero too, so the global fiscal multiplier will exceed a national open-economy multiplier that econometricians typically measure.

One the other hand, there are forces at work that may yield global fiscal multipliers that are disappointingly low. It is a mystery why anyone believed that stimulus multipliers observed during normal times would apply during abnormal times. If the capacity of the system to function has itself been weakened because of damage to the tendrils of supply, it may not be able to respond as promptly to demand-side medicine. Furthermore, any discretionary consumption is not as likely to respond strongly to attempted fiscal stimulus during calamities. Those who are repairing their balance sheets may not be providing a spending stimulus, but reducing the fragility of wealth and finance is still a useful thing.

ANTI-KEYNES RHETORIC: POSSIBLE ANTIDOTES

What is striking is that Keynesian ideas once regarded as routine and introductory are now widely regarded as being fallacious at best and dangerously imbecilic at worst. Clearly the critics of fiscal policy are baffled and frustrated by the widespread academic and expert acceptance of fiscal stimulus. They surely were right and they had the Nobel Prizes to prove it. And to explain things to Chicagoans and their sympathisers Paul Krugman needs to resort to publicising diagrams once prominent in textbooks.

The traditional Keynesian position is put by Krugman (2009), who draws a two-sector leakages-and-injections diagram. In this picture saving (S) plus taxes (T) equal investment (I) plus government spending (G), the accounting identity that both Eugene Fama and John Cochrane think vitiates fiscal policy – but it doesn't. See Cassidy (2010) and Cochrane (2009). An increase in G does not reduce I one-for-one, it shifts ($I + G$) upwards and instead increases GDP, which leads to higher realised aggregate S and T.

This comforting Keynesian conclusion stems from the key assumption that investment is autonomous, unaffected (not reduced) by the higher government spending. Other slope and intercept values are assumed constant. Given the assumptions, the Keynesian case is correct. The conversion of circular-flow analogy into its mathematical counterpart convinces nobody who rejects the validity of the thought experiment being modelled. No amount of formal mathematics will persuade a sceptic because they will simply reject the starting equations, the signs of functional relationships or the posited dynamics. They think we have deceived ourselves.

Our conclusion may sound too good to be true. In the Australian context, Tony Makin (2010) states: 'All spending must be funded one way or another, however, and the funds borrowed for that purpose exhaust funds that could finance other economic activity.' Henry Ergas (2009b) dismisses this (appropriating Bentham's metaphor, by the way):

> Ultimately, all government spending must be paid for from taxes that have high economic costs. To claim that Keynesian multipliers create magic puddings[5] that can make this all come good is nonsense on stilts. A dollar misspent is a dollar misspent, and reduces incomes by at least that amount. The employment 'created' by that dollar, when it could have been used for more worthwhile alternatives, is part of the waste, not a benefit.

The key ideas of Keynes's economics are fairly simple, but Keynesians have delighted in provocatively presenting them as paradoxical, and this may have been a bad rhetorical tactic. ('You have to be in a really clever minority, like me, to understand Keynesian economics.' And sometimes even we are not clever enough.[6]) There are times when, contrary to Keynes, words need to be a little mild. Otherwise Keynesians will find themselves lampooned for what they did actually say.

There is a catch that even Keynesians concede. The increase in G is soon self-funding,[7] but there is still the matter of covering the cyclical deficit created by the long and deep slump itself. For this, there will need to be a few subsequent booms to generate sufficient cyclical fiscal windfalls.

Ricardian Equivalence is sometimes regarded as the final nail in the Keynesian coffin. It has to be true in logic that sooner or later taxpayers will bear the burden. Both classical theory and untutored common sense (you can't get something for nothing) suggest the same thing. But the Australian public did not think about Ricardian Equivalence when cash payments were proposed to meet the crisis. Certainly there was no discussion of whether the tax cut was to be effected by printing money or funded by tax collections later. Cartoonists may be more perceptive observers and communicators than economists are. When the Australian government implemented a lump-sum cash-payments scheme, the Leader of the

Opposition was depicted as trampled down in the stampede of popularity (see Nicholson (2009)). Ordinary opinion suddenly became pliable and knows a good thing when it sees it.

A picture of money has shaped contemporary policy debates. Such money can sit in coffers. It is regarded as ammunition that can be fired only once. Governments should not use up their ammunition before the war is over. But when money is used, it is not used up. But even here the ammunition has not been used up; it has merely been moved from government coffers to private ones.

THE COMMON SENSE IN FISCAL POLICY

The most relevant aspects of the Keynesian vision reduce to these simplicities. If resources are left idle, output is lost forever. It is not stored up for later use. It is not correct to regard resources as storable stocks, just as it is not correct to regard loanable funds as storable in treasure chests. Classical economists make the same conceptual mistake and metaphorical mis-selection in both the real and the financial sector.

If the flow of services from inputs cannot be stored for future use, it is better to produce and consume now than not to produce at all. Compared with producing nothing, more consumption spending does raise GDP if a flow of resource utilisation is available. Our wealth is our ability to produce. Inactive capacity is less valuable than active capacity. Wealth rises when it is used. In a slump, a rise in effective demand brings supply back into operation and raises *effective wealth*.[8] And wealth effects themselves spur consumption. Demand and the health of the supply side are related. A chaotic and disrupted supply side need not respond to demand stimulus. Demand management may need to have one eye on repairing broken links in the supply chains of production and finance: this is classical-inspired activism. Derangement and disarray are not to be confused with efficient search equilibrium.

Waiting to activate a flow of services from labour and capital typically only reduces our wellbeing. Critics of Keynesianism often appear to regard resources as a stock. If you use something now, you can't use it later when it would have been more valuably allocated. Surely the analogy is revealed as false as soon as it is identified and stated. Pondering analogies helps us to catch the bungle. Capital and labour that are currently in existence need to be used now and used later. Their user cost (wear-and-tear through use) may often be negligible. Nothing is gained from not using them now but only using them later. Analogies with oil reserves, maturing bottles of wine or a growing forest are false. Production using what already exists cannot be wasteful if demand covers the variable cost of production. Sunk costs are not opportunity costs.

The same false analogy spreads across a range of critiques of fiscal stimulus. Suppose governments use idle resources to build roads that go nowhere in particular. All that is then left behind is a new road, and better a road that currently leads nowhere than no road at all. And it will probably lead somewhere one day. There is no more of a 'distortion' in allocation than if a natural event made transport easier than before. A road that is built, or a river that is navigable, is there to be used. If resources later are attracted to the river, there is no market 'distortion'. If resources are attracted to a road, likewise there is no distortion in allocation. A road that is built is largely a sunk cost. The only economic cost once the bridge is built is maintenance, and if it turns out that the marginal social benefit does not even cover this, then let it degrade. If the choice is between a road to nowhere and no output at all, the former involves greater aggregate economic wealth. At least the road is potentially useful.

In 1942 Keynes argued for post-war urban reconstruction. To confront the rhetorical question, 'Where is the money going to come from?' he said, 'anything we can actually *do* we can afford' (CW XXVII, p. 270). If all the resources are just sitting there going to waste, it is silly not to put them to some reasonable use instead. If the only thing holding production back is a temporary reduction in demand, then raise demand back towards its sustainable level.

TARGETED FISCAL POLICY

Standard renditions of Keynesian fiscal policy have high levels of aggregation. Priming the pump is sometimes regarded as sophistication in conservative fiscal policy. It was Keynesianism in a form that a practical farmer or engineer could understand and accept. Is it ever asked whether fiscal policies can alleviate blockages caused by failures in key private sector supply linkages brought about by crises?

Consider the housing glut in the US. Homes have been abandoned and large areas stand evacuated. There are people who want to live in houses, and who have some money. As individuals they do not want to live in an empty suburb, but there may be enough individuals scattered to fill a suburb. Houses are rapidly deteriorating, and markets currently are not able to marry those with the money to cover the net avoidable costs and cut the losses of both mortgagor and mortgagee. The assets are being physically destroyed by neglect, vandalism and crime. If governments could speedily initiate targeted rescue programmes, wealth would be preserved and protected. If these developments are too far from schools, build schools. If transport costs are too high for people to commute, provide a bus link. If an economy is a network, its links can be repaired with far-reaching benefits beyond the demand-side multiplier effects. If the fabric of supply and finance is shredded, private companies are even less likely to create entire communities complete with infrastructure. Governments can alleviate such effective supply failures and expand the size and scope of the viable network of production and exchange through time and space. Supply networks disrupted by broken links of finance, information and trust can be restored. Agility here requires vigilance and pre-approved funding; these government economists would be in a rapid response unit.

Something similar can apply to targeting demand. The information about particular pockets of lower-than-normal demand may be available. If you know from experience that normally 100 raincoats are bought and sold, but in a slump the figure is only 60, it is reasonably safe for a government to place an order for an extra 20 or 30. (Some will realise that this is offered to meet Hayek's notorious argument that raising the demand for raincoats would only deepen the structural crisis. Restoring normal demand is hardly likely to spur unwarranted investments in factories that make raincoats.) There could be a significant private notional demand across the economy for these raincoats, but unemployment has rendered this demand ineffective.

WHAT CAN WE LEARN FROM THE AUSTRIANS?

Austrians see pattern in complex systems. These patterns indicate to them that interventionist attempts to control these systems undermine the subtle control systems that have already evolved. Consequently Austrians limit the scope for government action, including fiscal policy. And they sometimes put their case with confidence, if not brashness. By contrast, textbook Keynesians explain how policy actions by a few properly trained macroeconomists (remarkably like themselves) can engineer a higher order in a system otherwise lurching out of control. Austrian stories of causation centre on how individual actions create spontaneous order. Keynesians explain how individual actions can generate widening and deepening disorder. It is conventional to regard these paradigms as incommensurable, but syntheses happen whether the protagonists like it or not.[9]

Keynesians have not taken seriously the argument money is never truly idle; it is part of the web of finance that permits a coherent allocation of resources at any time and over time.

IDLE THOUGHTS ON MONEY

Keynesians tend to aggregate and render homogeneity across the group. But critics of the logic of Keynesian demand stimulus claim that even if a resource or asset appears to be idle, it may be waiting for the efficient moment to become overtly active. What appears to be idleness is stillness poised to leap. The argument (if this is the right word) is used in connection with labour, capital and with financial assets. As an argument in the real sector, it lacks plausibility to those who regard involuntary unemployment as a valid concept. Unemployed workers would be resting, waiting, rethinking, relocating and retraining. But the parallel argument may have more merit in the financial sector. (Nothing here suggests that activity, even hyperactivity, in the financial sector is necessarily efficient though.)

It is neither obviously true nor obviously false that money is 'idle' in slumps and can be borrowed without much concern about side-effects now or later. This is a research topic to explore, not one to decide by edict as a core assumption. Of course, it is harder to believe rationally that resources are not really idle when they observably are, but this is nevertheless widely done by classical economists.

The Keynesian use of the term, 'idle', has probably misled many, including some Keynesians. Money held as wealth in the financial sector may be whizzing around from one financial market to the next. Money can be 'hot' and energetic or it can sit for a while in cold storage in a term deposit. The asset velocity of money may be extremely high, but its income velocity may be low. Funds churned furiously do not lead to the generation of currently produced goods and services. Asset prices (house prices, share prices) rise, but the production of new houses and new factories lags, or never eventuates.

Keynesians have unwisely dismissed the possible intricacies of the financial network. The Keynesian assumption that the financial sector can adapt rapidly to digest large volumes of government bonds should have been subjected to more critical scrutiny. Funds may not simply be there to be easily siphoned off. What Keynesians regard as mere liposuction of surplus fat, Austrians regard as the excision of crucial healthy specialised tissue.

Both the Austrian and the Keynesian positions are perfectly intelligible and each may be valid in a particular time or place. These judgements are central to the art of economics. Keynes's point was that the stock of saving is very large, and some of the money now churned in the financial sector can be borrowed by the government and disbursed without significantly reducing the ability of private investors to obtain funds for real investment. You can agree or disagree, but the point is whether you understand what economists are disagreeing about and why.

Keynesians often speak of idle money as the counterpart of idle resources. They argue that fiscal policy can impart stimulus if monetary policy cannot (the liquidity trap, for example). Idle savings (the stock partly held in the form of money) can be borrowed and re-injected into the circular flow. So if funding extra government outlays by printing new money is unacceptable, the necessary funds can be borrowed. The early Keynesian vision was of wealthy, do-nothing, coupon-clipping rentiers supposedly being rewarded merely for 'waiting'. Siphoning funds from them can do no harm to production; indeed, their gradual and automatic 'euthanasia' in a maturing economy is something to look forward to.

The Austrian View in tolerably truthful caricature is that saved funds return to the real economy as productive investment in due course after an efficient linking and networking of financial flows through space and time. Austrians argue that Keynesians are wrong to regard these funds as 'idle' and ripe for borrowing. The complex tendrils of asset and finance markets are too opaque and delicately structured to allow heavy macro-interventions, especially in the form of lorry loads of broadly homogeneous government paper being dumped in one part of the system, especially a part that may already be distressed and damaged.

The Keynesian approach to financial markets is as highly macro as its view of goods and factor markets: a rising financial tide raises all assets. Asset complementarities are restored. The fine microstructure of financial markets is no more crucial than the fine microstructure of the real economy. Markets will sort out compositional disturbances and absorb macro-interventions. Keynesians treat markets more roughly; they may have more faith in the resilience of markets than Austrians do.

Although the classical end of the spectrum bears the main brunt of criticism in this chapter, there is also a surprising high-handedness in how Keynesians respond to their critics. In particular, the effect of large sales of bonds on highly compromised financial markets appears to be of little concern to many Keynesians, if only because there may be no alternative and the problem can be sorted out later.

CONCLUSIONS

A slogan is indeed often more effective than a treatise. The art of rhetoric centres on controlling the focal point of the discussion. Metaphor and its cousins cut through the detail to the point of contention.

We may reject metaphor in our official pronouncements over proper method, but we soon resort to it in debate when we meet resistance. Analogies reveal what we are really talking about. Astute metaphors may enhance the quality of policy advice and foster scientific advance.

Metaphor is also a source of energy, a lubricant and a catalyst. The last is the least recognised and the most interesting. A metaphor permits clusters of ideas to click together or to come apart for re-combination elsewhere. We should take our own metaphors and those of others very seriously.

Analogies eventually break down, as we all have been sagely told. But this suggests that up to some point they in fact work. Exactly where the analogy breaks down may tell us something new about the problem we are studying.

Recent debates over the suitability of fiscal policy in part reflect an Austrian critique of the Keynesian approach. In some respects, the debate barely extends beyond assertion and crude metaphor. The different intuitions are in collision; they are not yet in exploratory engagement. This chapter is offered as a beginning step.

Post-Keynesians sometimes have a siege mentality and dream of escaping what is depicted as hostile encirclement by orthodoxy. There is sometimes a two-way lack of courtesy and respect.[10] The rhetoric needs to fit the reality: it is wise to be pleasant towards those bigger than you are and to target more precisely those widely recognised as at the radical fringe of orthodoxy.

It may be that economists need to speak to (not with, none of us does that) the public without using incomprehensible jargon. But we also need to converse more effectively with other economists. 'Fiscal stimulus' is close to oxymoronic in the eyes of its circle of hardline critics. Some may be too doctrinaire to participate, but others are genuinely baffled by what Keynesians are thinking, and comparing metaphors may help us at least start to communicate.

NOTES

1. The allusion is to Keynes's *General Theory* (1936, p. 297).
2. Helpful are Black (1962, ch. 3) and Lagueux (1999).
3. Jacob Bronowski has written penetrative though accessible books on these matters, e.g., Bronowski (1964).
4. I was tempted to use this question as the sub-title of the chapter. Good taste or something else prevailed.
5. Norman Lindsay's nimble-footed 'magic pudding' restores itself as it is eaten (an idea similar to Keynes's widow's cruse from the *Treatise on Money*). Such metaphors insinuate themselves into the public mind (e.g. by cartoons), and the connotations (praise or derision) matter greatly. I stress that the Australian anti-Keynesians I cite are highly

educated and have intelligent and enquiring minds. The seeming absurdity of 'self-funding' spending immediately suffices to discredit the Keynesian argument. Of course, a successful advertising campaign would recoup its own costs without magic. There are serviceable and familiar counter-analogies. In the Australian context, see Henry Ergas (2009a, 2009b), Steve Kates (2009a, 2009b) and Tony Makin (2009a, 2009b). There are real differences in nuance and degree, but the thrust of their objections is basic and conceptual.

6. The interplay of money, finance, the spending multiplier, saving and investment (scheduled and realised) can befuddle us still. Here we have moved from metaphor to the heuristic; leakages-and-injections is a basic model, but lying behind it is a thorny analytical and exegetical thicket.
7. Recall the standard two-sector model. Investment drives saving rather than saving leading to investment. This is easy on a diagram but it is hard to follow an adjustment process through to the end (finance motive for demanding money, revolving fund of credit, expenditure multiplier. . .). I cannot say that I understand the details myself. Even Keynes had problems during the interest rate controversy after the *General Theory*. Investment can initially be funded by bank credit. Depending on how you establish the exact transactions sequence (or structure: Leijonhufvud), a higher subsequent quantity of saving at the new income-equilibrium in effect re-finances the ongoing investment flow. Saving flows also restore bank liquidity in a way that depositing income cheques does not, which is why banks compete to attract 'idle' saving deposits. All this (if correct) is hard to reconcile in a step-by-step explanation of the process by which equilibrium is reached. If there is an instantaneous multiplier, these difficulties are skipped over.
8. Share prices rise, for example, as expected profits rise during recovery. The distinction between notional and effective is made in the works of Robert Clower and Axel Leijonhufvud and is extended here into the domain of wealth. See e.g., Leijonhufvud (1968, 81–83).
9. George Shackle sits between, perhaps above, the Austrians and the Keynesians. In Shackle there may be a workable synthesis at both the conceptual and the practical levels.
10. There are some Post-Keynesians whose scorn towards orthodoxy is open (a few of my own students pick up such a signal). But I still think there is something to be said for the claim that there is no Post-Keynesian Economics: economics is simply good or bad (perhaps more importantly, interesting or boring).

BIBLIOGRAPHY

Black, Max (1962), *Models and Metaphors*, Ithaca, NY and London: Cornell University Press.

Bronowski, Jacob (1964), *Science and Human Values*, Harmondsworth: Pelican Books.

Economist (2009), 'Debate: Keynesian Principles . . .We are All Keynesians Now', accessed March 15, 2013 at http://www.economist.com/debate/overview/140.

Cassidy, John (2010), 'Interview with Eugene Fama', posted January 13, 2010, accessed March 15, 2013 at http://www.newyorker.com/online/blogs/johncassidy/2010/01/interview-with-eugene-fama.html.

Cochrane, John H. (2009), 'Fiscal Stimulus, Fiscal Inflation, or Fiscal Fallacies?', February 27, 2009; accessed March 2013 at http://faculty.chicagobooth.edu/john.cochrane/research/Papers/fiscal2.htm.

Ergas, Henry (2009a), 'Five reasons a fiscal stimulus may not work', *The Australian*, February 9, p. 12.

Ergas, Henry (2009b), 'Rudd on road to disaster', *The Australian*, March 30, p. 8, available at http://www.onlineopinion.com.au/view.asp?article=8748 (posted April 3).
Garrison, Roger W. (1995), 'The Persistance of Keynesian Myths: A Report at Six Decades,' accessed March 15, 2013 at http://www.auburn.edu/~garriro/fk1hdale.htm.
Kates, Steven (2009a), 'The Dangerous Return to Keynesian Economics', *Quadrant Online*, February 3. Accessed March 15, 2013 at http://www.quadrant.org.au/blogs/qed/2009/02/the-dangerous-return-to-keynesian-economics.
Kates, Steven (2009b), 'Government spending spree has no real-world benefit', *The Age*, February 20. Accessed March 15, 2013 at http://www.theage.com.au/business/government-spending-spree-has-no-realworld-benefit-20090219-8clf.html.
Keynes, J. Maynard (1936), *The General Theory of Employment Interest and Money*, London: Macmillan.
Keynes, J. Maynard (1942), 'The Listener', in Donald Moggridge (ed.), *CW* XXVII (1980), 264–70.
Klamer, Arjo (1984), *The New Classical Macroeconomics: Conversations with New Classical Economists and Their Opponents*. Brighton: Wheatsheaf.
Krugman, Paul (2009), 'A Dark Age of macroeconomics (wonkish)', The Conscience of a Liberal, New York Times, available at http://krugman.blogs.nytimes.com/2009/01/27/a-dark-age-of-macroeconomics-wonkish/.
Lagueux, Maurice (1999), 'Do metaphors affect economic theory?', *Economics and Philosophy*, 15 (1), 1–22.
Leijonhufvud, Axel (1968), *On Keynesian Economics and the Economics of Keynes*, New York: Oxford University Press.
Makin, Anthony (2009a), 'Bad spend worse than no spend', *The Australian*, March 4, p. 12.
Makin, Anthony (2009b), 'Why extra pocket money won't stimulate the economy', *The Australian*, March 25, p. 12.
Makin, Anthony (2010), 'Saddled with legacy of fiscal extravagance', *The Australian*, August 30. Accessed March 15, 2013 at http://www.theaustralian.com.au/national-affairs/saddled-with-legacy-of-fiscal-extravagance/story-fn59niix-1225911594527.
Meltzer, Allan (2009), 'Audience Participation: Featured Guest', *Economist*, Debate, accessed March 2013 at http://www.economist.com/debate/days/view/280.
Moggridge, Donald (ed.) (1980), *The Collected Writings of John Maynard Keynes*, London: Macmillan.
Nicholson, Peter (2009), 'Turnbull opposes Rudd bonus 600', February 5, available at http://nicholsoncartoons.com.au/.
Reddy, Sudeep (2009), 'The new old big thing in economics: J.M. Keynes', *The Wall Street Journal*, January 8, accessed March 15, 2013 at http://online.wsj.com/article/SB123137373330762769.html.
Runes, Dagobert D. (1966), *Treasury of Thought*, Philosophical Library, New York.
Vercelli, Alessandro (1991), *Methodological Foundations of Macroeconomics; Keynes and Lucas*, Cambridge: Cambridge University Press.

8. Teaching macroeconomics: seeking inspiration from Paul Davidson

Finn Olesen

INTRODUCTION

As it is known from the history of economic thought, Post Keynesianism is heterodox in so far that, according to Arestis (1996), it consists of at least three main traditions (a Keynes-like, a Kaleckian and an Institutional one). However, Post Keynesianism is in many ways fundamentally linked to the writings of John Maynard Keynes; for example, Eichner and Kregel (1975) and Chick (1995). Primarily it has to do with the kind of economic understanding that Keynes presented in his *A Treatise on Probability*, published in 1921, and in his seminal work *The General Theory of Employment, Interest and Money* from 1936.

One of the most prominent economists within the Keynes-like tradition of Post Keynesianism is Paul Davidson. Throughout almost all of his writings, Davidson has repeatedly argued that to understand the relevant economic processes of a modern monetary entrepreneurial macro economy you have to acknowledge and to take into account the fundamental conclusions of Keynes. Based on this understanding, theoretically as well as methodologically, he has rightfully criticized neoclassical thinking, which is basically the theoretical foundation behind much of the modern macroeconomic mainstream, for its lack of relevance to conduct a thoroughly macroeconomic analysis. However, he has done more than just criticize the mainstream. He has also tried to put forward, from the very beginning of his career, some alternative and opposing views to the mainstream understanding. Given the influence of Sidney Weintraub, from early on Davidson recognized the importance of conducting macroeconomic analysis within the framework of the macroeconomic model presented in Chapter 3 of *The General Theory*: 'The Principle of Effective Demand'.[1]

The present chapter aims partly to present some views on Davidson's interpretation of Keynes – in essence, the argument made by Davidson claiming that Keynes rejected three crucial axioms of the neoclassical mainstream understanding of the 1930s – and partly to discuss how macroeconomics could be taught seeking inspiration from the writings of Paul Davidson. Finally, the chapter closes with some concluding remarks.

CORE STATEMENTS OF DAVIDSON

According to Davidson, Keynes rejected three very restrictive and crucial axioms of the neoclassical paradigm of his day when he put forward his new macro model of *The General Theory*.[2] In doing so, Keynes made his economic reasoning to be quite different from the macroeconomic mainstream, then as now. Contrary to this kind of understanding, given 'The Principle of Effective Demand' Keynes was able to show how a macroeconomic outcome of involuntary unemployment could emerge and seemingly become a catastrophically and perhaps almost a stationary phenomenon of economic life for a very long period of time, as history repeatedly has shown us.

First, Davidson would point out, money is never neutral in the sense that money actually does affect real economic variables in the short run as well as in the longer run. As such, Keynes rejected the neutrality of money axiom and broke away from the economic reasoning that has to do with the understanding imbedded in what is termed the 'classical dichotomy'. Acting economically, households as well as firms have to take financial matters into account when they decide what to do in an economic environment characterized by a fundamental kind of uncertainty; and, as pointed out by Asensio (2012), the introduction of fundamental uncertainty is *the* seminal innovation of Keynes in his *General Theory* which allowed him to put forward his general macroeconomic theory. Thereby, the existence of money represents a kind of link between the present and the truly unknown future which is of immense importance. Furthermore, it has to be remembered that the elasticity of the production of money is zero as no businessman would or could 'produce' money when the demand for money goes up. According to Holt et al. (1998:498), arguing along the guidelines given by Davidson, money therefore represents:

> a 'sink-hole' of purchasing power: if expectations about the future become pessimistic, liquidity preferences rises, raising the demand for money and lowering the demand for the products of labor. Since money is not produced using labor, the fall of demand for commodities produced by labor is not offset when money demand rises.

Or, as Davidson explains it himself in Davidson (2007:29):

> Once the neutrality of money is rejected . . . then an organizing principle for studying the level of employment and output in a market economy involves:

> (1) comprehending the role of money as a means of settling contractual obligations and (2) understanding the essential role that liquidity plays in determining the flow of production and employment in the economic system in which we live.

From the very beginning of his career, Davidson had a strong feeling of the importance of the finance motive to the Keynesian analysis; for example, Davidson (1965, 1967). As he pointed out: 'Sidney's aggregate supply plus the finance motive was what broke the code of the *General Theory* for me. Those two things together were really what made me a post-Keynesian' (King 1994:364).

Secondly, according to Davidson, Keynes rejected the axiom of gross substitution, as Davidson terms it. Quite contrary to the classical economic understanding, to Keynes and to Post Keynesians in general, no change in relative prices is capable in itself of moving the economy back into a position of full employment. Such changes would not automatically establish an optimal macroeconomic outcome in the economy. As a general rule, markets are not going to clear simultaneously. Economic behaviour of the individual household and/or firm and the way the processes of economic adjustment unfold themselves within the economy are determined by many other things than just by changes in relative prices. Or, as Davidson puts it:

> a basic axiom of Keynes's logical framework is that nonproducible assets that can be used to store savings are not gross substitutes for producible assets in savers' portfolios. . . . Consequently, relative price changes via a flexible pricing mechanism will not be the cure-all 'snake-oil' medicine usually recommended by many neoclassical doctors for the unfortunate economic maladies that are occurring in the real world.(Davidson 1984:567, 568–9)[3]

Thirdly, as Davidson sees it, Keynes understood the macroeconomic system as a system that was functioning in a non ergodic manner. Focusing on the behaviour of households and firms, Keynes made it clear that economic agents always act on their expectations when they have to decide what to do in the future. But their expectations are not rational in the modern macroeconomic understanding of the concept. Of course, households and firms try to achieve the best economic outcome they possibly can. That is, individuals have to formulate their expectations on the basis of imperfect knowledge about a truly uncertain future in an economic system that is dynamic, changeable and path-dependent. Therefore, households and firms are almost bound to be mistaken in their decision-making processes, at least to some degree. According to Asensio (2012:22), although they make use of all the information that is available to them, 'whatever the kind of probabilistic or non-probabilistic tools they use, true uncertainty makes it possible for expectations to be eventually systematically wrong: the past events never give enough information about what the future will be'.[4]

As such, the macro economy does not behave as a simple deterministic functioning system. Rather than being a closed and a stationary system, the macro economy should be understood as an open, changeable and a path-dependent social system where households and firms act according to their free will, which makes it possible for them to change their minds up to the very moment when they decide what to do economically. The macroeconomic system then often undergoes a significant change when the economy moves from an irrevocable past to an unpredictable future; for example, Davidson (2003–4, 2005).[5] This is so because, as pointed out by Davidson (1984:572), 'Keynes (1936, Ch. 12) rejected this view that past information from economic time series realizations provides reliable, useful data which permit stochastic predictions of the economic future'. This means that the future is truly unknown in any statistical sense.[6] Individual households and firms have to act under the conditions of fundamental or strong or ontological uncertainty, most often with a less than precise and certainly almost imperfect kind of knowledge as the future economic outcomes have yet to be created by today's actions; for example, Davidson (1982–3, 1991b). Therefore, 'Keynes's nonergodic uncertainty and animal spirits concepts . . . mean that although we can have perfect hindsight, there is no lens that can provide corrected vision regarding the future. Entrepreneurial vision of the future is not faulty, but is, instead, based on dreams or nightmares' (Davidson 2003–4:253).[7] As a consequence of this fact, it becomes very important to understand the crucial role played by money contracts in the economy. It is by agreeing upon such contracts that the individuals try to hedge themselves against the potential negative effects of future economic outcomes that manifest themselves sometime in the years ahead.

TEACHING MACROECONOMICS

Seeing himself as a 'Keynes-Post Keynesian' as stated in Holt et al. (1998), Davidson has repeatedly argued that the relevant macroeconomic framework is that of 'The Principle of Effective Demand' given by Keynes in Chapter 3 of *The General Theory*. As such, together with Eugene Smolensky he published in 1964 a textbook in macroeconomics that presented itself as an alternative to the prevailing mainstream interpretation of macroeconomics using 'The Principle of Effective Demand' as its macro model. Contrary to the advice of the publisher[8] Davidson and Smolensky

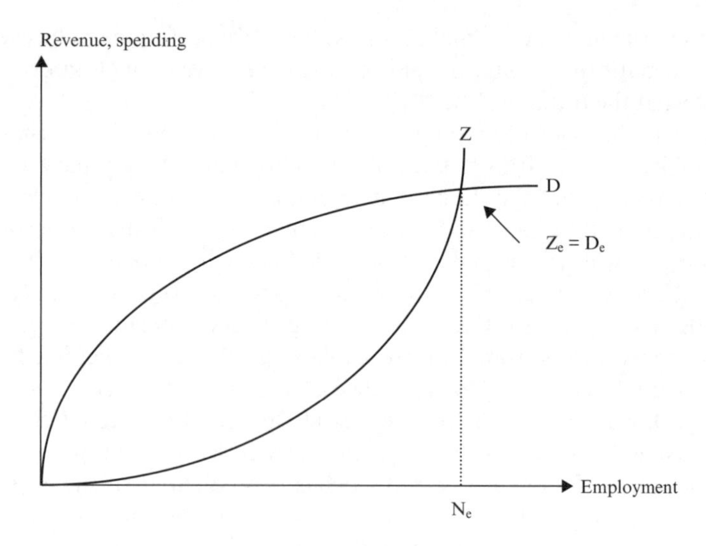

Figure 8.1 The principle of effective demand

insisted on having it titled *Aggregate Supply and Demand Analysis.*[9] Unfortunately for the authors, this book never became a big success. Davidson recognized this himself, as he states that the book: 'was designed to be *the* fundamental Post Keynesian macroeconomic textbook. I could never understand why economists who professed to be Post Keynesians, refused to read it, much less use it as a basic macrotext' (Davidson 2003–4:255). Not being a success, the book never sold more than approximately 3000 copies in total (King 1994:364).

However, in what follows some selected elements of this book are highlighted as the book has manifested itself as an early contribution to the Post Keynesian teaching of macroeconomics. As such, throughout the book there is a very strong emphasis upon the fact that the economic behaviour of both households and firms is conducted in a macroeconomic environment characterized by uncertainty. That is, economic behaviour of the individual is based on expectations of an unknown future.

In the macroeconomic framework of Davidson and Smolensky, the outcome of the macro economy is, as seen in Figure 8.1, determined by the intersection of the aggregate supply and the aggregate demand functions, Z and D, where the expected revenues are drawn as a rising convex curve with an increasing slope and the demand expenditures are drawn as a rising concave curve with a declining slope. The intersection of the two curves determines the level of the effective demand in the economy: 'It represents an equilibrium level of spending, where entrepreneurial expectations are just being realized, so that there is no inducement to change hiring policy' (Davidson and Smolensky 1964:6). However, based on expectations of a truly uncertain future, it is not given that agents' individual behaviour in total would be able to bring about a macroeconomic outcome that guarantees full employment. Not surprisingly, then, the main focus in the economic analysis of Davidson and Smolensky, as pointed out above, is on the two core elements: expectations and uncertainty. As they pinpoint:

> In the real world, however, uncertainty is important and affects all economic activity. Many of the institutions of our modern economy would have no function in a world of certainty. . . . The supply function is usually thought to be based on short-term expectations, while the demand for investment goods is based on long-term expectations. . . . Both long- and short-term expectations are relevant for the hiring decisions. Actual sales are irrelevant except to the extent that they modify present or future expectations. (Davidson and Smolensky 1964:7, 8)

Aggregate Supply and Demand Analysis is organized as follows. In Part II of the book the focus is on the demand side. While Chapter 3 has to do with the consumption function in a traditional 45° diagram setting, Chapters 4 and 5 deal with the investment function (the schedule of the marginal efficiency of capital and the acceleration principle). As investment purchases can be very volatile as they depend upon expected future returns even many years ahead of now, investment decisions might easily trigger an economic expansion or contraction. This follows from the fact that decisions to invest or not are primarily dependent upon whether or not the marginal efficiency of capital is above or below the rate of interest. That is, investment decisions have to do with matching expected and uncertain future returns with present real costs:

> Belief that the purchase of so long-lived a good will be profitable, therefore, involves a bold plunge into an unforeseeable future. . . . But investment decisions must be made, and they are made. They are made with one-third fact and two-third animal spirits. These animal spirits largely depend on the mood of the business community. (Davidson and Smolensky 1964:51, 52)

In Chapter 6 the CI/LM macroeconomic model of Davidson and Smolensky is presented. Although this model in many ways looks a lot like the IS/LM model, there are at least two distinct differences between the two. First, the CI/LM model explicitly incorporates the liquidity trap as a horizontal part of the LM curve. Secondly, as the CI curve is dependent upon the marginal efficiency of capital, this curve implicitly has entrepreneurs' expectations built into its functional relationships. Furthermore, it is not given with certainty that the intersection of the two curves will automatically bring about a situation of full employment. If total output is below that of full employment the government might want to induce a change in economic policy in order to try to stimulate aggregate demand and raise the level of output and employment (monetary and fiscal policies are discussed in Chapters 7 and 8).

Part III of the book is devoted to the supply side of the macro economy. Chapters 9 and 10 give us the aggregate supply and demand functions, where the aggregate supply function 'links expected sales revenue to employment' (Davidson and Smolensky 1964:118). It is an upward sloping curve that is primarily dependent upon the money wage rate. Likewise, the aggregate demand function is made dependent upon four factors: consumption, investment, governmental purchases and foreign trade. The intersection of the two curves determines the level of effective demand, as illustrated in Figure 8.1.[10]

In Chapter 11 the money wage rate is endogenously determined using a demand curve for labour that could look like: a) the traditional downward sloping curve representing classical thinking; b) a vertical perfect inelastic curve representing the thinking of Keynes; or c) an upward sloping curve representing the scenario with a situation of underconsumption. Likewise, the supply curve of labour is given as a normal upward sloping one.

Having put the labour market in place, Chapter 12 introduces three basic types of inflation. The price level could rise due to movements along a given aggregate supply curve. This phenomenon is termed diminishing returns inflation. Then inflation could occur when the Z function shifts upward. In this case, we have profits inflation (due to a higher degree of monopoly power) and wage-price inflation. Furthermore, inflation could also occur as a consequence of changes in the level of aggregate demand. When the D function is shifted upward we have inflation based on two factors: a combination of diminishing returns and wage-price inflation.

In Chapter 13 the complete equilibrium model is presented. Equilibrium in the goods markets as well as financially are given by relations (1) and (2) respectively, where F is income payment to rentiers (assumed to be fixed), w is the money wage rate, N is the level of total employment and i is the interest rate. Finally, the quantity of money, M^S, is exogenously determined by the banking system.

$$Z(w,N) = D_C(F,w,N) + D_I(i,w,N) \tag{8.1}$$

$$M^S = M^D = L_1(w,N) + L_2(i) \tag{8.2}$$

Quite similarly to the analysis of Keynes's *General Theory*, the aggregate demand is split into consumption spending, (D_C), and investment expenditures, (D_I), as consumption decisions are primarily based on short-term expectations whereas investment decisions are primarily based on long-term expectations. Likewise, the money demand is, as traditionally, divided between the demand for transactions and precautionary balances and the speculative demand for money. From this, Davidson and Smolensky derive two functions which, given the assumption of an exogenously fixed money wage rate, simultaneously determine the level of employment and the interest rate.

In sum, the macroeconomic analysis of Davidson and Smolensky is one that is firmly based upon expectations. Entrepreneurs decide what to supply based on what they expect would maximize their profits. Likewise, households consume according to what they expect their incomes to be. However, the expectations of both entrepreneurs and households may not be fulfilled as the macroeconomic environment is one characterized by uncertainty. Therefore, the macroeconomic outcome is not normally one of optimality; rather, economic crisis may be present from time to time, thereby making involuntary unemployment a troublesome phenomenon of real life. Finally, in quite a modern way, Davidson and Smolensky deal not only in detail with the demand side of the economy but also put a lot of emphasis on understanding the working of the supply side of the economy (e.g. how the money wage rate might be determined endogenously and how to deal with the complicated questions of inflation).

As stated earlier, *Aggregate Supply and Demand Analysis* never took off as a macroeconomics textbook.[11] However, that did not make Davidson give up writing books on macroeconomic matters. On the contrary, over the years he has delivered a number of books to the public. As such, in 2011 a revised edition of his *Post Keynesian Macroeconomic Theory* was published as a modern macroeconomics textbook addressing not only questions of a theoretical nature but also discussing actual economic problems of the real world.[12] In what follows, some selected elements of this textbook are presented and discussed.

Not surprisingly, in his opening chapter Davidson starts out by giving the background to Keynes's revolution. As Davidson has explained repeatedly in almost all of his writings, Keynes found that the classical mainstream macroeconomics of his day was unable convincingly to explain the facts of real life. Keynes believed that 'the fatal flaw of the classical system lay in the special unrealistic axioms that were necessary to demonstrate the self-correcting tendency of an unfettered competitive economic system' (Davidson 2011:4). That is, the mainstream understanding was unable to explain the existence of involuntary unemployment. Economists needed an alternative and this was given by Keynes in 1936 as he 'developed the economic theory analogue to non-Euclidean geometry where three fundamental classical axioms were overthrown' (Davidson 2011:5). Unfortunately, as Davidson points out, the message of Keynes has not had that much influence on macroeconomics as the modern macroeconomic mainstream is still hinged on the above mentioned fundamental three classical axioms that Keynes revolted against in his *General Theory*.[13] However, there is an alternative to the mainstream economic understanding, as Davidson tries to unfold in the remaining chapters of his book.

As such, in Chapter 2 Keynes's 'Principle of Effective Demand' is presented and Davidson explains why the theory of Keynes is more general than classical theory, which is fundamentally based on Say's Law.[14] Stressing the importance of uncertainty – while the classical kind of uncertainty is an epistemological concept, the uncertainty in Keynes's theory is an ontological concept making the macroeconomic system to be a non ergodic system[15] – and the role played by expectations when individuals decide how to act economically, Chapters 3 and 4 deal with private consumption and investment.

After a short chapter on government spending the scene is set for an analysis of the financial sector of the economy in Chapters 6–9. As explained by Davidson, in a classical world of perfect certainty and perfect markets, money has a very limited role to play. However, in the Keynes story where the economic environment is characterized by fundamental or ontological uncertainty, the functions that money performs are crucial to the understanding of how a modern monetary economy functions.[16] How do individuals try to cope with such a kind of uncertainty? They make contractual commitments and these contracts are money contracts: 'It is the synchronous existence of money and money contracts over an uncertain future that is the basis of the monetary system that we are all familiar with' (Davidson 2011:98). That is, the liquidity preference is of vital importance to the understanding of how the real sector and the financial sector interact as interdependent sectors. As such, Davidson provides a thorough presentation and discussion of the different motives for holding money, including the finance motive.

Finally, Davidson discusses the importance of the banking system as 'an increase in the demand for money induces an endogenous increase in supply *if bankers are willing and able to expand under the rules of the game* that regulate banking operations' (Davidson 2011:141). As we have experienced recently, financial institutions can be very innovative, as shown by, for example, all the new financial products created and offered to the public in the years leading up to the international financial crisis. However, although some financial innovations clearly make the financial sector more efficient, to the benefit of society, for example more liquidity offered to the public at lower costs, not every kind of innovative behaviour from this sector is beneficial to society, as the international financial crisis has so vividly illustrated. Economic greed is never the best way to call forward a macroeconomic outcome of optimality. Or, as Davidson (2011:150) tells us: 'In times of either euphoria or fear of the future, there are no market "fundamentals" that determine the market price of the equities of any specific enterprise' (or the price of any other financial product for that matter).[17]

In Chapter 10, Davidson discusses the causes and cures of inflation. We are told that inflation has elements of what Davidson terms 'diminishing returns inflation',[18] 'degree of monopoly or profits inflation',[19] 'wage inflation' and 'import inflation or deflation'. That is, in this perspective inflation is not normally a monetary phenomenon as is the case when you apply the quantity theory of money which dichotomizes the economy in a real sector and a financial sector that interact as independent sectors. To Post Keynesians, as Davidson points out, 'inflation can only occur in economies that use money (and money contracts) to organize production and exchange processes . . . inflation is a symptom of a fight over the distribution of current income' Davidson (2011:174). As such, an appropriate cure for inflation could be to introduce the right kind of incomes policies, for example Tax-based Incomes Policy.[20]

Chapters 13–17 address various aspects of the international economy. That is, a) some facts about balance of payment accounting and the degree of openness (Ch. 13); b) a discussion of trade imbalances and how to try to overcome them seen from the perspective of the classical process of real adjustment which Davidson critically evaluates (Ch. 14); c) Thirlwall's Law (Ch. 14); d) the law of comparative advantages (Ch. 14); e) fixed versus flexible exchange rates (Ch. 15); f) the problems of how to recycle finance from trade surplus nations to trade deficit nations (Ch. 16); g) export-led growth (Ch. 17); and h) how to reform the international payments system in order to be able to promote global growth in a more appropriate way than what is presently the case (Ch. 17).

Finally, the book is closed with a chapter on Keynesianism. Discussing especially Old Keynesianism and New Keynesian Economics, Davidson points out that Keynesianism, be it 'Old' or 'New', really has nothing to do with the fundamental core elements of Keynes's macroeconomic understanding. Whereas Keynesianism in general is more or less a discussion about the speed of various adjustment processes,[21] the economics of Keynes is about a quite different macroeconomic universe:

> Keynes insisted there is a fundamental analytical distinction between a money-using production economy where even 'in the long period' money is not neutral and the real exchange economy of classical economics where money is presumed neutral as a matter of faith. There can be no necessary logical connection between the New Keynesian analysis that sees non-flexible prices as the essential characteristic explaining fluctuations and Keynes's analysis where non-neutral money and unemployment can co-exist even with perfect price flexibility in both the short and the long run. (Davidson 2011:330)

CONCLUDING REMARKS

Teaching macroeconomics on a permanent basis makes you sometimes wonder what has happened to the modern macroeconomic mainstream of today. Although the various models in themselves are very cogently formulated in their uniform mathematical clothing, they all appear somehow to be concerned with a kind of macroeconomic environment that is artificial and not of this world.[22] Is a representative agent that optimizes his intertemporal consumption pattern applying rational expectations really the best and most relevant way to portray actual economic behaviour? Do households and firms only focus on relative price relationships when they plan what to do economically for the coming periods? And what about financial matters? Which role do these crucial aspects play in modern macroeconomics? As we have all witnessed since 2008, if financial markets dry up, so to speak, when banks cannot deliver the necessary amount of liquidity, it can have quite catastrophic consequences for the individual household as well as the individual firm. And how do we conduct economic policy the right way? Of course, we have to take supply-side effects into account when we evaluate a given policy proposal but could these effects do the trick by themselves and make the macroeconomic outcome in the longer run one of perfection? That is, is it really safe to rely on dynamic supply effects as the only remedy to call forward an overall equilibrium situation of full employment in the longer run? Does supply really create the necessary amount of demand by itself? Doesn't Say's Law break down, as Keynes pointed out decades ago, when in a modern monetary economy it is no longer the same people with the same motives that perform the desire to save and the desire to invest? Shouldn't demand be given a more active and important role to play on the scene of macroeconomics than is normally the case in modern economic analysis, especially as almost every economic decision made by households as well as firms is taken in a macroeconomic environment of uncertainty?

However, the macroeconomic universe of Paul Davidson is a quite different one. He proposes an alternative to the modern mainstream understanding by focusing, as Keynes did, on 'time, money, and uncertainty'. He acknowledges that every economic act is an act that is carried out in historical time by individuals of their own free will, which makes them able to change their minds up to the very last moment before their plans become actual economic decisions. And such plans are made in a macroeconomic environment of uncertainty where the individuals have to make expectations about outcomes in the future based on more or less imperfect information. As such, they are almost bound to make mistakes not only of a stochastic but also of a more systematic nature, as the kind of uncertainty with which they are confronted is of both an epistemological and an ontological character. Therefore, the individuals engage in making contracts as they try to cope with and hedge themselves from an unknown future. And these contracts are money contracts as money is *the* way to insure yourself against the future negative effects of uncertainty. Therefore, money is of course never neutral in either the short or in the longer run. Money does affect the way individuals plan and act economically. Likewise, individual behaviour is dependent upon the given set-up of institutions. And these institutions may change, even radically, as time goes by.

In sum, stated alternatively, the macroeconomic universe of Paul Davidson is a universe that has to do with the real life phenomena with which households, firms and governments are faced daily. Therefore, the macroeconomics of Paul Davidson is the economics of the real world. As such, he still offers some very important messages to modern students of economics, theoretically as well as methodologically, if they want to learn more about how to perform economics the right way when they themselves are acting as economists in the years to come.

NOTES

1. As Davidson said himself in an interview with Colander: 'coming under the influence of Sidney Weintraub at exactly the right time structured the rest of my career' (Colander 2001:87). Especially important in this respect was the contribution made by Weintraub (1958). As Davidson pointed out in another earlier interview with King: 'I understand Keynes from that book more than from Keynes. If you don't read that book, you don't really understand Keynes' (King 1994:362).
2. Some very good introductions to Davidson – his career and his writings – are given in Colander (2001), Holt et al. (1998), Rotheim (1996) and King (1994).
3. 'If the axiom of gross substitution is not . . . imposed . . . then the theory cannot demonstrate that all markets (including the labor market) will clear simultaneously even if all prices are instantaneously flexible' (Davidson 2007:31).
4. Or as stated in Davidson (1991a:32): 'Post Keynesians emphasize the fallibility of human nature and the fact that unfettered human decisions do not necessary automatically result in the best of all possible worlds. The developing economic system is an

evolutionary process where human expectations regarding an uncertain and an unpredictable future will have unavoidable and significant effects on economic outcomes.'

5. Or in Rotheim (1996:30): 'Actions today become based on the expectation of future, uncertain streams of income, and the cumulative path taken by an economy becomes dependent upon, rather than being independent of, the totality of those very individual decisions at every moment in time.'
6. Therefore, you have to acknowledge, as Davidson argues, that: 'Keynes' uncertain future involves a creative economic reality in the sense that the future can be permanently changed in nature and substance by actions of individuals, groups (e.g., unions, cartels), and/or governments, often in ways not completely foreseeable by the creators of change. . . . In a nonergodic environment . . . this existing market information does not, and cannot, provide reliable data for forecasting the future' (Davidson 1996:482).
7. So, as pointed out by Davidson (1984:574): 'when one is dealing with human activity and institutions, one may be, in the nature of things, outside the realm of the formally precise. For Keynes as for Post Keynesians the guiding motto is "it is better to be roughly right than precisely wrong!"'. Therefore, as stated in Davidson (1991a:64): 'The Post Keynesian model of the economic system may not have the same rigorous mathematical beauty of the neoclassical model, but it is a better description of reality.'
8. As Davidson states in Colander (2001:90): 'I remember that when we submitted the manuscript to a number of publishers, they all disliked the title. We sent it out, and everybody said, "Change it to Macroeconomics" or something like that. We insisted on the title. . . . When it didn't sell the editor and the publishers said, "We told you so!".'
9. As stated in the Preface to the book: 'What this book offers, which other texts do not, is a treatment of Keynesian theory into which price theory has been directly incorporated. . . . Once a bridge between micro- and macroeconomics is established, it becomes possible to call upon all the theoretical concepts and generalizations of microtheory to increase our understanding of price level and employment phenomena' (Davidson and Smolensky 1964:xi, xii).
10. And, as pinpointed by Davidson and Smolensky (1964:145, 146): 'When entrepreneurial expectations of revenue equal Z_e, they will hire N_e workers, and will discover that the concomitant demand outlays (D_e) are such that their expectations are just fulfilled. At that point, *ceteris paribus*, there will be no inducements to change the employment level. . . . The value of total spending as given by the aggregate demand function where it is intersected by the aggregate supply function is called *effective demand.* Effective demand is the point where aggregate spending equals aggregate expectations of sales; it represents an equilibrium level of expenditures, where entrepreneurial expectations are just being realized so that there is no inducement to change hiring policy.'
11. Perhaps this has to do with the fact, as pointed out by Cummins (1964:156), that a rather high level of abstraction is maintained throughout this very short textbook, requiring students to have 'considerable intellectual maturity and a solid background in price theory' to be able to gain from reading the text.
12. Actually, Davidson's book, together with Jesper Jespersen's *Macroeconomic Methodology: A Post-Keynesian Perspective* (Edward Elgar Publishing, 2011), and some articles were used as readings in a macroeconomic course at Aalborg University, Denmark, in the autumn of 2011 and 2012.
13. 'Today, most economists, especially at our most prestigious university economics departments, are even more rigorously trained in the mathematical formalisms of classical axiomatic value theories than earlier generations. These mainstream economists' theories, therefore, are still wedded to the axioms of classical analysis. . . . Accordingly, textbook mainstream macroeconomic models are still founded on the special classical axioms. The resulting policy implications are, as Keynes noted, "misleading and dangerous" if applied to the real world in which we live' (Davidson 2011:7).
14. In Chapter 11 of the book, Davidson describes in detail how the aggregate supply function is derived, whereas Chapter 12 analyses the demand and supply of labour.
15. 'Once the theorist recognizes that the economic environment involves a nonergodic

stochastic process where the future can not be reliably predicted, then the role of money, the savings decision and the reason why Say's Law is not a "true" law for such a system can easily be demonstrated' (Davidson 2011:39).

16. 'It is only in a world of uncertainty and disappointment that money comes into its own as a necessary mechanism for deferring decisions' (Davidson 2011:102).
17. For example, Davidson (2011:151): 'the US housing bubble of the early twenty-first century encouraged mortgage originators to search out possible home buyers, even if a thorough investigation of the three Cs – collateral, credit history, and character – of such subprime borrowers would have suggested the borrowers were not good credit risks'.
18. 'Economic expansion can lead to increasing costs not only because of the classical law of diminishing returns but because labour and capital inputs are really not equally efficient. Increasing production flows often involves the hiring of less-skilled workers, and the utilization of older, less-efficient standby equipment' Davidson (2011:167).
19. 'When entrepreneurs believe that the market conditions have changed sufficiently so that it is possible . . . for them to increase the mark-up of prices relative to costs, the economy will experience a profit inflation' Davidson (2011:168).
20. 'This policy must be considered a necessary supplement to monetary and fiscal policies that would *guarantee* continuous full employment. In return for this guarantee of full employment and high production levels, labour would be required to restrict its wage demands to, at most, rises in average productivity, while business must hold profit mark-ups constant' Davidson (2011:182).
21. 'The entire controversy amongst New Classical, New Keynesians and Old Keynesians is a tempest in a tea pot involving different assumptions about the length of time it takes prices as compared to output to adjust to an exogenous change in demand' (Davidson 2011:332).
22. As Kay (2011:7) has stated: 'Economic models are no more, or less, than potentially illuminating abstractions. . . . The economic world, far more than the physical world, is influenced by our beliefs about it. . . . Information is reflected in prices, but not necessarily accurately, or completely. There are wide differences in understanding and belief, and different perceptions of a future that can be at best dimly perceived.' These facts make some economists very critical of the use of mathematical models, as in the case of, for instance, Tony Lawson: 'The essence of my criticism of the modelling emphasis is simply that the twin presuppositions of economic modellers that (i) empirical regularities of the sort required are ubiquitous, and (ii) social reality is constituted by sets of isolated atoms, are simply erroneous. . . . If event regularities hardly occur in the social realm, it does not take too much reflection to see that the second presupposition is also invalid, that the constituents of social reality can rarely be aptly portrayed as systems of isolated atoms' (Lawson 2009:764). Others are not as opposed towards the use of mathematics; for example, Davidson (2012:64, 65) has pointed out: 'Mainstream economists are not wrong in the need for rigor in economic theorizing. It is not rigor and the use of mathematics *per se* that creates the useless economic models that make mainstream economists look so poorly . . . it is perfectly acceptable to have rigor and even math in economic models. . . . But the axioms underlying the model must be thoroughly examined to see if they are applicable to the real world.'

REFERENCES

Arestis, Philip (1996): 'Post-Keynesian economics: towards coherence', *Cambridge Journal of Economics*, 20(1), pp. 111–35.

Asensio, Angel (2012): 'On Keynes's seminal innovation and related essential features: revisiting the notion of equilibrium in *The General Theory*', from the book

Keynes's General Theory Seventy-Five Years Later, edited by Thomas Cate, Cheltenham: Edward Elgar Publishing, pp. 19–34.
Chick, Victoria (1995): 'Is there a case for Post Keynesian economics?', *Scottish Journal of Political Economy*, February, pp. 20–36.
Colander, David (2001): 'An interview with Paul Davidson', *Eastern Economic Journal*, Winter, pp. 85–114.
Cummins, Gaylord (1964): 'Aggregate supply and demand analysis', *Southern Economic Journal*, October, pp. 156–7.
Davidson, Paul (2012): 'Is economics a science? Should economics be rigorous?', *Real-World Economics Review*, no. 59, pp. 58–66.
Davidson, Paul (2011): *Post Keynesian Macroeconomic Theory, Second Edition*, Cheltenham: Edward Elgar Publishing.
Davidson, Paul (2007): *John Maynard Keynes*, Great Britain: Palgrave Macmillan.
Davidson, Paul (2005): 'Responses to Lavoie, King, and Dow on what Post Keynesianism is and who is a Post Keynesian', *Journal of Post Keynesian Economics*, Spring, pp. 393–408.
Davidson, Paul (2003–4): 'Setting the record straight on *A History of Post Keynesian Economics*', *Journal of Post Keynesian Economics*, Winter, pp. 245–72.
Davidson, Paul (1996): 'Reality and economic theory', *Journal of Post Keynesian Economics*, Summer, pp. 479–508.
Davidson, Paul (1991a): *Controversies in Post Keynesian Economics*, Cheltenham: Edward Elgar Publishing.
Davidson, Paul (1991b): 'Is probability theory relevant for uncertainty? A Post Keynesian perspective', *Journal of Economic Perspectives*, Winter, pp. 129–43.
Davidson, Paul (1984): 'Reviving Keynes's revolution', *Journal of Post Keynesian Economics*, Summer, pp. 561–75.
Davidson, Paul (1982–3): 'Rational expectations: a fallacious foundation for studying crucial decision-making processes', *Journal of Post Keynesian Economics*, Winter, pp. 182–98.
Davidson, Paul (1967): 'The importance of the demand for finance', *Oxford Economic Papers*, July, pp. 245–53.
Davidson, Paul (1965): 'Keynes's finance motive', *Oxford Economic Papers*, March, pp. 47–65.
Davidson, Paul and Smolensky, Eugene (1964): *Aggregate Supply and Demand Analysis*, New York: Harper & Row.
Eichner, Alfred S. and Kregel, J.A. (1975): 'An essay on Post-Keynesian theory: a new paradigm in economics', *Journal of Economic Literature*, December, pp. 1293–314.
Holt, Richard, Rosser, J.B. and Wray, L.R. (1998): 'Neglected prophets – Paul Davidson: the truest Keynesian?', *Eastern Economic Journal*, Fall, 495–506.
Kay, John (2011): 'The map is not the territory: an essay on the state of economics', *Institute for New Economic Thinking*, September 26, http://ineteconomics.org/sites/inet.civicactions.net/files/kay-john-state-of-economics-v11.pdf, last accessed 12 March 2013.
King, J.E. (1994): 'A conversation with Paul Davidson', *Review of Political Economy*, 6(3), pp. 357–79.
Lawson, Tony (2009): 'The current economic crisis: its nature and the course of academic economics', *Cambridge Journal of Economics*, 33(4), pp. 759–77.
Rotheim, Roy (1996): 'Paul Davidson' from the book *American Economists of the*

Late Twentieth Century edited by Warren Samuels, Cheltenham: Edward Elgar Publishing, pp. 18–43.

Weintraub, Sidney (1958): *An Approach to the Theory of Income Distribution*, Westport, CT: Greenwood Press Publishers.

9. What about the mainstream critique of American principles of economics textbooks?

Poul Thøis Madsen

INTRODUCTION

The financial crisis and the subsequent recession have been a real challenge to economists as well as to economic theory. In the media a blame game has been going on and economists and their theories have been portrayed as one of the main culprits. A repeated message has been that, had economic theories been of more relevance, we might have avoided the crisis, or at least not been taken so much by surprise.[1] The economics textbook – as one important representative of economic theory – has also come under closer scrutiny and criticism due to the financial crisis (cf. Blinder 2010).

Criticisms of economics textbooks do, however, go way back – certainly among non-mainstream economists, but perhaps more surprisingly, also among mainstream economists. I document in this chapter that a debate on modern textbooks has been going on for decades, culminating in the period 1987–1993, among mainstream economists who either write mainstream textbooks or teach from them. As self-criticism constitutes an important source of change for future editions of principles of economics textbooks we need to understand the character of the self-criticism, as well as why it has largely evaporated – as documented below.

First I briefly pose some questions concerning why we should care about the theme raised in this chapter. Secondly, a number of methodological considerations related to my study are discussed, especially concerning operationalization and delimitation. Thirdly, I present the results of my analysis. Next, I discuss whatever happened to the mainstream critique of textbooks. Finally, I try to answer the question of why heterodox as well as mainstream economists should care about the results.

WHY SHOULD ECONOMISTS CARE ABOUT MAINSTREAM SELF-CRITICISM – PART I?

Let me first answer this question by posing a number of other questions which implicitly demonstrate why *I* care. First of all I stumbled across some mainstream critique by accident. It made me curious and led me to speculate about the following questions:

a. How much mainstream criticism is there out there? (Next to nothing was my guess.)
b. Is the mainstream critique essential? (Mainly minor points I guessed.)
c. How does the critique raised by mainstream economists differ from that of heterodox economists? (Hugely I guessed – as a consequence of b).)
d. Has it had any impact? (I regarded mainstream textbooks as somewhat immutable.)
e. Could the critique be used as a platform for heterodox economists trying to change mainstream textbooks?
f. Why should mainstream economists care about mainstream criticism of textbooks?

Based on the following analysis, answers to these questions are attempted in part II below.

Problems of Operationalisation and Solutions to These

In the following I have to spend some time on methodological issues because the study is complicated but some of these issues are also results in their own right. Several factors make it difficult to identify the mainstream debate on textbooks. First, the debate tends to be invisible. Even in academic books covering discussions on textbooks terms like 'textbook' or 'principles of economics textbooks' are often not used as entries. One gets the impression that textbooks are somehow the money-making 'black sheep' of the family not having any academic interest. Textbooks tend to get less academic respect among mainstream economists than their importance might warrant, also as the products of eminent economists.

A second complicating feature is that the most visible overall disagreement in the literature is over the validness of mainstream economic theory rather than over textbooks. In these discussions it is often unclear whether problems caused by, for example, the lack of reality are supposed to concern research only or also textbooks. Therefore, in order to make the analysis operational, only explicit debates on textbooks are dealt with in my analysis.

Thirdly, a parallel debate is on how to teach economics, often involving the question of textbooks (which to choose, how to use them, etc.). It is troublesome to separate this debate from the general debate on economics, as in, for example, Shiller (2010).

Fourthly, a number of articles actually deal explicitly with textbooks, but descriptively, without really evaluating their content (e.g. Brazelton 1977; Brue 1996; Elzinga 1992; Watts 1987) – despite the fact that at least two of the references have rather polemic titles.

A fifth, related identification problem concerns articles that might be considered critical towards textbooks, but one cannot be certain. When, for example, Brazelton (1977) describes, without judging, a development in textbooks which some other economists might consider unfortunate, does he then consider this development to be a problem or not?

Sixthly, the analysis has also been complicated by articles in which explicit criticisms are found, but the critic is unidentified. This problem and the previously mentioned leave an interpreter in a dilemma: it should be the author – not the interpreter – who explicitly formulates and forwards the criticism. To avoid misinterpretation, authors should be attributed a specific point of view only when this is undoubtedly so.

A seventh, fundamental problem concerns the category or concept 'mainstream economist', which is not something well defined or delineated. It makes more sense to operate within a continuum of 'mainstream economists' ranging from those highly self-critical to those who do not (or will not) criticize anything in textbooks (the 'truth' of the content of textbooks is taken for granted).[2,3] What unifies these at times very different economists is a fundamental acceptance of the archetypical textbook – often characterized as 'neoclassical' by non-mainstream economists.[4] This might explain why the self-criticism presented below is either rather limited or why the authors are so hesitant in drawing too radical conclusions – even when airing somewhat devastating criticisms.

The eighth and final problem of operationalization also relates to problems of generalization. Is it defensible to talk about principles textbooks as a homogenous whole? The argument for upholding this abstraction is twofold: a) the contributions cited below also follow this procedure; and b) most introductory textbooks are still strikingly similar, as already argued by Stiglitz (1988).

Delimitations

Apart from addressing these problems of operationalization it has also been necessary to make certain delimitations in order to make the whole analysis operational. The focus is on *academic* criticism as articulated in scientific articles and books. This delimitation reduces the potential number of contributions significantly – it does not give much credit to mainstream economists to contribute to the academic critique of textbooks (in contrast to non-mainstream economists or non-economists for whom textbook-bashing is part of their academic game).

Another kind of criticism is also left out – internal self-criticism in textbooks. American textbooks are currently under (re)construction triggered by a number of sources: the self-criticism of authors but also by feedback from a number of internal reviewers and users (students and teachers) and probably also from publishers. The focus of this chapter is, however, primarily on textbooks as seen from the outside rather than from the inside, as it is more likely for outsiders to raise essential criticisms and to articulate these explicitly.

The analysis rests on an extensive literature research using different methods (among those analysing literature lists in leading articles) and different databases (e.g. econlitt and google.scholar), while the *Journal of Economic Education* has been searched issue by issue to find relevant discussions of textbooks. As the mainstream debate on textbooks is so wide-ranging and often practically invisible, it can by no means be claimed that I have found all relevant contributions. One could, however, argue that possibly overlooked contributions would, at most, have led to only slight modifications of the results presented below. The rationale underlying this argument is that the already identified criticisms share some common features: they are few, superficial and tend to abstain from drawing radical conclusions. This striking similarity indicates that any overlooked contributions would probably share some of the same features.

As mentioned, the focus is on the limited and often very brief critique of introductions. Limited as this critique is, the point is that critique exists, and that this critique is much more decisive than the far more lengthy critique by non-mainstream economists. It is more likely that change will come from mainstream economists but partly triggered by external shocks such as the financial crisis. It should be noted, though, that one of the results is that it has not been possible to find more than a few more recent academic mainstream critiques of textbooks. This of course raises two questions: why the critique has evaporated and whether this also implies that the previous critique has been taken into account.

Analysis

I have (only) managed to identify 20 mainstream publications criticizing the mainstream textbook. The first of these was published in 1951 – the most recent in 2010 – but the majority of criticism was published in the period between 1987 and 1993. The relatively high number of critical contributions in 1988 can be attributed to the special issue of the *Journal of Economic Education* on textbooks.

The critical points contained in these 20 publications can be divided into three major problems typically found in expositions of standard principles of economics textbooks: (1) fundamental and general problems with most of the content; (2) problems due to the changes that general development textbooks undergo from edition to edition; and (3) specific and less general problems with parts of the content. For obvious reasons there is some overlap between the different categories of criticism.

Fundamental problems

One can identify three different fundamental points raised by mainstream economists who critique textbooks in general. The first of these concerns the relation between the textbook and actual economic reality. Textbooks often pretend directly or indirectly to make a representation of the world we live in. Some mainstream economists question how successful textbooks are in this effort because they find that actual economic reality is gradually being squeezed out. Less and less contextual and historical knowledge, as well as history of economic ideas, is to be found in textbooks (Shackelford 1991), while at the same time textbooks tend to omit helping students to operationalise the often very abstract concepts and theories into 'relevant facts' (Bell 1988, 137). In consequence, textbooks have dire problems in 'transmitting real knowledge of the economy' (Boulding 1988, 123) to students.The second fundamental critical point is the implicit notion of 'objectivity' of textbooks which manifests itself in at least two ways. This notion tends to crowd out discussions of disagreement among economists, as these are downplayed or not mentioned at all (Boskin 1988; Stiglitz 1988, 177). Closely related to this point, one easily finds textbooks by authors trying to be politically neutral and believing this to be possible (Shackelford 1991; Watts 1987). But claiming objectivity and political neutrality is merely another way of getting rid of reality. In the real world economists disagree and political neutrality is unattainable.

The third fundamental problem for some economists is a perceived bias towards Keynesianism: 'many Principles book authors have placed the Keynesian theory at centre stage for too long. There is something to this view' (Maxwell 1999, 124). This is a criticism also raised by economists outside the mainstream, such as free-market economists (cf. libertarians such as Buckley 1951 and Bolton and Taylor 1982), while leftwing economists tend to notice a neoliberal bias. Such disagreements demonstrate the impossibility of being objective. In this context, disagreement concerning the choice of the underlying theoretical framework is regarded as a fundamental and unsolved challenge to textbooks, as it implies disagreement on how the actual economy fundamentally works.

Problems with the direction of development

Mainstream textbooks are not something static – they have changed considerably since the launch of Samuelson's famous textbook immediately after the Second World War, which book itself has developed significantly from edition to edition (Brazelton 1977; Elzinga 1992). These analyses have led to some of the critical comments presented below. In addition, a number of mainstream economists have, in passing, commented on what they perceive as problematic developments in textbooks in general.

A first critical point is that the books become ever thicker (Maxwell 1999, 125–127; Stiglitz 1988, 173). This could in part be ascribed to the fact that textbook writers are hesitant to eliminate even out-dated material (Boskin 1988, 160).

A second critical development is the tendency to eliminate some aspects of economics, which are seen as highly relevant by some economists, such as the already mentioned contextual knowledge and the history of economic ideas.

And third, the leading textbooks tend to become more and more similar. According to Stiglitz (1988, 173), this could be ascribed to monopolistic competition within the textbook market – a market form that is suspected of promoting imitation and inhibiting innovation.[5]

Problems with content of a less general nature

Criticisms of parts of content are of a less fundamental character than the three stated above but have a certain overlap with some of those already mentioned. They may refer to important issues regarded as inadequately treated in textbooks or even, in a few instances, to inconsistencies and mistakes. Critiques of content tend to list critical points rather than deal with possible implications of remedying them. The critical points are:

1. Mainstream textbooks rely heavily on the assumption of perfect competition. Stiglitz (1988, 175) points out that this kind of competition has become ever more irrelevant, but that this fact is not reflected in textbooks.
2. Textbooks might be 'one of the last places where shifts in economic method are realized' (Hoass 1993, 223).

3. Principles of economics textbooks are divided into micro- and macro-level sections and they are unsuccessful in integrating the two (Stiglitz 1988, 175).
4. Stiglitz (1988, 172–175) views as problematic that textbooks are so similar and demonstrate lack of innovativeness.
5. The dominant mainstream critique of content concerns important omissions:
   a. There is too little mention of:
      i. technological change (Boskin 1988, 162; Stiglitz 1988, 175);
      ii. 'information and uncertainty' (Stiglitz 1988, 176);
      iii. how economists do research (in different editions of textbooks by Samuelson according to Elzinga 1992, 876);
      iv. the international dimension (a standard criticism of American textbooks raised by Bell 1988; Boskin 1988; and Stiglitz 1988);
      v. economic history (Giedeman and Lowen 2008).[6]
   b. There is a whole literature (with Susan Feiner as fulcrum) criticizing the low priority given to questions of race and gender in textbooks (Bartlett 1997; Cherry and Feiner 1992; Feiner 1993; Feiner and Morgan 1987; Feiner and Roberts 1990; Folbre 1993).
   c. Introductory textbooks have problems handling actual monetary policy especially because they tend to operate with models having one interest rate only (Blinder 2010, 386; Harck 2009).[7]
   d. Recent principles of economics textbooks fail 'to give students even imperfect answers' as to what caused the financial crisis of 2008 (Blinder 2010, 385).

Whatever Happened to the Mainstream Critique of Textbooks?

It is striking that the mainstream critique seems to have almost vanished (in the literature list there are only three articles criticizing principles of economics texts published during 2000–2010). One can conceive of three explanations:

1. There is not much merit in criticizing textbooks.
2. There is no perceived need for change. Allan Blinder (2010, 390) claims that 'the basic framework . . . remains solid'. If textbook writers generally believe that the basic framework is solid, it follows that the incentive for changing textbooks – more than through the usual incremental changes and small additions – is very small.

3. Textbooks have responded to the most important part of the criticisms and been changed accordingly – leaving most of the critical points raised out of date.

The answer to the question raised in the heading is probably to be found in a combination of the three explanations. Concerning the third explanation, one can observe some changes in modern textbooks substantiating the idea that textbooks have actually changed:

- According to Harck (2009), one can find advanced textbooks today giving a more adequate presentation of monetary policy, and Blinder is about to do so in his textbook (Blinder 2010). And, already for some time there have been introductory texts on the market with a more satisfactory presentation of monetary policy (e.g. Burda and Wyplosz 2009; Lipsey and Chrystal 2007).
- Some of the more recent textbooks have also dealt with some of the minor queries above, such as:
    - helping students to operationalize abstract concepts by placing 'boxes' in the text, thus more directly confronting the issue at hand (e.g. O'Sullivan, Sheffrin and Perez 2010);
    - the size of the books has stagnated at around 800–900 pages[8] (and additional articles are typically posted on the internet);
    - US textbooks have generally become less Keynesian (according to – and to the regret of – Blinder 2010, 386);
    - future textbooks will probably take the financial crisis more seriously. They will 'have a full article devoted to crises[9] and also will likely reorganize the macroeconomics presentation to better explain the crisis' (Colander 2010b, 383).

The above implies that some of the criticisms have been taken into account, but most of the fundamental criticism – too little relation to reality and a false objectivity – remains valid. This is of course not easily documented, but my guess would be that most teachers using textbooks – if pressed – would be in agreement. Furthermore, it should be noted that even some of the smaller problems remain unresolved, partly because they are linked to these more fundamental problems. It should, however, be noted that most textbook writers have responded to the 'lack of reality' criticism by working hard on making textbooks *appear* to be related to reality by time and again relating theoretical element to reality, especially in boxes. But I would argue that in essence the theoretical parts are still highly abstract and unrelated to reality.

WHY SHOULD ECONOMISTS CARE ABOUT MAINSTREAM SELF-CRITICISM – PART II?

I can now return to the questions raised at the beginning of the chapter.

a. How much mainstream criticism is there out there?

It is well known that often criticism has to pile up before it can have an impact. In this case it is to be noted that the criticisms are limited in quantum and not widely shared by a number of different economists. Furthermore, criticism has more or less evaporated from the academic debate. In sum, next to no mainstream debate is going on these days.

b. Is the mainstream critique essential?

c. How does the critique raised by mainstream economists differ from that of heterodox economists?

To my surprise some of the critique has been fundamental and has great similarity with criticisms raised by heterodox economists. What makes it less surprising is that some of these mainstream economists share views common to those of heterodox economists (Stiglitz, Blinder and Boulding). The qualitative difference between mainstream and heterodox critiques is that mainstream economists tend to single out minor critical issues without relating to the totality of the textbook.

d. Has it had any impact?

I have argued above that the self-criticism seems to have had some limited impact on the content of textbooks but that essentially textbooks are the same as always. This leads to the next question:

e. Could the critique be used as a platform for heterodox economists trying to change mainstream textbooks?

The results suggest that a dialogue on how to make textbooks more realistic and pluralist is possible with *some* mainstream economists. If we could link the analysed rather dated self-criticism with the financial crisis it might become possible to reinvigorate mainstream self-criticism. It is striking that the financial crisis does constitute a piece of reality which textbooks have to cope with (cf. Blinder 2010) but also that this crisis is very much about disagreements among economists. In other words, if textbooks are to take the financial crisis seriously they have to link more to reality and different theoretical views on economic reality. The self-criticism demonstrates that there have been mainstream economists who would like to change textbooks quite a bit. What heterodox economists might start discussing is how to help them rather than yelling at them. It does not contribute to a constructive dialogue that heterodox economists tend to assume that mainstream economists are completely unaware of any limitations from which mainstream theory might suffer.

f. Why should mainstream economists care about mainstream criticism of textbooks?

Writers and users of mainstream textbooks ought to have a keen interest in possible weaknesses in the books – to improve future editions as well as teaching. But they can also use the results to reflect upon what a textbook is and what we can require from textbooks. Nowadays there is a tendency among mainstream economists to take the present textbooks for granted. Textbooks are textbooks and they are not easily changed. The results can be used to formulate some critical questions to mainstream economists which are posed in the conclusion. One of my aims with this study is to reinvigorate the mainstream debate on textbooks and hence contribute to the improvement of future textbooks. Regrettably, *Journal of Economic Education* rejected an article based on these results mainly because the criticisms are dated which, rather than being a weakness, is a result in its own right.

CONCLUSION: WHY SHOULD WE CARE ABOUT MAINSTREAM SELF-CRITICISM?

This chapter identifies a limited but lively debate about textbooks in the academic literature among mainstream economists. A few of the economists referred to are fundamentally in disagreement with mainstream textbooks because of what these critiques perceive as a lack of relation to the real economy and a mistaken quest for objectivity. More are worried about the current development of textbooks, but the major part of the critical voices only find one or two minor issues that need to be dealt with to a greater extent. The second major result is that the mainstream debate has largely disappeared. I have tried to explain why but I would like to hear an explanation from mainstream economists. Just as puzzling as the existence of a mainstream self-critique is its disappearance.

Why do I think that these results should interest mainstream as well as heterodox economists? First, mainstream economists might use the results to ponder one fundamental question: what would I like to improve in textbooks and in my introductory teaching? Suppose some mainstream economists say that no change is really needed – it would be obvious to ask them why they disagree with some of their fellow economists. Their answer could be interesting. Secondly, they might use some of the critical points raised here as a source of inspiration for amending the textbooks, making them more realistic and including more debate – thereby increasing the interest of their students.

Heterodox economists might use the results to argue that some of their criticisms are in complete correspondence with claims made by mainstream economists. Furthermore, they might use the results to formulate a criticism which is less offensive to mainstream economists and, hence, easier to accept. Somehow we have to work on how to make our criticisms irrefutable not only to heterodox but also to mainstream economists.

NOTES

1. A number of economists actually did – partly based on economic theory – expect a crisis similar to the one we have experienced, but of course they had problems in predicting the actual timing of the crisis (cf. Bezemer 2009).
2. This limitation implies that a central non-mainstream work on economics textbooks (Aslanbeigui and Naples 1996) acknowledged by some mainstream economists falls outside the scope of my analysis.
3. A further complication is non-mainstream economists publishing in mainstream journals and criticizing mainstream textbooks on mainstream premises. For this reason Hill and Myatt's (2007) pertinent but non-mainstream criticism of the treatment of perfect competition in textbooks has not been included in the analysis.
4. In this context David Colander is a very important figure for several reasons. He is one of the few mainstream economists still insisting on criticizing textbooks and has done so in a number of articles (e.g. Colander 2005). At the same time his own textbook (Colander 2010a) has explicitly tried to take into account a great deal of the criticisms presented below. Furthermore, he explicitly calls his book 'not neoclassical' (Colander 2010a, ix). One could, hence, be tempted to categorize him as non-mainstream. He is, however, a borderline case for two reasons. First, on the other hand he calls explicitly himself and his own textbook 'mainstream' (Colander 2010a, xxiii). Secondly, at least one non-mainstream economist regards Colander as being methodologically mainstream (e.g. Lawson 2009), while mainstream economists would probably tend to regard Colander as somewhat unorthodox. I have however chosen not to include Colander in the analysis, as this would tend to blur otherwise very clear results.
5. A more systematic analysis of the apparent similarity reveals great differences between mainstream textbooks but also a number of similarities (cf. Shackelford 1991).
6. This criticism is formulated in a positive vein: 'a ripe area for improvement in introductory economics textbooks' (58).
7. The most important criticisms are the use of one interest-rate model, but also the confusing emphasis on long-term interest rates in monetary policy discussions.
8. This development had already been observed by Carvellas, Kessel and Ramazani (1996) and by a textbook author, McEachern (1996).

9. Colander's own textbook (2010a) was the first of the most-sold principles of economics textbooks to have a full chapter on the financial crisis. A more recent textbook (Arnold, 2011) has also one chapter on the financial crisis.

BIBLIOGRAPHY[10]

Arnold, R.A. 2011. *Principles of Economics*, 10th edition. Mason, OH: South-Western Cengage Learning.

Aslanbeigui, N. and M.I. Naples (eds.) 1996. *Rethinking Economic Principles. Critical Essays on Introductory Textbooks*. Chicago, IL: Irwin.

Bade, R. and M. Parkin 2010. *Foundations of Economics*, 5th edition Boston, MA: Addison-Wesley. International Edition.

*Bartlett, R.L. 1997. *Introducing Race and Gender into Economics*. London: Routledge.

*Bell, C.S. 1988. The Principles of Economics from Now until Then. *Journal of Economic Education* 2:133–147.

Bezemer, D.J. 2009. 'No One Saw This Coming': Understanding Financial Crisis Through Accounting Models. *MPRA Paper* No. 15892. Germany, München.

*Blinder, A. 2010. Teaching Macro Principles *after* the Financial Crisis. *Journal of Economic Education* 4:385–390.

*Bolton, C. and J.B. Taylor (eds.)1982. *American Economics Texts: A Free Market Critique*. Reston: Young America's Foundation.

*Boskin, M.J. 1988. Observations on the Use of Textbooks in the Teaching of the Principles of Economics. *Journal of Economic Education* 2:157–164.

*Boulding, K.E. 1988. What Do We Want in an Economics Textbook? *Journal of Economic Education* 2:113–132.

*Brazelton, W.R. 1977. Some Major Changes in the Principles of Economics as Exemplified by the Principles of Economics of Paul Samuelson, 1948–1973. *American Economist* 2:3–11.

*Brue, S.L. 1996. Controversy and Change in the American Economics Curriculum. *American Economist* 2:44–51.

*Buckley, W.F. 1951. *God and Man at Yale. The Superstitions of Academic Freedom*. Chicago, IL: Regnery Publishing.

Burda, M. and C. Wyplosz 2009. *Macroeconomics: A European Text*. Oxford: Oxford University Press.

Carvellas, J., H. Kessel and R. Ramazani 1996. Counting Pages: The Evolution of the Economic Principles Text. *Aslanbeigui and Naples 1996* 215–224.

*Cherry, R. and S. Feiner 1992. The Treatment of Racial and Sexual Discrimination in Economics Journals and Economics Textbooks: 1972 to 1987. *Review of Black Political Economy* 2:99–118.

Colander, D. 2005. What Economist Teach and What Economist Do. *Journal of Economic Education* 3:249–260.

Colander, D. 2010a. *Economics*, 8th edition. Boston, MA: McGraw-Hill/Irwin. International Student Edition.

Colander, D. 2010b. Introduction to Symposium on the Financial Crisis and the Teaching of Macroeconomics. *Journal of Economic Education* 4:383–384.

Colander, D. et al. 2009. The Financial Crisis and the Systemic Failure of

Academic Economics. *Discussion Papers* 09-03. University of Copenhagen, Department of Economics.
*Elzinga, K.G. 1992. The Eleven Principles of Economics. *Southern Economic Journal* 4:861–879.
*Feiner, S.F. 1993. Introductory Economics Textbooks and the Treatment of Issues Relating to Women and Minorities, 1984 and 1991. *Journal of Economic Education* 2:145–162.
*Feiner, S.F. and B.A. Morgan 1987. Women and Minorities in Introductory Economics Textbooks: 1974–1984. *Journal of Economic Education* 4:376–392.
*Feiner, S.F. and B. Roberts 1990. Hidden by the Invisible Hand: Neoclassical Economic Theory and the Textbook Treatment of Race and Gender. *Gender and Society* 2:159–181.
*Folbre, N. 1993. How Does She Know? Feminist Theories of Gender Bias in Economics. *History of Political Economy* 1:167–184.
*Giedeman, D.C. and A. Lowen 2008. The Use of Economic History in Introductory Economics Textbooks. *Journal of Economics and Economic Education Research* 3:47–66.
*Harck, S. 2009. Til kritikken af den økonomiske lærebog – en replik. *Nationaløkonomisk Tidsskrift* 2:254–261.
Hill, R. and A. Myatt 2007. Overemphasis on Perfectly Competitive Markets in Microeconomics Principles Textbooks. *Journal of Economic Education* 1:58–77.
Hoass, D.J. 1993. A Historical Narrative of Methodological Change in Principles of Economics Textbooks. *Journal of Economic Issues* 1:217–230.
Keynes, J.M. 1936 [1973]. *The General Theory of Employment, Interest and Money*. The Collected Writings of John Maynard Keynes vol. VII. Edited by Donald Moggridge. Cambridge: Macmillan Cambridge University Press.
Lawson, T. 2009. The Current Economic Crisis: Its Nature and the Course of Academic Economics. *Cambridge Journal of Economics* 33:759–777.
Lipsey, R.L. and A. Chrystal 2007. *Economics*, 11th edition. Oxford: Oxford University Press.
Maxwell, P. 1999. The Economic Principles Text: Its Evolution and Influence in Australia. *Journal of Economic and Social Policy* 2:117–132.
McEachern, W.A. (1996). Principles of Economics Textbooks: Coping with Scarce Resources and Unlimited Wants. *Aslanbeigui and Naples 1996*: 215–224.
*Shackelford, J. 1991. One-Semester Introductory Economics Textbooks: Echoes and Choices. *Journal of Economic Education* 1:55–87.
Shiller, R.J. 2010. How Should the Financial Crisis Change How We Teach Economics? *Journal of Economic Education* 4:403–409.
*Stiglitz, J.E. 1988. On the Market for Principles of Economics Textbooks: Innovation and Product Differentiation. *Journal of Economic Education* 2:171–177.
O'Sullivan, A., S. Sheffrin and S. Perez 2010. *Economics. Principles, Applications and Tools*, 6th Edition. Upper Saddle River, NJ: Pearson. International Edition.
*Watts, M. 1987. Ideology, Textbooks, and the Teaching of Economics. *Theory into Practice* 3:190–197.

10. * indicates a publication containing critique of mainstream textbooks.

10. Teaching Keynes's theory to neoclassically formed minds

Angel Asensio

INTRODUCTION

Keynes's theory is difficult to teach partly because it is not the first (economic) language with which people have to deal. Students first spend hours and hours learning neoclassical language, including the flawed neoclassical approach to Keynes's theory, with the result that neoclassical economics tends to become their 'natural' way to think and speak about economics. Hence the teaching of the genuine Keynes theory requires dealing with two intellectually related heavy tasks: first, unlearn or deconstruct the 'natural language' (recognize, for example, that price flexibility does not necessarily involve market clearing, that competitive forces do not involve market efficiency in general, that public intervention is not necessarily the devil. . .), and, secondly, start learning a new economic language from the beginning.

One difficulty is that both neoclassical and Keynes's economics often refer to common words with different meanings. Both Keynes's and neoclassical theory deal with the economy in terms of a market system, with individuals and firms drawing supply and demand plans in a (more or less) competitive way. But theories, as languages, are made of concepts rather than words, that is, of word meanings, so that common words may mean different things depending on the methodological framework. As Keynes emphasized the methodological importance of true uncertainty, the way individuals take *rational* decisions in his theory differs sharply from the mainstream's inter-temporal optimization principle, with the result that the market functioning and the whole system properties also differ sharply. In the same spirit, psychological and sociological factors do influence rational decisions in the face of true uncertainty, while rationality merely amounts to optimization in risk contexts; competitive equilibrium does not mean a cleared labour market in Keynes's theory, while it does in neoclassical theory; unemployment does not necessarily involve either voluntary unemployment or imperfect competition in Keynes's theory, while it does in neoclassical theory. . . The first challenge therefore, as far as the teaching of *The General Theory* is concerned, is to avoid rejecting the useful words whose neoclassical meaning is rejected,[1] for *The General Theory* could hardly be taught if, instead of restating Keynes's genuine meaning of such words as individual plans/decisions, supply and demand, market, equilibrium. . ., the words were just rejected along with their neoclassical meaning.

A second challenge, then, is to restate the proper Keynesian meaning of the deconstructed words, together with the genuine meaning of the other innovative concepts of *The General Theory*, like 'liquidity preference', 'the state of confidence', 'the effective demand' or 'the shifting equilibrium'. . . But concepts per se do not constitute a theory, just as word meanings do not constitute a discourse. Concepts must be articulated to one another, according to some methodological principle, in order to produce sensible propositions and theoretical outcomes capable of providing a coherent explanation of the functioning of the real economy. Keynes suggested that thinking of economics under uncertainty was the seminal innovation, the new methodological principle that had to deliver a different theory.[2] Uncertainty indeed operates at every level of the theory: the way the individuals take *rational* decisions, the way they interact in markets and the way the whole system accordingly behaves. At every stage, uncertainty makes common words have a different meaning in Keynes's theory as compared with a risk context. It is the aim of this chapter to offer an exposition of the macroeconomics of competitive equilibrium that is based on both the deconstruction of neoclassical theory and the restatement of *The General Theory* proper meaning and proper articulation of concepts at every level.

The next section first considers the way both approaches deal with uncertainty and rational decisions. It presents Keynes's theory as a genuine economics of uncertainty which remains unsurpassed, in spite of the recent efforts of the mainstream to deal with uncertainty more consistently. The third section then argues that the modern theory of decision in uncertainty supports Keynes's approach. Because of the absence of reliable knowledge with respect to future outcomes, individual subjectivity is necessarily involved in all decisions that carry substantial long-run implications. *The General Theory* accordingly introduced concepts such as 'liquidity preference' and 'marginal efficiency of capital' in decision theory, and revealed the role of psychological and sociological determinants such as 'conventions', the 'propensity to consume' and 'animal spirits', which have also received support recently in the field of neural science. The fourth section argues that *The General Theory* revolutionized macroeconomics because these renewed micro-foundations drastically changed both the related aggregate supply/demand functions and the macro-markets interaction. The result was a transmutation of the competitive equilibrium analysis, with money non-neutrality, leading role of 'effective demand', failure of competitive forces to remove unemployment and even potential instability. The next two sections put forward the potentially destabilizing forces of competitive markets and the institutional stabilizers that must behave endogenously if an equilibrium is to be the logical outcome of the individual's decisions under uncertainty. The chapter concludes by emphasizing the different meaning of the notion of equilibrium and other key concepts that are involved both in the mainstream and in Keynes's theory, and which is the cause of *The General Theory* still being very confusing for neoclassically formed minds.

IRRATIONAL OPTIMIZATION AND RATIONAL DECISION MAKING UNDER UNCERTAINTY

There have been events that carried strong economic consequences but were nevertheless strictly unpredictable, as they were just unthinkable, before they happened. What, for example, was the probability of a revolutionary breath across northern Africa, or the probability of a nuclear disaster in Japan, or terrorist attacks on the World Trade Center. . .? And to the extent that we are conscious of our incapacity to foresee the future consequences of current decisions, our decisions do not simply depend on the forecast we make, they 'also depend on the *confidence* with which we make this forecast, on how highly we rate the likelihood of our best forecast turning out quite wrong' (Keynes 1936, p. 148). Yet in the standard mainstream model, the so-called DSGE,[3] individuals do maximize their expected earnings/utility, based on probabilities they firmly believe in, in spite of the fact that they can hardly ignore that these probabilities have no objective foundation. The rationality of such behaviour is questionable in general, although it could be acceptable in a context where expectations have not been deceived for a long time, so that individuals no longer doubt their forecasts. But in a system which is subject to unpredictable mutations, it is rational to have a limited confidence in one's predictions.

Econometrics has been a powerful instrument of the academic domination of the neoclassical way of thinking, but the abundant literature on 'time varying' relations, 'shifting'/'switching' regimes, structural change,. . . is now becoming a major source of its weakening, for it carries strong methodological questions even from the mainstream's own point of view (Hendry 2002; Kurmann 2005; Hinich, Foster and Wild 2006). As Nobel Prizewinner Edmund Phelps pointed out in the *American Economic*

Review: 'if an economy possesses dynamism . . . and its structure is ever-changing, the concept of rational-expectations equilibrium does not apply and a model of such an economy that imposes this concept cannot represent at all well the mechanism of such an economy's fluctuation' (Phelps 2007, p. 548). Experimental economics also attest that 'when the environment changes continually, . . . the learning process may never reach a stationary point' (Sunder 2007, p. 96). According to Frydman and Goldberg, 'contemporary economics' insistence on sharp predictions has misdirected research and impeded its progress'(Frydman and Goldberg 2008, p. 68).

As a matter of consequence, non-Keynesian theorists admit larger definitions of uncertainty nowadays, with the result that they do not consider adaptive learning and expectations as irrational (Sargent 1999; Farmer 2002; Evans and Ramey 2006; Preston 2006; Hansen 2007). It is time, indeed, to recognize that uncertainty matters. It could possibly oblige researchers to adopt less ambitious ways of modelling in terms of their predictive capacity, but it does not prevent theorization and modelling at all. For example, the Rational Beliefs Equilibrium modelling (Kurz 1994; Kurz and Motolese 2001; Wu and Guo 2003) rests on a theory of nonstationary (therefore nonergodic[4]) systems, where individuals' rational expectations change according to their changing beliefs/theory about the economic system functioning. The Imperfect Knowledge Economics promoted by Frydman and Goldberg (2008) also wishes to deal with strong uncertainty. But these approaches, though they unquestionably improve the role of uncertainty in the theory by allowing for nonergodicity, still assume that agents are always confident about their expectations in spite of the fact that their theory is likely to be wrong in the future.

This is an unfortunate assumption that dispossesses uncertainty of its very effects, for, as shown in the next section, the 'state of confidence' may influence decisions considerably when individuals are unsure. Whereas this concept looks irrational within the restrictive approach to uncertainty that the mainstream uses, it is in fact the principle of optimization that lacks rational foundations in the face of true uncertainty. Optimization would be a rational basis for inter-temporal decisions if individuals could reasonably trust in their views about the future, that is, if there was not true uncertainty, or if individuals could rationally behave 'as if' there were not. But insofar as true uncertainty really does matter, it is not that rational to make decisions based on such a fragile foundation as a subjective distribution of probabilities. Hence, as stated in Table 10.1 (see p. 177), the meaning attached to the notion of rationality strongly differs according to the methodological approach to uncertainty. In particular, while the notion of confidence does not play any rational role in risk contexts, it crucially takes part in rational decision making under uncertainty.

MICRO-FOUNDATIONS AND AGGREGATE RELATIONS

Keynes's economics, on the other hand, allowed for psychological and sociological determinants that, far from being irrational, actually supersede the restrictive view of the mainstream with respect to individual decisions.[5] This is why Keynes introduced new concepts like the 'fundamental psychological law', the 'psychological incentive to liquidity' and the 'psychological expectation of future yield from capital assets'. Mainstream economists may feel uneasy with the way Keynes deals with concepts like the 'inducement to invest' or the 'propensity to consume' in *The General Theory*, instead of their usual producer and consumer optimal plans. The meaning of these concepts, however, is very clear when decisions are considered in a context of true uncertainty. For example, while the consumer optimal plan would require a reliable knowledge of all the individual future revenues, along with a reliable distribution of probabilities related to a reliable set of possible future events (plus a complete market structure), that is, while the consumer optimal plan would require something highly unrealistic as far as true uncertainty is considered, Keynes invokes the 'fundamental psychological law' according to which individuals have a rather stable, though potentially changing, propensity to consume out of their current revenue. Actually, Keynes's recurrent focus on individual psychology and sociological determinants is very much in accordance with the psychological science findings of the late 20th century, which established that the optimization principle does not provide a good explanation of rational decisions: 'More generally, decision makers are often influenced by emotional, social and political factors, and this can give the appearance of "irrational" decision making' (Eysenck 2001, p. 348).[6] *The General Theory* (ch. 12) therefore refers to the market conventional valuation of asset prices because there is no objective basis which could help to compute what a 'natural' level should be. According to Epstein and Wang (1994, p. 283), 'uncertainty may lead to equilibria that are indeterminate, that is, there may exist a continuum of equilibria for given fundamentals. That leaves the determination of a particular equilibrium price process to "animal spirits" and sizable volatility may result.'[7] Hence, since the assets valuation cannot but rest on subjective views, their equilibrium price is conventional in character (remember Keynes's famous 'beauty contest'). The equilibrium price is the one which, given the information delivered by the past and current context, the market expects to be durable. If the current market price is higher/lower than the conventional market price, and if it is expected to decrease/increase accordingly, then the demand in effect decreases/increases so that the market rate eventually meets the convention. The market convention therefore provides an anchor for expectations, which would be undetermined otherwise, as asset prices would be. It happens consequently that, at the aggregate level, the higher is the prospective yield of assets, the higher is aggregate investment, since rational behaviour commands that all projects having a 'marginal efficiency of capital' higher than the rate of interest must be realized. Hence the global amount of productive investment corresponding to a given interest rate is not unique; it actually depends on 'the schedule of the marginal efficiency of capital', that is, on how optimistic/pessimistic the prospective yield of capital assets is.

As *The General Theory* caused much trouble within the neoclassical way of thinking, orthodox economists attempted to provide a rationale for Keynes's critical concepts within their own restricted definition of uncertainty. For example, when empirical evidence against the single transaction-money theory called for a theoretical response to Keynes's suggestive 'speculative motive' for demanding money, Tobin (1958) introduced his famous portfolio optimal trade-off between interest and risk, thereby justifying an interest-rate elastic demand for money. Another crucial example is given by the marginal efficiency of capital, which meaning was cautiously distinguished by Keynes from the marginal productivity of capital precisely because of uncertainty. But Keynes's theory of the inducement to invest, which proved to be better than the traditional function of the interest rate, was translated in terms of 'Tobin's *Q*' deviations from the neoclassical equilibrium value (that is, 1) within a stationary model (Brainard and Tobin 1968, p. 105), although Keynes's *Q* clearly departed from the ergodic vision of the world, as attested in *The General Theory* chapter 11 (section 2) and chapter 21 (section 1).

As a matter of consequence, in Tobin's framework the money demand and investment decisions were basically determined by means of optimization, irrespective of any degree of confidence or animal spirit. Yet, as Knight (1921, p. 227) had also emphasized,

> the 'degree' of certainty or of confidence felt in the conclusion after it is reached cannot be ignored, for it is of the greatest practical significance. The action which follows upon an opinion depends as much upon the amount of confidence in that opinion as it does upon the favorableness of the opinion itself. The ultimate logic, or psychology, of these deliberations is obscure, a part of the scientifically unfathomable mystery of life and mind.

The point is formally attested in modern decision theory under uncertainty (Chateauneuf, Eichberger and Grant 2007). In their model, Nishimura and Ozaki (2004) showed that, while an increase in risk ('mean preserving spread of the wage distribution the worker thinks she faces') increases the reservation wage, an increase in Knightian uncertainty ('a decrease in her confidence about the wage distribution') reduces the reservation wage. Although their analysis is not about financial decisions, the intuitive reason clearly recalls Keynes's arguments regarding the liquidity preference and the inducement to invest: when uncertainty increases, people aim to reduce it by accepting a job and cancel a future search (that is, by preferring a certain amount of money today rather than an uncertain amount in the future[8]). The authors also showed in a recent paper that 'an increase in Knightian uncertainty makes the uncertainty-averse decision-maker more likely to postpone investment to avoid facing uncertainty' (Nishimura and Ozaki 2007), in a way similar to Keynes's views about the effects of a decrease in confidence on the marginal efficiency of capital. In the same vein, Gomes (2008) found that 'an uncertainty averse agent saves more than a risk aversion agent and this gap increases with the degree of uncertainty aversion'.

As a matter of fact, while in the mainstream's approach to 'inter-temporal optimal choices' psychological and sociological determinants are confined to the making of individual preferences, Keynes's economics points out how usefully they can also contribute to explain (rational) decisions themselves in the face of uncertainty. Therefore, in spite of the mainstream's attempts to integrate such notions as the inducement to invest or speculative demand for money, they cannot have the same meaning. And the money demand and investment functions accordingly, as well as the other functions related to decisions involving uncertain long-term outcomes, cannot but strongly differ too. Also, in Keynes's theory conventional behaviour proves to be a powerful concept with crucial implications for the economic system as a whole as far as the determination of asset prices (and interest rates; see below) is concerned, whereas it simply does not make sense in an inter-temporal optimization framework.

DISRUPTIVE UNCERTAINTY AND EFFECTIVE DEMAND

As no complete-markets system can be imagined which could allow for a complete set of insurance contracts against capital losses, Keynesian uncertainty gives to money a role as a hedge against the potential losses that could occur if savings were invested in financial markets, while the demand for money is essentially related to the transaction motive in mainstream macroeconomics. Of course, provided the rate of interest is attractive enough to push savers to part with money and buy non-money assets instead, the liquidity preference that logically results from uncertainty aversion can be compensated for. But the critical point is that the function of the interest rate is not to reward savings, but to reward the acceptance of non-insurable risks in Keynes's economics. It is first of all an incentive for lending out of a given amount of savings, not an incentive for saving out of the revenue or global wealth. The equilibrium rate of interest, accordingly, is determined by the supply and demand for money (as a hedge against uncertainty), not by the supply and demand for savings; in such a way that the competitive adjustment of the rate of interest is not aimed at equalizing aggregate saving and investment, which does invalidate 'Say's law'.[9]

In mainstream economics, an insufficient aggregate demand of goods, or, equivalently, an excess of full-employment saving over investment could not be a stable situation, for it would trigger a decrease in the rate of interest, thereby clearing both the market for goods and the market for saving simultaneously. And since the supply of goods therefore cannot be constrained by the demand side, firms can freely hire until the marginal product of labour is made equal to the real wage.[10] Hence, in the mainstream analysis of competitive markets, unemployment simply cannot result from a deficient aggregate demand. But in the presence of strong uncertainty, on the other hand, the long-term interest-rate decrease caused by a depressed aggregate demand, and the real-balance effect as well, may meet various obstacles. First, if the money supply decreases along with the demand for money, as stated in the Post Keynesian endogenous money approach, then the rate of interest does not decrease.[11] Secondly, it may be that the depressive forces harm the state of confidence in such a way that people increase the liquid-assets share in their portfolio, which could inhibit both the Keynes and Pigou effects even if the authorities were prepared to let the interest rate decrease by means of a weaker decrease in the money supply. Thirdly, even if the interest rate decreased, the worsening business climate could deter investments (the schedule of the marginal efficiency of capital goes down) in such a way that unemployment would not decrease (and could even increase, as Keynes put forward in *The General Theory* chapter 19, p. 263).

Why cannot mainstream theory consider these obstacles? The answer is clearly because true uncertainty is never considered, but risk. When a depression arises, people do not increase the liquid-assets share in their portfolio if the depression is merely considered a 'white noise'. In the same spirit, a depression does not change the long-run expected return on capital and the related inducement to invest. That is to say, 'uncertainty' proves to be inoffensive when Tobin's semantic shift operates within the common syntax.

But if, in accordance with *The General Theory*, the equilibrium interest rate involves the money market, instead of the 'loanable funds' market, and the supply of goods therefore does not create its own demand, then firms cannot decide their demand of productive factors nor their production plans without considering the expected demand of the goods they are deciding to produce, the effective demand. The effective demand is essentially determined by the global propensity to consume (including public expenditures) and, as regards the demand for investment goods, by the subjective and potentially changing 'views about the future', since these views determine both the expected return on investment and the equilibrium rate of interest. Hence if, given the global propensity to consume, expectations are not optimistic enough to stimulate the effective demand sufficiently, firms cannot but limit their demand for labour. As the resulting equilibrium unemployment may be higher or lower depending on the subjective 'views about the future', Keynes's notion of equilibrium involves an important difference as compared with the mainstream's, since the latter only deals with a unique, predetermined ('natural') equilibrium the individuals just have to compute.

Another important issue with respect to the signification of equilibrium is related to the discussion of whether or not unemployment decreases in case of a downward pressure on wages, since, according to the mainstream, flexible wages should remove unemployment in competitive markets. Until chapter 19 of *The General Theory*, the money wage is taken as constant (chapter 3) or independent (chapter 18) 'to facilitate the exposition' (p. 27), the case for endogenous changes in wages being properly discussed in chapter 19. Keynes then considers the possible effects of wage decreases, which mainly operates through distributional effects on the global propensity to consume, and through expectations effects on both the schedule of the marginal efficiency of capital and the rate of interest.[12] The conclusion is that wages decreases could arm effective demand further and depress the economy even more, instead of clearing the labour market. There is therefore an additional questioning the theory has to deal with, for the effective demand depends both on individuals' expectations that have no objective anchor, and on the level of wages that competitive forces do not anchor in general. Does this mean that there is an inherent indeterminacy of equilibrium in *The General Theory*?

POTENTIAL INSTABILITY AND INSTITUTIONAL ENDOGENOUS STABILIZERS

Keynes put forward strong arguments that allowed him to develop the theory of a system which, 'whilst it is subject to severe fluctuations in respect of output and employment, is not violently unstable' (Keynes 1936, p. 249). Those arguments were based on the meaningful idea that institutions and conventional behaviour actually anchor the system in spite of potential indeterminacy. Crotty (1994) accordingly suggested that a stable set of conventions and institutions allows for stability in Keynes' theory.

However, the meaning of stability is ambiguous in the literature on economic institutions, for it is not always clear whether it is referring to the equilibrium outcome of some offsetting forces at a point in time (say static stability/instability), or to the dynamic outcome of these forces (dynamic stability/instability). Minsky (1986) and Cornwall and Cornwall (2001) offered a penetrating analysis of how institutions can repel or limit dynamic instability and/or support macroeconomic performances through the control they have on some factors that do influence the succession of the short-run equilibrium positions (e.g. financial regulation, 'socialization of investment'. . .). But institutions cannot be considered from a dynamic point of view only, for they also play a crucial role in the determination of the equilibrium solution at any point in time, that is, before the dynamics of equilibrium can even be considered.

On this issue, Rotheim (1993, p. 215) noticed that 'given the conventional behaviors that followed from the social interactions of individuals, Keynes sought not indeterminacy', while Hodgson (1989, p. 116) pointed out that in Keynes's theory 'markets function coherently *because* of institutional rigidities and "imperfections", and not *despite* them as neoclassical theorists presume'. Now, insofar as market forces would produce 'violent instability' in the absence of institutional stabilizers but do not show indeterminacy in general, one is led to the conclusion that the system itself must generate endogenously the institutions/conventions' stabilizing response, for otherwise there would be no equilibrium solution. *The General Theory* deals more explicitly with 'conditions of stability' from the dynamic point of view (Keynes 1936, pp. 250–254) than from the 'static' point of view, but it deals obviously with the critical question of static stability or instability (indeterminacy) when it refers to the role of trade unions and wage rigidity as a hedge against potential cumulative depression (Keynes 1936, chs 19, 21),[13] a kind of indeterminacy, and when it refers to the conventional nature of the rate of interest (Keynes 1936, ch.15, pp. 202–204) or to the conventional valuation of the prospective yield of capital assets as a way to anchor expectations and decisions (chapters 12 and 15). It happens, then, that according to Keynes, there could not be, strictly speaking, any flex-price competitive equilibrium with Keynesian unemployment, for, with flex-prices, competitive wages would either adjust effectively to full employment (provided the effective demand is not hindered), or unemployment would increase continuously as a result of the negative effects on the effective demand that would continuously put the pressure on wages. . .. The alternatives, accordingly, are either full employment or cumulative depression. As Keynes himself stated:

> If . . . money-wages were to fall without limit whenever there was a tendency for less than full employment, . . . there would be no resting-place below full employment until either the rate of interest was incapable of falling further or wages were zero. In fact we must have *some* factor, the value of which in terms of money is, if not fixed, at least sticky, to give us any stability of values in a monetary system. (Keynes 1936, pp. 303–304)

Of course, although rigidities are required if Keynesian unemployment is to be an equilibrium solution, this is not to say that rigidities cause unemployment. By contrast with the Benassy (1984)–Malinvaud (1980a,b) range of models, where it was argued that flexible prices would eventually lead the economy towards the Walras outcome,[14] money-wage rigidity in Keynes's theory expresses a form of endogenous resistance to further wage decreases when it becomes clear that wage flexibility does not reduce unemployment. It is the necessary stabilizing response of institutions like trade unions, regulation, wage bargaining and demand policies[15] to cumulative depressive forces; a response failing which no equilibrium would even exist. Hence, in Keynes's theory, wage rigidity is not a competitive distortion responsible for unemployment as the mainstream considers it, it is the endogenous outcome of institutional stabilizers that take part of the adjustment to equilibrium at any time.The section 'Micro-foundations and aggregate relations' above also showed the critical role of conventions as an anchor for subjective views about the future with respect to the assets' prospective yields and equilibrium prices. Chapter 15 of *The General Theory* accordingly also deals with the equilibrium long-term interest rate in terms of convention. It is true that there are two approaches to the equilibrium long-term interest rate in the book, but they are reconciled when Keynes argues that the convention finally commands the market equilibrium rate. Indeed, although in the section above the rate of interest appeared to be determined by the supply and demand of money, Keynes's theory also suggests that if the current market rate is higher/lower than the convention and the rate of interest therefore is expected to decrease/increase, the demand for money alters so that the current rate eventually meets the convention. The long-term rate of interest therefore:[16]

> is a highly conventional . . . phenomenon. For its actual value is largely governed by the prevailing view as to what its value is expected to be. *Any* level of interest which is accepted with sufficient conviction as *likely* to be durable *will* be durable; subject, of course, in a changing society to fluctuations for all kinds of reasons round the expected normal. (Keynes 1936, p. 203)

Hence, in *The General Theory*, there are counter forces such as institutions and conventional behaviour that prevent the system from indeterminacy in spite of the deleterious effects of uncertainty. These forces, which operate in the labour market, in the goods market and in the financial and monetary sector, lead to a very different meaning of the notion of equilibrium in Keynes's theory as compared with the mainstream.

EQUILIBRIUM AT ANY POINT IN TIME

Because of true uncertainty, the theoretical representation of the economic process is essentially dynamic: expectations determine individual choices that in turn influence the current and future (unpredictable) outcomes, which, afterwards, cause changes in expectations (Figure 10.1). In such a system, expectations in general cannot be fulfilled but fortuitously (which does not preclude the possibility that expectations are fulfilled for a period --which length however would be unpredictable – and therefore the possibility that they do not change during that period). Hence, the adequate notion of equilibrium necessarily differs from that which is based on the requirement that expectations are fulfilled. Since economic decisions involve future outcomes over a long period of time, such a definition of equilibrium would only make sense if there was any reliable way of predicting the long-term outcomes; if the future was predetermined. As he denied this, Keynes provided a method of thinking about an intrinsically dynamic economic system.

According to Kregel (1976) and Chick (1983), the method rests on taking expectations as given, in spite of the fact that they are subject to endogenous change. Therefore, in 'the static model of a dynamic process', the authors pointed out, expectations influence the individual economic decisions and, thereby, the aggregate solution, while the aggregate solution's

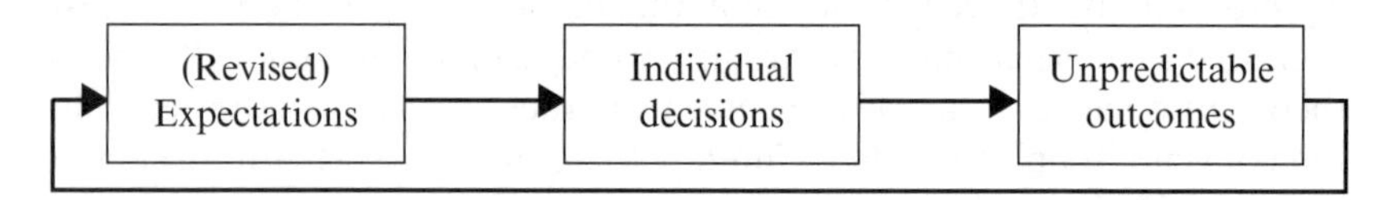

Figure 10.1 A theoretical representation of the economic process

influence over expectations is provisionally ignored. This amounts to neutralization of the feedback effects of the system on expectations, so that it becomes possible to draw a temporary solution, the motion of which can be analytically assessed as a function of the state of expectations.[17,18]

Two important consequences follow on the methodological ground. First, as it would hardly be acceptable to suppose that expectations could remain unchanged for a while in an ever-changing economic system, Keynes's equilibrium has to be related to the very short run: 'Our present object is to discover what determines at any time the national income of a given economic system' (Keynes 1936, p. 247).[19] Secondly, although it may be useful, for the sake of analytical purpose, to consider expectations as a given variable, they are nevertheless an endogenous variable that has to be considered in equilibrium at any point in time, failing which the system would simply be indeterminate. The same point arises when the endogenous determination of wages comes under consideration: wages have to be taken as given in spite of the fact that they will change endogenously in the future. Now, in what sense can expectations' and wages' 'given' values at every point in time be considered in equilibrium in spite of their ephemeral nature? This is the critical aspect of Keynes's equilibrium theory that requires the stabilizing action of conventions and institutions. Conventions and institutions do counter endogenously the potential chaos that unbridled competitive forces otherwise could produce; they provide the system at any point in time with an anchor for the valuation of asset prices as well as for the interest and wage rates, in such a way that the production and transactions just become possible.[20] These institutional stabilizers are the very reason why, in spite of the absence of any predetermined 'natural' anchor, the system does not go anywhere.[21]

DISCUSSION

Keynes's *General Theory* and mainstream economics differ from one another in so many aspects that it makes communication between the two strands of thought almost impossible when the debate starts from theoretical results rather than methodological grounds. Conversely, setting uncertainty at the centre of the methodological debate reveals the very reason for the theoretical oppositions.

As Keynes did adopt the widest approach to uncertainty, he was led to micro-foundations that had to be corroborated in psychological science, neural science and decision theory decades after he published *The General Theory*, while the mainstream's restricted definition of uncertainty became more and more questionable. Those micro-foundations in turn changed dramatically the theoretical properties of the competitive equilibrium. In particular, in the absence of any objective anchor for expectations, the collective outcome of individuals' decisions continuously depends on changing views about the future. Keynes's theory accordingly delivers a different (competitive) equilibrium for every state of 'views concerning the future', while the mainstream only reckons a mythic efficient solution. This is why *The General Theory* is more general and realistic than mainstream economics. Keynes's equilibrium accordingly involves both a wider role for institutions and a richer concept of equilibrium which admits the possibility that all markets do not clear: in a competitive system, the wage and interest rates do not adjust so that the labour market, the loans market and the goods market clear, as in mainstream theory; they adjust in such a way that the induced/endogenous response of institutions and conventional expectations does stabilize the system at any time in spite of the potentially destabilizing competitive forces. The very anchoring of the system is not a predetermined 'natural' one, to which relative prices would be spontaneously driven thanks to the markets' competitive forces; it operates through the attraction of the rate of interest towards the conventionally expected rate, through the institutionalized resistance of wages to further decreases in case of unemployment and often through public support to the aggregate demand (even in countries where macroeconomic policy is usually supply-side oriented).

These 'revolutionary' findings only make sense provided true uncertainty is considered. Unfortunately, the mainstream has been accustomed for too long to the belief that no economic theory is possible under true uncertainty, or that it is not a useful concept. Hence most economists have been used to thinking with a restricted definition of uncertainty according to which the meanings of the key concepts differ sharply from those Keynes had in mind (Table 10.1 summarizes the meanings attached by the mainstream and Keynes's economics to words as common as rationality, equilibrium, unemployment. . .).This is why *The General Theory* remains so confusing for neoclassically formed minds nowadays, in spite of the fact that, even compared with the recent sophisticated attempts to elaborate a macroeconomics of uncertainty, *The General Theory* still provides the most coherent and relevant conceptual framework. Unfortunately, as the mainstream language is the first that students learn and practise abundantly, while there are scarce opportunities to learn and practise alternative theories, they tend spontaneously to attach the mainstream's meaning to the key concepts in the face of these alternative discourses. The result is a rather confused comprehension. Teaching Post Keynesian economics therefore requires the concepts being first deconstructed, if the Post Keynesian discourse is to be really understood. This chapter hopefully offers helpful material to proceed in this way.

Table 10.1 The meaning of key concepts according to the context considered

	Mainstream economics Risk: objective/reliable probabilities	*The General Theory* Uncertainty: subjective/unreliable probabilities
Rationality	– Decisions based on inter-temporal optimization	– Inter-temporal optimization not reliable; confidence matters – Decisions based on psycho/sociological factors.
Equilibrium	– Inter-temporal – Fulfilled expectations	– Provisional (a point in time). Influenced by the endogenous response of institutions, conventions and economic policy to potentially destabilizing competitive forces
Simplified market structure (aggregate level)	– Four macro-markets (money is neutral in the long run) – Represents a 'complete markets structure' in the case of perfect competition	– Four macro-markets – A 'complete markets structure' is a fiction, so that the notion of 'incomplete markets structure' is not relevant either
General competitive equilibrium	– Unique, Pareto-optimal (given preferences, capital stock, technology), but the system may temporarily deviate in case of unexpected changes (white noise) – All markets clear	– A different equilibrium for every state of the 'views about the future' (given technology, preferences, capital stock, institutions. . .) – Inter-temporal 'Pareto optimality' is a fiction, so that the notions of inter-temporal second best, third, fourth. . . are not relevant either – Labour market may clear or not
Adjustment process /stabilizers	– Competitive forces drive relative prices so that all markets clear	– Competitive forces are potentially destabilizing (relative prices do not ensure that all markets clear) – Institutions/conventions provide stability endogenously
Involuntary unemployment	– Imperfect competition in the labour market	– Insufficient expected demand for goods (no matter whether competition is perfect or not in the labour market or elsewhere)

Note: The 'Rational Beliefs Equilibrium' theory and 'Imperfect Knowledge Economics' are not considered in the table since, as mentioned in the text, they have a serious issue with respect to the rationality of the individual decisions.

NOTES

1. Some Post Keynesians have been tempted to throw the baby out with the bath water, by rejecting the use of mathematics as a formal language, the notion of equilibrium, the notion of market. . ., instead of only rejecting the neoclassical misuse of mathematics and the neoclassical meaning of such and such useful word.
2. 'Or, perhaps, we might make our line of division between the theory of stationary equilibrium and the theory of shifting equilibrium – meaning by the latter the theory of a system in which changing views about the future are capable of influencing the present situation. . . . We can consider what distribution of resources between different uses will be consistent with equilibrium under the influence of normal economic motives in a world in which our views concerning the future are fixed and reliable in all respects; – with a further division, perhaps, between an economy which is unchanging and one subject to change, but where all things are foreseen from the beginning. Or we can pass from this simplified propaedeutic to the problems of the real world in which our previous expectations are liable to disappointment and expectations concerning the future affect what we do to-day' (Keynes 1936, pp. 293–294).
3. See Benassy (2007) for a stylized version.
4. Ergodicity is defined as the dynamic stability of a stochastic process; see Vercelli (1991, pp. 40, 154) and Davidson (2002, pp. 39–69). In a nonergodic dynamic, the past events never give enough information about what the future will be. Nonstationarity is not a necessary condition for nonergodicity, although it is a sufficient one.
5. 'We are merely reminding ourselves that human decisions affecting the future, whether personal or political or economic, cannot depend on strict mathematical expectation, since the basis for making such calculations does not exist; and that it is our innate urge to activity which makes the wheels go round, our rational selves choosing between the alternatives as best we are able, calculating where we can, but often falling back for our motive on whim or sentiment or chance' (Keynes 1936, pp. 162–163).
6. Huettel et al. 'identified brain regions that showed a selective increase in activation to decision making under ambiguity, compared to decision making under risk' (Huettel et al. 2006, p. 770). See Davidson (2010) for a comment.
7. These results were obtained with Knight's definition of uncertainty, which remains narrower than that adopted by Keynes and, therefore, does not fully capture Keynes's view. See Davidson (1996).
8. This converges with neural scientists' statement that, 'People often prefer the known over the unknown, sometimes sacrificing potential rewards for the sake of surety' (Huettel et al. 2006, p. 765).
9. Aggregate saving and investment are always equal, of course, but it is through the level of output, not the rate of interest, that saving is equalized to investment. The term 'adjustment' in this text is used in a logical sense. The adjustment or adjustment processes mentioned therefore can take place instantaneously in historical time, as a result of instantaneously revised decisions.
10. In the monetary version of the theory, the fourth market, namely the money market, also contributes to the support of aggregate demand through the real-balance effect and the – not that Keynesian – 'Keynes effect'.
11. Notice that monetary policy is involved in the adjustment to the equilibrium solution.
12. In an open economy the external demand effects of a wage cut should be considered as well. But it is not guaranteed nevertheless that the effective demand could lastingly be stimulated, for the negative effects in foreign countries would produce unemployment and wage cuts abroad, which would tend to offset the initial advantage of the first country.
13. 'it would be much better that wages should be rigidly fixed and deemed incapable of material changes, than that depressions should be accompanied by a gradual downward tendency of money-wages, a further moderate wage reduction being expected to signalize each increase of; say, 1 per cent in the amount of unemployment' (Keynes 1936, p. 265).

14. In Malinvaud (1980a), nevertheless, prices flexibility could produce a cumulative depression in case of unemployment, but that result was obtained within a two-market economy (labour and goods), where the cumulative process resulted from the assumption that the decrease in prices produced by the supply excess of goods is stronger than the decrease in wages (hence the real wage increases, so that firms reduce the production level). Hence Malinvaud overlooked the stabilizing 'Keynes effect' that would have been triggered if the neoclassical money market had been considered too in a complete model of the economy.
15. To the extent that an aggregate demand stimulus does limit unemployment, it can also be considered a counter force against wage decreases.
16. For a recent discussion on the role of monetary authorities with respect to the determination of the long-term rate of interest in *The General Theory*, see Asensio (2011).
17. Kregel (1976) pointed out that Keynes does refer to three (distinct but related) notions of equilibrium in his *General Theory*, depending on whether the short-term expectations, the long-term expectations or both remain stable. Every type of model is of interest to study some specific aspect of the whole theory: if long-term expectations are stable, it is possible to consider the dynamic effects of variable short-term expectations (as in *The General Theory* chapter 5); if long-term and short-term expectations are stable, we have Keynes's static model, and if short-term expectations are stable while long-term expectations are allowed to vary, we have Keynes's 'shifting equilibrium'. It is of course the latter which is the object of the theory, the other being analytical intermediate tools.
18. See the simplified formal statement of Keynes's equilibrium in the Appendix to this chapter. For a more detailed presentation, see Asensio (2011) and Asensio, Charles and Lang (2012).
19. Mark Hayes (2006, p. 6) pointed out that 'The day is Keynes's quantum unit of time, "the shortest interval after which the firm is free to revise its decision as to how much employment to offer. It is, so to speak, the minimum effective unit of economic time" (GT, 47, n1).'.
20. This is distinct from the dynamic approaches mentioned above, where the institutions' endogenous responses refer to something quite different. Minsky, for example, argued forcefully that massive liquidity pumping and public deficit are the necessary/endogenous responses to the intrinsic bias of capitalism towards 'financial fragility'. See Delli Gatti, Gallegati and Minsky (1994) for an attempt at modelling the dynamics that may emerge from this approach.
21. Endogenous institutional stabilizers are not necessarily triggered with the conscious goal of stabilizing the economy. They may be defensive responses which turn out to be stabilizing and may therefore anchor the system in a more or less unfavourable position. These considerations offer a way to explain heterogeneity in macroeconomic performances which might usefully complete the existing literature, where performances are rather related to some deliberate institutional and policy arrangements aimed at improving efficiency, but where little attention is paid to the defensive actions aimed at countering destabilizing forces continuously.

REFERENCES

Ambrosi, G.M., 2009, *Keynes, Pigou and the General Theory*, revised manuscript (25 January) of the 'Keynes Seminar' lecture, held at Robinson College, Cambridge, 22 October 2008.

Asensio, A., 2011, 'Equilibrium interest rate and financial transactions in Post Keynesian models – pointing out some overlooked features', *Intervention – European Journal of Economics and Economic Policies*, 8(2), 385–400.

Asensio, A., 2012, 'On Keynes's seminal innovation and related essential features:

revisiting the notion of equilibrium in *The General Theory*', in T. Cate (Ed.), *Keynes' General Theory: Seventy-five Years Later*, Cheltenham: Edward Elgar Publishing pp. 19–34.

Asensio, A., Charles, S. and Lang, D., 2012, 'Post-Keynesian modeling: where are we, and where are we going to?', *Journal of Post Keynesian Economics*, 34(3), 393–412.

Benassy, J.P., 1984, *Macroéconomie et théorie du déséquilibre*, Paris: Dunod.

Benassy, J.P., 2007, 'IS–LM and the multiplier: a dynamic general equilibrium model', *Economic Letters*, 96, 189–195.

Brainard, W.C. and Tobin, J., 1968, 'Pitfalls in financial model building', *American Economic Review*, Papers and Proceedings of the Eightieth Annual Meeting of the American Economic Association, 58, no. 2.

Chateauneuf, A., Eichberger, J. and Grant, S., 2007, 'Choice under uncertainty with the best and worst in mind: neo-additive capacities', *Journal of Economic Theory*, 137, 538–567.

Chick, V., 1983, *Macroeconomics after Keynes*, Cambridge, MA: MIT Press.

Chick, V. and Tily, G., 2007, 'Transfiguration and death: Keynes's monetary theory', *Association of Heterodox Economics 9th Conference*, University of the West of England, Bristol, 13–15 July.

Cornwall, J. and Cornwall, W., 2001, *Capitalist Development in the Twentieth Century: An Evolutionary Keynesian Analysis*, Cambridge: Cambridge University Press.

Crotty, J., 1994, 'Are Keynesian uncertainty and macrotheory compatible? Conventional decision making, institutional structures, and conditional stability in Keynesian macromodels', in Robert Pollin and Gary Dymski (Eds), *New Perspectives in Monetary Macroeconomics*, Ann Arbor, MI: University of Michigan Press, pp. 105–139.

Davidson, P., 1996, 'Reality and economic theory', *Journal of Post Keynesian Economics*, 18(4), 479–508.

Davidson, P., 2002, *Financial Markets, Money and the Real World*, Cheltenham: Edward Elgar Publishing.

Davidson, P., 2010, 'Behavioral economists should make a turn and learn from Keynes and Post Keynesian economics', *Journal of Post Keynesian Economics*, 33(2), 251–254.

Delli Gatti, D., Gallegati, M. and Minsky, H., 1994, 'Financial instability, economic policy and the dynamic behavior of the economy', Working Paper no. 126, Annandale-on-Hudson, New York, The Levy Economics Institute of Bard College.

Epstein, L.G. and Wang, T., 1994, 'Intertemporal asset pricing under Knightian uncertainty', *Econometrica*, 62(3), 283–322.

Evans, W.G. and Ramey, G., 2006, 'Adaptive expectations, underparameterization and the Lucas critique', *Journal of Monetary Economics*, 53, 249–264.

Eysenck, M.W., 2001, *Principles of Cognitive Psychology*, New York: Psychology Press Ltd (2nd ed.)

Farmer, R.E.A., 2002, 'Why does data reject the Lucas critique?', *Annals of Economics and Statistics*, 67–68, 111–129.

Frydman, R. and Goldberg, M.D., 2008, 'Macroeconomic theory for a world of imperfect knowledge', *Capitalism and Society*, 3(3), 4–76.

Gomes, F.A.R., 2008, 'The effect of future income uncertainty in savings decision', *Economic Letters*, 98, 269–274.

Hansen, L.P., 2007, 'Beliefs, doubts and learning: valuing macroeconomic risk', AEA Papers and Proceedings, *American Economic Review*, 97(2), 1–30.
Hayes, M.G., 2006, *The Economics of Keynes: A New Guide to The General Theory*, Cheltenham: Edward Elgar Publishing.
Hendry, D.F., 2002, 'Forecast failure, expectations formation and the Lucas critique', *Annals of Economics and Statistics*, 67–68, 21–40.
Hinich, M.J., Foster, J. and Wild, P., 2006, 'Structural change in macroeconomic time series: a complex systems perspective', *Journal of Macroeconomics*, 28, 136–150.
Hodgson, G., 1989, 'Post-Keynesianism and Institutionalism: the missing link', in John Pheby (Ed.), *New Directions in Post Keynesian Economics*, Aldershot: Edward Elgar Publishing, pp. 94–123.
Huettel, S.A., Stowe, C.J., Gordon, E.M., Warner, B.T. and Platt, M.L., 2006, 'Neural signatures of economic preferences for risk and ambiguity', *Neuron*, 49, 765–775.
Keynes, J.M., 1936, *The General Theory of Employment, Interest and Money*, London: Macmillan.
Knight, F.H., 1921, *Risk, Uncertainty and Profit*, New York: Harper.
Kregel, J.A., 1976, 'Economic methodology in the face of uncertainty: the modelling methods of Keynes and the Post-Keynesians', *Economic Journal*, 86, 209–225.
Kurmann, A., 2005, 'Quantifying the uncertainty about the fit of a new Keynesian pricing model', *Journal of Monetary Economics*, 52, 1119–1134.
Kurz, M., 1994, 'On the structure and diversity of rational beliefs', *Economic Theory*, 4, 877–900.
Kurz, M. and Motolese, M., 2001, 'Endogenous uncertainty and market volatility', *Economic Theory*, 17, 497–544.
Lawson, T., 1985, 'Uncertainty and economic analysis', *Economic Journal*, 95, 909–927.
Malinvaud, E., 1980a, *Réexamen de la théorie du chômage*, Paris: Calman Levy, first published as *The Theory of Unemployment Reconsidered*, Oxford: Basil Blackwell, 1977.
Malinvaud, E., 1980b, *Profitability and Unemployment*, New York: Cambridge University Press with Editions de la Maison des Sciences de l'Homme.
Minsky, H.P., 1986, *Stabilizing an Unstable Economy*, New Haven, CT: Yale University Press.
Nishimura, K.G. and Ozaki, H., 2004, 'Search and Knightian uncertainty', *Journal of Economic Theory*, 119, 299–333.
Nishimura, K.G. and Ozaki, H., 2007, 'Irreversible investment and Knightian uncertainty', *Journal of Economic Theory*, 136, 668–694.
Palley, T., 1996, *Post Keynesian Economics: Debt, Distribution, and the Macro Economy*, London: Macmillan.
Phelps, E.S., 2007, 'Macroeconomics for a modern economy', *American Economic Review*, 97(3), 543–561.
Preston, B., 2006, 'Adaptive learning, forecast-based instrument rules and monetary policy', *Journal of Monetary Economics*, 53, 507–535.
Rotheim, R., 1993, 'On the indeterminacy of Keynes's monetary theory of value', *Review of Political Economy*, 5(2), 197–216.
Sargent, T.J., 1999, *The Conquest of American Inflation*, Princeton, NJ: Princeton University Press.

Sunder, S., 2007, 'What have we learned from experimental finance?', in Sobei H. Oda (Ed.), *Developments on Experimental Economics: New Approaches to Solving Real-World Problems*. Lecture Notes in Economics and Mathematical Systems 590. Berlin: Springer, pp. 91–100.

Tobin, J., 1958, 'Liquidity preference as behavior towards risk', *Review of Economic Studies*, 25, 65–86.

Vercelli, A., 1991, *Methodological Foundations of Macroeconomics: Keynes and Lucas*, Cambridge: Cambridge University Press.

Wu, H.M. and Guo, W.C., 2003, 'Speculative trading with rational beliefs and endogenous uncertainty', *Economic Theory*, 21, 263–292.

APPENDIX

A formal statement of Keynes's equilibrium conditions.

Modern mainstream models are aimed at representing a 'complete market structure' which allows for inter-temporal optimization. On the other hand, Keynes's macroeconomics breaks with the microeconomic approach à la Walras–Arrow–Debreu because the concept of complete markets simply does not make sense when the future is truly uncertain. Accordingly, inter-temporal optimization cannot provide the essential motive for individual decisions. Both theories nevertheless refer to macro-markets, which in a simplified closed system are the goods market, the labour market, the money market and the bonds market (aimed at representing the 'financial market'). Equilibrium is determined given the exogenous variables (like technology, the stock of productive capital, individual preferences, the legal and institutional framework), which may vary in the long period, but while the mainstream delivers a unique and Pareto-optimal stable solution (provided gross substitution holds), Keynes's theory delivers a different equilibrium for every state of the 'views about the future'.

Basically, a model is a set of conditions involving supply and demand sides in every macro-market. These conditions express individual decisions and constraints in which compatibility is ensured at any time by the adjustment of prices and quantities to equilibrium values. In mainstream economics, decentralized competitive forces drive the adjustment process, while in Keynes's approach, endogenous institutional stabilizers take part of the process. Table 10A.1 summarizes the way equilibrium values emerge in Keynes's theory.

The level of output depends on the rate of interest (which involves the liquidity preference function) along with the schedule of the marginal efficiency of capital (E), and on the public and private components of the global propensity to consume (the suspension points in the aggregate demand function). Unemployment happens when, given the global propensity to consume, the conventional interest rate (as compared with the schedule of the marginal efficiency of capital) does not allow for a sufficient amount of investment. In this case, there is no systematic force that could spontaneously eliminate unemployment, since N^* does not depend on wages in the neoclassical way. The only way wages could influence output in this simple model is through the demand-side effect of an expected change of wage which would impact on the schedule of the marginal efficiency of capital, rather negatively according to chapter 19 of *The General Theory* (though the possibility that a positive impact leads to full employment is not discarded as a special case). But as far as institutions

Table 10A.1 *Competitive equilibrium conditions (equilibrium prices and quantities in bold)*

Goods market	*Demand*: $Y_d = C + I + G = Y_d(i, E, \ldots)$ The effective demand (Y_d^e) is (approximately) equal to Y_d.[1] *Supply*: equal to effective demand: $Y_s = Y_d^e$, ➔ (1) $\mathbf{Y^*} = Y_d(i^*, E, \ldots)$ The market may clear on different positions, according to the 'views about the future' (which influence I, E and therefore Y_d^e and Y^*). The competitive price level is determined so that the real wage is equal to marginal productivity of labour, given the equilibrium employment level (see below) and the technology ($Y = f(N,K)$, diminishing marginal returns)[2] (2) $w/p = f'_N \rightarrow \mathbf{p^*} = w^*/f'_N$
Labour market	*Demand*: $Y = f(N,K) \rightarrow N_d = g(Y^*, K)$ *Supply*: rationed, $N_s = N_d$ ➔ (3) $\mathbf{N^*} = g(Y^*, K)$ In the face of unemployment, flexible money-wage would be destabilizing through the negative effects on E, Y_d. . . ➔Institutional and social forces stabilize the money-wage: $\mathbf{w^*} \equiv w_{I\&M}$
Money market	*Demand*: $L(Y, p, i)$ *Supply*[3]: $M_s(i)$ (4) $M_s^*(i^*) = L(Y^*, p^*, i^*) \rightarrow \mathbf{M^*, i^*}$ Rmk: L (and M^*) would shift if i^* differed from the convention so that i^* actually 'gravitates' around a long-run solution: $\mathbf{i_{LR}}^* = i_{conv}$ ➔The market may clear on different positions according to the liquidity preference and the capacity of monetary authorities to influence the convention.
Financial market	Implicit (aggregate balanced budgets).[4]

Notes:

'e'	superscript denotes the expected value of a variable.
Y	output, 'volume'[5]
Y_d^e	effective demand, 'volume'
C	consumption, 'volume'
I	investment, 'volume'
G	government expenditures (here exogenous), 'volume'
N	employment
M	quantity of money
K	capital stock (given)

Table 10A.1 (continued)

p	output price
w	money-wage
$w_{I\&M}$	money-wage that market and institutional forces lead to (given)
i	long-term interest rate
i_{conv}	conventional long-term interest rate (given, but authorities may have some influence)[6]
E	marginal efficiency of capital schedule[7] (given)

1. Keynes's model abstracts from possible differences between the effective (expected) demand and the realized aggregate demand. The reason is discussed in *The General Theory*, chapter 5, which concludes: 'there is a large overlap between the effect on employment of the realised sale-proceeds of recent output and those of the sale-proceeds expected from current input' (Keynes 1936, p. 51).
2. Notice that competitive imperfections, such as monopoly power, are not necessary for a mark-up relation to appear. For example, with the familiar Cobb–Douglas technology: $f(N, K) = AN^{\alpha}K^{1-\alpha}$, $0 < \alpha < 1$, we get immediately $\frac{w}{f'_N(N, K)} = \frac{1}{\alpha}\frac{wN}{Y}$, where $\frac{1}{\alpha}$ represents a mark-up on the unit labour cost.
3. In the Post Keynesian pure horizontalist case, perfect accommodation makes *Ms* independent of i, so that the money supply adjusts to the demand endogenously. See Asensio (2011) for a detailed discussion.
4. See Asensio (2011) for a formal statement.
5. One cannot disregard the difficulty of measuring such a heterogeneous aggregate (the same applies to the capital stock (K) and, accordingly, the output price (p) also raises difficulties). However, measuring in wage units, as Keynes did, does not really solve the problem (see Hayes 2007 and Ambrosi 2009 for a recent discussion). As it has become usual and it is not the 'bone of contention between Keynes and Pigou', (Ambrosi 2009), we do refer to the 'volume' of output, the capital stock and the price index. Notice that the volume of output equals real income insofar as producers' expectations of aggregate demand are correct (see Chick and Tily 2007, p. 8, footnote 9).
6. This expected rate of course includes the expected inflation, so that a conventional real rate r^* can be deduced from $i^* = r^* + (dp/p)^e$.
7. Notice that the money-wage expected change is likely to influence E. This is an important feature of the dynamics of Keynes's equilibrium, along with expectations, technology. . .. It is omitted here for the sake of simplicity (as at equilibrium, institutions are deemed to have stabilized the money-wage at a given level).

do stabilize $w_{I\&M}$ against the destabilizing pressure of unemployment, any change of wages is to be considered the result of some combined institutional and market forces. This is to consider the active role of institutions *at any time*, besides the influence of the institutional framework on the long-run dynamics.

A salient feature of Keynes's 'static model of a dynamic process' is that i^* and w^* are not modelled. These variables undoubtedly are endogenous to the economic system, but their equilibrium level depends on expectations and human institutions that cannot be modelled with a high degree of generality in a context of uncertainty. The conventions' and institutions' responses are context-dependent variables that can only be modelled in specific cases. The 'static model' accordingly delivers a genuine 'shifting equilibrium', insofar as there is no objective anchor for E, i^* and w^*, with the result that, at any given time, there is a continuum of possible equilibria, of which expectations, conventions and institutions determine the unique solution.

Keynes's 'static model' is essential to the study of any dynamic aspect of the theory, for it provides the equilibrium value of the key variables as a function of the set of given variables (expectations, wages, but also the capital stock, the productivity, income distribution. . .), so that the functional relations involved by the determination of the effective demand can be considered in a tractable way. Once those relations have been identified, and the related equilibrium solution is determined, it becomes possible to consider the dynamics of the equilibrium by considering the effects of a change in such and such variable which was taken as given until then. It is the aim of Post Keynesian cycle and growth models to explore the related features.

11. Neoclassical and Keynesian macro models: thinking about the 'special case'

Marco Missaglia*

> It is self-contradictory to discuss a process which admittedly could not take place without money, and at the same time to assume that money is absent or has no effects. (F.A. von Hayek, *Pure Theory of Capital*, 1941, p. 31)

> we need to learn several things from the mainstream consensus. . . . I believe that the edifice of mainstream economics is an important model for the construction of an alternative . . . we cannot afford to avoid methods on account of our distaste for the way the method has been used in the past (D. Foley, *Notes on Ideology and Methodology*, 1989, pp. 3 and 6)

INTRODUCTION

The purpose of this chapter is to propose a reflection on an old and fundamental topic in economic theory, i.e. the degree of 'generality' of the neoclassical rather than the Keynesian macro model: is it true, as stated by the proponents of the so called Neoclassical Synthesis, that *The General Theory* is nothing but a 'special case'?

The chapter is organized as follows. The next section illustrates the standard neoclassical macro model. In this section there is nothing essentially new; it only serves the purpose of setting the stage for the subsequent arguments. This model will be written in its 'complementarity format', which is the best way to show the strong *formal* similarities between the neoclassical and the Keynesian (*General Theory*) macro model. Along these lines, the third section shows how Keynesian models may be written in the same way as a neoclassical model. The following section will use these formal similarities as a starting point for a deeper discussion on the issue of 'generality' of neoclassical and Keynesian macro models. The fifth section concludes.

A NEOCLASSICAL GENERAL EQUILIBRIUM MODEL IN ITS COMPLEMENTARITY FORMAT

Mathiesen (1985b) demonstrated that an Arrow–Debreu general equilibrium model (for the sake of argument let us call it a 'neoclassical' macro model) may be formulated as a complementarity problem, i.e. as a system of three classes on nonlinear inequalities: a) zero-profit conditions impose that in equilibrium no sector gains 'extra-profits': the cost of producing one unit of output must be greater than or equal to the price of that unit. Should this relation be satisfied as a strict inequality, the relevant activity would close off; b) market clearance imposes that, for each commodity and factor, supply must be greater than or equal to demand. Again, whenever this relation is satisfied as a strict inequality, the price of the relevant commodity falls to zero (free commodity); c) income balance imposes that each agent's expenditures (in present and future goods – savings are included in the picture) must equal the value of her factors' endowment.

A bit of algebra may help the reader to understand the issue at stake. Without any loss of generality, the spirit and the logic of a neoclassical (henceforth, NC) general equilibrium model may be summarized in the simplest case of an economy with one sector, two factors (capital and labour), no government and no relations with the rest of the world:

$$C(w,r) \geq QV \text{ zero-profit condition} \tag{11.1}$$

$$V \geq \frac{CONS}{QV} + INV \text{ market clearance} \tag{11.2}$$

$$LS \geq \frac{\partial C(w,r)}{\partial w} V \text{ market clearance} \tag{11.3}$$

$$KS \geq \frac{\partial C(w,r)}{\partial r} V \text{ market clearance} \tag{11.4}$$

$$CONS = w.LS + r.KS - QV.INV \text{ income balance} \tag{11.5}$$

Expression (11.1) says that the cost C of producing one unit of output, expressed as a function of the wage rate w and the rental rate of capital r,[1] must be greater than or equal to the unit price of that output, QV. This is nothing but the zero-profit condition we mentioned earlier. Expression (11.2) is the equilibrium condition on the product market. It says that total supply V must be greater than or equal to total demand, the latter being the sum of consumption and investment. The variable $CONS$ refers to nominal consumption expenditures, whereas INV represents the real investment level. Expressions (11.3) and (11.4) are the equilibrium conditions on the factor markets. LS and KS represent, respectively, labour and capital supply. On the right-hand-side of expressions (11.3) and (11.4), labour and capital demands are expressed using Shepard's lemma. Finally, expression (11.5) is simply the budget constraint for this simple economy: consumption expenditures are by definition equal to the difference between total income (labour plus capital incomes) and total savings, the latter being *ex ante* equal to investments (a neoclassical world).

For the sake of comparison with the Keynesian alternatives we will describe below, let us assume for the time being that real investment expenditures are given (which is not that different from assuming, as is usually the case with more sophisticated dynamic neoclassical models, full employment plus a given intertemporal elasticity of substitution). In the model (11.1)–(11.5) there are therefore five endogenous variables: w, r, QV, $CONS$ and V, whereas labour and capital supply, LS and KS, are given by demography and history of capital accumulation respectively.[2] In the neoclassical model (11.1)–(11.5) Say's law holds and 'supply creates its own demand': if, say, LS (KS) goes up, then the factor price w (r) would fall, firms would hire more people (rent more capital), real output would increase and that extra output would be certainly bought thanks to the extra incomes distributed by firms.[3] Supply creates its own demand and something like an 'aggregate demand deficiency' is ruled out by definition. It is perfectly possible to introduce unemployment in such a framework without changing its underlying representation of the world. Just add a third curve in the labour market diagram – the so called 'wage curve' – to represent those institutional rigidities (unions, legislation on minimum wages) or entrepreneurial choices dictated by asymmetric information (efficiency wage considerations) or, again, workers' choices driven by their expectations (Harris–Todaro movements of the labour force[4]) which prevent labour demand from staying in line with supply. System (11.1)– (11.5) should be modified as follows. A sixth relation is to be added, representing the specific unemployment theory at hand. In relatively general terms we could write.

$$w \geq w(V;\beta), \tag{11.6}$$

to indicate the specific constraint on wage flexibility which causes unemployment. β is the set of relevant parameters (the minimum wage rather than the psychological cost of migrating, and so on), whereas real output V is introduced among the arguments of the wage curve simply because several mainstream unemployment theories reasonably make the degree of wage flexibility dependent on how things are going around in the economy. Obviously, (11.3) and (11.5) are to be changed accordingly:

$$LS.er \geq \frac{\partial C(w,r)}{\partial r}V \qquad (11.3')$$

$$CONS = w.(LS.er) + r.KS - QV.INV, \qquad (11.5')$$

where '*er*' indicates the employment rate. A seventh relation is to be added to impose an upper bound on the employment rate (one if, for the sake of simplicity, frictions, mismatching and similar complications are assumed away):

$$er \leq 1 \qquad (11.7)$$

It is worth stressing that this version of the model modified to take unemployment into account is still 'intrinsically neoclassical', which means – let us insist on this point – that Say's law is believed to hold and therefore aggregate demand may never be deficient.

THE COMPLEMENTARITY FORMAT OF A KEYNESIAN MACRO MODEL

A 'Keynesian' model, in essence, is a theoretical scheme in which unemployment does not originate in the labour market. Its causes are to be found in the product market, where aggregate demand deficiencies may prevent full employment being reached even if wages and prices are perfectly flexible. This is so because Say's law does not hold, which is in turn explained by the intrinsically *monetary* nature of capitalistic production and the deep difference between risk and uncertainty (Keynes, 1936; Pasinetti, 1993). Sure, several 'Keynesianisms' have been populating the economic literature panorama. Here, for the sake of argument, we will concentrate on two variants of Keynesianism, namely the bastard-Keynesian[5] and the post-Keynesian. As far as the post-Keynesian paradigm is concerned, we will illustrate both a 'structuralist' post-Keynesian model and a simple example of the so called 'stock-flow consistent' (SFC) models.

A Bastard-Keynesian Model

A bastard-Keynesian model (henceforth, BK) combines some features of the standard, neoclassical general equilibrium model with some Keynesian element. Factor demand curves are still downward-sloping and factors' returns are determined by their marginal productivity – this is the neoclassical part of the story – but the position of these curves depends on aggregate demand through the standard Keynesian multiplier effect. There is more than that. As we have just stressed, unemployment is essentially related to what happens in the product market. Any increase in aggregate demand provokes a contraction of unemployment (until full employment is reached) and vice versa. The theoretical core of the BK model may once more be described with reference to a closed economy with no government. In its complementarity format, the BK system is:

$$C(w,r) \geq QV \tag{11.8}$$

$$V \geq \frac{CONS}{QV} + INV \tag{11.9}$$

$$LS.m \geq \frac{\partial C(w,r)}{\partial w} V \tag{11.10}$$

$$KS \geq \frac{\partial C(w,r)}{\partial r} V \tag{11.11}$$

$$CONS = w(LS.m) + r.KS - QV.INV \tag{11.12}$$

$$CONS \leq (1 - s) QV.V \tag{11.13}$$

$$m \leq \overline{m} \tag{11.14}$$

One can immediately see, with a simple visual inspection, how deep are the formal similarities between the neoclassical model with unemployment and the BK system. At the formal level, '*er*' and '*m*' are two different names for the same thing,[6] whereas the only (big!) difference lies in the two constraints (11.6) and (11.13). The production side of the economy is the same (profit maximization, Shepard's lemma, etc.) – in a sense we are sticky to Keynes's own acceptance in *The General Theory* of 'the first classical postulate' according to which the real wage equals the marginal product of labour under a regime of decreasing returns to additional employment. To understand the difference between the two systems one has to look at expression (11.13), where s is the average propensity to save.[7] Expression (11.13) says that consumers' nominal expenditures are a fraction of nominal GDP (remember this is a closed economy with no government) – the standard Keynesian textbook's assumption which gives rise to the well-known Keynesian 'multiplier'. Imagine there is an exogenous increase in the real investment level INV – good mood in Keynesian 'animal spirits'. *Ceteris paribus*, the extra demand will push V upward in relation (11.9), which in turn will increase nominal consumer spending ($CONS$) in equation (11.13): both components of GDP increase, even if consumption does so at a lower rate than investment because a fraction s of extra output is saved. The increase in GDP is only possible in that the extra labour demand by firms (the right-hand-side of relation (11.10)) may meet a corresponding labour supply: this is the meaning of the multiplier m attached to LS. The upper bound on m set by equation (11.14) means that sooner or later firms' extra demand of labour will not be met because full employment has been achieved. In that case any further improvement in animal spirits will not translate into GDP growth, relation (11.13) will be satisfied as a strict inequality and, as is the case with the standard neoclassical model, more investment (savings) will simply mean less consumption (equation (11.12)). Clearly, the value of the upper bound on m will depend on the unemployment rate of the economy and, say, on the 'employability' of jobless people, but this is not the issue we want to discuss here. Rather, we want to stress once more that the two systems, which are so radically different in terms of their economics, may be written the same way.

A Structuralist, Post-Keynesian Model

A similar argument may be applied to the post-Keynesian variant of Keynesianism, sometimes labelled as 'structuralism' for reasons which will become apparent later (see Taylor (1983, 1990, 2004) and Lavoie (2009)).[8] Without bothering the reader too much, some of the defining characteristics of structuralism/post-Keynesianism (henceforth SPK) are illustrated briefly to help us understand the subsequent arguments. As schematically as possible, the SPK theoretical edifice is built around four main pillars. First, possibilities of substituting primary factors are only there in the medium to long run. If their relative price changes, it will take time to combine productive factors differently. It follows that the only reasonable production function in the short run is a Leontief production function, and its coefficients are to be updated from period to period according to some dynamic, relative price-dependent – and context-specific – rule. Secondly, rather than being governed by technology (marginal productivities), the functional income distribution is a social fact. So, for instance, the wage rate is to be considered exogenous, somewhat determined by the specific structure of the economy at hand, its conflicts and institutions. Thirdly, at least some markets are not perfectly competitive and producers make prices as a markup over direct costs.[9] Fourthly,

Say's law does not apply and aggregate demand matters. These pillars may be translated into the following SPK system, expressed again in its complementarity format:

$$C(w,\tau) = (1+\tau)\mathbf{w.b} \geq QV \qquad (11.15)$$

$$V \geq \frac{CONS}{QV} + INV \qquad (11.16)$$

$$LS.m \geq \mathbf{b}V \qquad (11.17)$$

$$r = \frac{\tau}{(1+t)} \cdot \frac{V}{KS} \qquad (11.18)$$

$$CONS = w(LS.m) + r.KS - QV.INV \qquad (11.19)$$

$$CONS \leq (1-s)QV.V \qquad (11.20)$$

$$m \leq \overline{m} \qquad (11.21)$$

Some explanation is required. The markup rate on variable cost, τ, is taken to be exogenous (see note 10) until the full capacity bound has been reached; b is the fixed (Leontief) labour–output ratio. The profit rate is expressed in relation (11.18) as the product between the profit share $\tau/(1+\tau)$ and the output–capital ratio V/KS (a proxy for the degree of capacity utilization). The other symbols have already been explained. When the economy is below full capacity, the SPK system solves for the five unknowns QV, V, m, $CONS$ and r. The wage rate w is usually assumed to be given for the reasons already stressed. When full capacity has been reached ($m = \overline{m}$), V becomes *de facto* exogenous and the markup rate in that case may be treated endogenously.[10]

It is important to draw the attention of the reader to one important difference between the neoclassical and the BK model on the one side and the SPK model on the other. In order to stress the formal equivalences of the three models written in their complementarity format, we have used the symbols '*KS*' and '*r*' in all cases. However, their meaning is not exactly the same. In the neoclassical and BK models, r is the user cost of capital and KS is the *flow* of capital services supplied to the market. In the SPK model, r is the macroeconomic profit rate and KS is the capital *stock* of the economy. Sure, it is always possible to fix units of measurement in such a way that one unit of flow emanates from one unit of stock. This, coupled with the mainstream assumption that there cannot be anything like 'unused capacity',[11] allows a modeller to use a dynamic rule for the evolution of the capital *stock* such that

$KS(t) = KS(t-1) + I(t-1)$ (assuming depreciation away) also in a model where KS is essentially a flow.

A Stock-Flow Consistent, Post-Keynesian Model

For the sake of illustration, we will only concentrate on the simplest possible SFC model – as a matter of fact what follows is nothing but a way of rewriting in its complementarity format the model 'SIM' presented by Godley and Lavoie in their comprehensive book on post-Keynesian economics (2007). It is really an extremely simple model – production requires only labour and only one asset, cash, may be accumulated – yet it already includes all those conceptual elements which allow us to write *any* SFC model in a much more parsimonious complementarity format. It is not only a matter of parsimony. Indeed, once a model is conceptualized in its complementarity format, it becomes possible to write it in MPSGE,[12] software which makes the inclusion of several *productive* sectors (on top of the *institutional* sectors which traditionally characterize SFC models) very much easier. As a consequence, one can easily enlarge the set of policy experiments usually associated with SFC models – not only macro policies, but trade and industrial policies as well. In its complementarity format, model 'SIM' will look this way:

$$C(w_t) = \mathbf{w_t b_t} \geq QV_t \tag{11.22}$$

$$V_t \geq \frac{CONS_t + GOVT_t}{QV_t} \tag{11.23}$$

$$LS_t.m_t \geq \mathbf{b_t} V_t \tag{11.24}$$

$$CONS_t = w_t(LS_t.m_t)(1 - \theta) + PH(H_{t-1} - \mathbf{H_t}) \tag{11.25}$$

$$GOVT_t = w_t(LS_t.m_t)\theta - PH(H_{t-1} - \mathbf{H_t}) \tag{11.26}$$

$$CONS_t \leq \alpha_1 QV_t V_t (1 - \theta) + \alpha_2 PH.H_{t-1} \tag{11.27}$$

$$GOVT_t = QV_t G_t \tag{11.28}$$

$$m_t \leq \overline{m} \tag{11.29}$$

Most symbols and relations of this model (where wages are assumed to be exogenous since distribution is socially determined) have already been explained, but some clarification may help. $GOVT_t$ is nominal government expenditure at time t; H_t and H_{t-1} represent the stock of cash at the end and at the beginning of period t, respectively; PH is the (constant) price of this asset;[13] υ is the direct tax rate; G_t is real public expenditure. Budget constraints (11.25) and (11.26) make it clear that cash is held by the households and issued by the government to finance its deficit. Relation (11.27) is, again, what we previously called a 'Keynesian constraint': a function according to which current consumption expenditures depend positively on both current disposable income and the stock of cash (wealth) available at the beginning of the period (α_1 and α_2 are the relevant parameters). Here households save and no one invests, but this does not last forever. In the steady state, to which the model converges smoothly (without oscillations) provided that $\alpha_1 > \alpha_2$ and, as typically (sometimes tacitly . . .) assumed by most post-Keynesians, $\overline{m} = +\infty$, savings are also nil.[14] In this extremely simple model, the steady-state value of GDP, $V^* = G/\upsilon$, only depends on fiscal parameters, whereas straightforward calculations show that the steady-state value of the stock of wealth (here, cash) is also affected by the consumption function parameters. In any case, what matters here is, once again, the methodological point: all sorts of Keynesian models may be written in a format, the complementarity format, which is then much more general than usually believed. We have already stressed the big advantages of this format compared with the traditional nonlinear programming-style in which Keynesian models are usually written. Let me go a bit deeper. What we are talking about is a more powerful and general format – usually applied to the fictitious mainstream world where the social fabric is seen as the outcome of a set of constrained optimization problems – which may be used to represent a much more realistic Keynesian world with its broader view on citizenship and politics. In his *Notes on Ideology and Methodology* (1989), Duncan Foley is right in claiming that the edifice of mainstream economics is an important model for the construction of an alternative.

To conclude this section. Any model, also those which are intrinsically non-Arrow–Debreu general equilibrium schemes, may be formulated and solved in the same format. The trick lies in understanding the nature of relation (11.13) in the BK model ((11.20) in the SPK model, (11.27) in the SFC model). We are used to calling it 'aggregate consumption function', a definitely Keynesian jargon. There is nothing wrong with this: relation (11.13), when read as an equality, is an aggregate consumption function. However, when read as a weak inequality, relation (11.13) may be given a different interpretation. It is nothing but a constraint whose *formal* nature is absolutely the same as that of a constraint like (11.6): a constraint with an associated slack variable which in turn, in both cases, operates as a multiplier attached to the quantity of labour. To put it differently: any unemployment theory may be expressed this way. Neoclassical unemployment theories, i.e. different views on the reasons why the wage rate is not fully flexible, can be represented by a relation like (11.6); Keynesian unemployment theories, i.e. different views on the reasons why there might be an aggregate demand deficiency, can be represented by a relation like (11.13). Is there a case which is more general than the other? We have to look behind those formal similarities.

NEOCLASSICAL VERSUS KEYNESIAN MODELS: WHAT IS THE SPECIAL CASE?

The Fisherian/Wicksellian Macroeconomics

Let us now switch to a more profound comparison between the neoclassical and the Keynesian macro models. A good starting point is the 'pure' neoclassical macro model. Such a model is intertemporal in nature – neoclassical people, endowed with perfect foresight, maximize their objective functions over their lifetime. To keep things as simple as possible without losing any generality, let us remain within the boundaries of a two-period economy. Output in the first period is simply given (manna from heaven), whereas in the second it is obtained through a traditional production function with the usual properties. Consumers maximize their lifetime (two-period) utility, firms maximize their discounted flow of profits. Labour supply is fixed, the economy is closed to the rest of the world and there is no government. This neoclassical world may be represented through the following system of equations:

$$Y_1 = \overline{Y} \tag{11.30}$$

$$u'(c_1) = (1+r)\beta u'(c_2) \tag{11.31}$$

$$C_2 = \omega L_2 + (1+r)(Y_1 - C_1) \tag{11.32}$$

$$F_K(K_2, L_2) = r \tag{11.33}$$

$$Y_1 = C_1 + K_2 \tag{11.34}$$

$$F_L(K_2, L_2) = \omega \tag{11.35}$$

$$L_2 = \overline{L} \tag{11.36}$$

$$Y_2 = F(K_2, L_2) \tag{11.37}$$

$$Y_2 = C_2 - K_2 \tag{11.38}$$

Equation (11.30) fixes first-period output. (11.31) is the well-known Euler condition, according to which the representative consumer gets her best when the ratio between marginal utilities of consuming today ($u'(c_1)$) and consuming tomorrow ($\beta u'(c_2)$) is equal to the associated relative price (r is the real interest rate). In this condition β represents the parameter of intertemporal preference – the higher β the more 'patient' is the consumer. Equation (11.32) is a standard consumer budget constraint. (11.33) and (11.35) are the standard conditions of profit maximization – the marginal product of capital must be equal to the real interest rate and the marginal product of labour must be equal to the real wage ω. In the neoclassical world income distribution is a technological issue and everyone gets what she deserves. Labour and capital produce the second-period output through the standard production function (11.37). Standard properties on marginal productivities apply. Equation (11.34) represents the equilibrium between aggregate supply and aggregate demand in the first period (in the first, manna-from-heaven period the capital stock is nil, this is the reason why first-period investment equals second-period capital stock). (11.36) defines the equilibrium between labour demand and supply, the latter being taken as exogenous. Finally, (11.38) establishes the aggregate demand–supply balance in the second period, when the level of investment is negative, $I_2 = -K_2$, since it would not make sense to leave some productive capacity for a future which does not exist.

The system (11.30)–(11.38) is fully determined. There are eight independent equations (Walras's law) and eight endogenous variables: Y_1, Y_2, C_1, C_2, r, ω, L_2, K_2. They all are real variables, which means that the real macro equilibrium has no relation whatsoever with what is going on in the monetary sphere of the economy. In particular, the real interest rate is already determined by the system (11.30)–(11.38). It follows that any expansionary monetary policy decided by the central bank can only push up the inflation rate. This is nothing but the quantitative theory of money, which is therefore a corollary (or a premise: it just depends on the perspective) of the neoclassical macro model:

$$M_1^d V = P_1 Y_1 \tag{11.39}$$

$$M_2^d V = P_2 Y_2 \tag{11.40}$$

$$M_1^d = M_1^s \tag{11.41}$$

$$M_2^d = M_2^s \tag{11.42}$$

In these equations concerning the financial sphere of the economy the four corresponding endogenous variables are prices and money demands in each of the two periods. V – money velocity – is considered fixed over the two periods and money supply is a policy variable decided by the central bank through the manoeuvre of base money (high-powered money). In the neoclassical macro model (11.30)–(11.42) – it could be named the 'Fisherian' macro model due to the fundamental contributions of Irving Fisher (1907, 1911, 1930) in developing the idea of macro as 'aggregated micro' – money is neutral. If in the first or in the second period the central bank decides to expand money supply, real variables will remain unaffected, already determined by the real sub-system (11.30)–(11.38). The only outcome will be higher prices, and we do not discuss here the real costs of inflation.[15]

It may also be noted that the sub-system (11.30)–(11.38) incorporates the so called *loanable funds theory*, which is again attributable to Fisher (1930). Indeed, provided that the marginal product of capital is decreasing ($F_{KK} < 0$), (11.33) gives rise to an investment demand which is inversely related to the real interest rate. On the savings side, the Euler condition (11.31) together with the budget constraint (11.32) make the savings flow an increasing function of the real interest rate, provided that the substitution effect dominates the income effect. The usual picture will emerge where the real interest rate adjusts so as to equate saving supply with investment demand. Macro causality runs from savings to investment: first, investment will never exceed the pool of loanable funds whose amount is decided by the savers; secondly, any act of saving will translate into a corresponding act of investment. The meaning of this saving-driven nature of neoclassical macroeconomics may be better understood by looking at what happens when, say, in the first period firms and consumers-savers expect a positive technological shock to take place in the second (in a sense, this is good mood in Keynesian animal spirits). Firms would like to invest more, but savers, who are willing to smooth consumption, will save less. The real interest rate will certainly go up, whereas the effect on savings and investment is ambiguous.[16] Investment plans do not have any traction on the economy.

It is important to stress that in this neoclassical/Fisherian world only one asset is traded in the financial market, namely the bonds (or equities; this is nothing but an institutional detail which does not modify the neoclassical discourse) issued by firms and subscribed by the savers. Money is not an asset; it only serves to facilitate transactions (this is the meaning of the exchange equations (11.39) and (11.40), where the volume of transactions has been assumed equal to GDP: which is not generally true but, again, this is an innocent simplification).

The Macroeconomics of *The General Theory* (From a Neoclassical Perspective)

In *The General Theory* (1936), the role of money constitutes the central departure from the Fisherian macro scheme. This is due to a different vision of the nature of uncertainty. In the neoclassical macro scheme uncertainty (better: risk) may be dealt with using tools of financial mathematics and probability theory. The probability distribution of risky events is known and therefore it is always possible, at least in principle, to design and trade bonds which are specifically tailored to the prevailing structure of risk.[17] Sure, in the real world these financial products may not materialize, but this is nothing more than a market failure (a 'missing market' in the mainstream vocabulary). It will suffice to fill the gap, to create the appropriate bonds and the markets where they can be traded. In *The General Theory* the approach to uncertainty is completely different. There are so many events whose probability distribution is simply unknown and there is no possibility to create the appropriate bond or (equivalently) find an insurance company willing to protect people against those negative events. In all those cases the only reasonable sheltering strategy is holding money or, to use the extraordinarily powerful Marxian wording, *general* purchasing power. That's why money is an asset. Savers will have to decide whether holding their wealth in money – whose rate of return is equal to minus the (expected) inflation rate – or in bonds, whose rate of return is equal to the nominal interest rate minus the (expected) inflation rate. Because of the reasons just explained the two assets are not perfect substitutes at all and the public will hold both of them in a proportion which depends on the nominal interest rate and people's 'liquidity preference'. As Keynes put it in *The General Theory*, the nominal interest rate is 'the premium which has to be offered to induce people to hold wealth in some form other than hoarded money'. Roughly speaking, and for the sake of argument, one could argue that, however crucial, this role of money as a store of value is the only relevant difference between the Fisherian and the *General Theory* macroeconomics. Keynes himself, as we have already stressed, admitted to accepting the other 'classical [read: neoclassical] postulates'. On top of this, he gave clear indications of how a neoclassical system as (11.30)–(11.42) should be modified to put money at the centre of the stage:

> The conviction . . . that money makes no real difference except frictionally and that the theory of production and employment can be worked out (like

Mill's) as being based on 'real' exchanges with money introduced perfunctorily in a later chapter, is the modern version of the classical tradition. Contemporary thought is still deeply steeped in the notion that if people do not spend their money in one way they will spend it in another. . . . These conclusions may have been applied to the kind of economy in which we actually live by false analogy from some kind of non-exchange Robinson Crusoe economy, in which the income which individuals consume or retain as a result of their productive activity is, actually and exclusively, the output *in specie* of that activity. . . . Those who think in this way . . . are fallaciously supposing that there is a nexus which unites decisions to abstain from present consumption with decisions to provide for future consumption. (Keynes, 1936, pp. 19–21)

Now, the crucial point made by mainstream authors – a point which has never been emphasized sufficiently in the literature – is the following: even if one accepts the idea of money as a store of value (an idea which in any case is not accepted by neoclassicists), the orthodox argument according to which 'the theory of unemployment requires a non-Walrasian model in which there is no Walrasian auctioneer continuously clearing commodity and labor markets' (Phelps, 1968, p. 30) is not invalidated. There is more than that: if one accepts the idea of money as a store of value and puts it in an otherwise fully Fisherian macro model, an increase in liquidity preference may move aggregate demand and supply in both directions.

Let's try to see why with the help of a 'bastard neoclassical' model where money also serves as a store of value. I want to be as clear as possible. The model which follows does not constitute my way of reading *The General Theory*. Rather, it constitutes the way a neoclassical author inclined to accept the idea of liquidity preference would read it. If we want to understand the reasons why *The General Theory* was not understood as a genuinely general scheme, this is exactly the kind of vision we have to look at.

The representative agent enjoys goods and leisure, and her lifetime utility function is $u(C_1,L_1) + \beta u(C_2,L_2)$. As before, L denotes labour and therefore the relevant partial derivative is negative, i.e. $u_L < 0$ for both periods. In the first period the representative agent will have to decide how to split her available cash $M_0 + P_1Y_1$, where M_0 denotes money balances in her hands at the beginning of the story (previously hoarded money), between consumption of present goods (P_1C_1), bonds (consumption of future goods) and money balances (M_d). The latter, let us stress this point once more, is again a decision of consuming future goods, but this preference, contrary to what happens with the decision to subscribe bonds, is not revealed to the market. Money guarantees the freedom not to choose. It may be noted that $(M_d - M_0)$ is the flow of hoarded money in the first period. In nominal terms, the lifetime budget constraint of the representative agent is to be written as:

$$P_2C_2 = w_2L_2 + (1 + i)[M_0 + P_1Y_1 - P_1C_1] - iM_d \qquad (11.a).$$

In words: future consumptions will be equal to future nominal wage income (w is the nominal wage) plus the capitalized value of current savings (i is the nominal interest rate) minus the opportunity cost of hoarding money.[18] For the sake of argument, one can write this budget constraint in real terms. The result is:

$$C_2 = \omega_2L_2 + (1+r)\left(\left(\frac{M_0}{P_1} + \right)Y_1 - C_1\right) - \left(\frac{iM_d}{P_2}\right) \qquad (11.b),$$

from which it becomes transparent that, compared with a pre-Keynesian world, the representative consumer incurs a real loss, expressed in units of second-period output, of (iM_d/P_2). This is the real price she decides to pay to deal with genuine uncertainty.

Straightforward calculations show that consumers' behaviour may be summarized by the following optimality conditions (on top of the budget constraint, obviously):

$$u'_{c_1}(C_1, L_1^s) = (1 + r)\beta u'_{c_2}(C_2, L_2^s)$$

$$u'_{L_1}(C_1, L_1^s) = -\omega_1 u'_{c_1}(C_1, L_1^s)$$

$$u'_{L2}(C_2, L_2^s) = -\omega_2 u'_{c_2}(C_2, L_2^s).$$

The first relation is the standard Euler condition we have already commented on above. The second and third conditions govern the labour–leisure choice in the first and second period respectively (L^s denotes labour supply). The economic rationale is the usual one – two goods are demanded in such a way that the ratio of their marginal utilities equates their relative price (here, the real wage ω).

As to the production side of the economy, let us assume that capital is only needed in the second period, whereas in the first labour is the unique productive factor, i.e. $Y_1 = F(L_1)$ and $Y_2 = F(L_2,K_2)$. The usual properties on marginal products apply, $K_1 = 0$ and technology $F(.)$ does not change. The optimization problem of firms (held by the consumers) – making as much money as they can – is basically the same as before, the only difference is that they have to demand labour in the first period as well.

All in all, if we accept the view according to which money as a store of value is the only truly new element introduced in *The General Theory* and for what remains '[neo]classical postulates' are to be accepted, the following macro system emerges:

$$Y_1 = F(L_1^d) \quad (11.43)$$

$$Y_2 = F(K_2, L_2^d) \quad (11.44)$$

$$F_L(L_1^d) = \omega_1 \quad (11.45)$$

$$F_L(K_2, L_2^d) = \omega_2 \quad (11.46)$$

$$F_K(K_2, L_2^d) = r \quad (11.47)$$

$$u'_{c_1}(C_1, L_1^s) = (1+r)\beta u'_{c_2}(C_2, L_2^s) \quad (11.48)$$

$$u'_{L_1}(C_1, L_1^s) = -\omega_1 u'_{c_1}(C_1, L_1^s) \quad (11.49)$$

$$u'_{L_2}(C_2, L_2^s) = -\omega_2 u'_{c_2}(C_2, L_2^s) \quad (11.50)$$

$$C_2 = \omega_2 L_2^s + (1+r)\left(\left(\frac{M_0}{P_1} + \right)\omega_1 L_1^s - C_1\right) - \left(\frac{iM_{dH}}{P_2}\right) \quad (11.51)$$

$$M_{dH}^1 = L(i;\alpha) \quad (11.52)$$

$$i = (1+r)\left(\frac{p_2}{p_1} - 1\right) \quad (11.53)$$

$$M_{dT}^1 V = P_1 Y_1 \quad (11.54)$$

$$M_{dT}^2 V = P_2 Y_2 \quad (11.55)$$

$$L_1^d = L_1^s \quad (11.56)$$

$$L_2^d = L_2^s \quad (11.57)$$

$$Y_1 = C_1 + K_2 \quad (11.58)$$

$$Y_2 = C_2 - K_2 \quad (11.59)$$

$$M_{dT}^1 + M_{dH}^1 = M_1^s \quad (11.60)$$

$$M_{dT}^2 = M_s^2 \quad (11.61)$$

Equations (11.43) to (11.50) have been explained already, the others deserve to be briefly commented upon. (11.51) is the budget constraint we have already introduced, where M_{dH} is the first-period 'hoarding' component of money demand. Obviously, in the second period (the last one) people do not wish to hoard money. (11.52) makes this component of money demand a negative function of the nominal interest rate (see above) and a positive function of a parameter α which is intended to capture liquidity preference. (11.53) is nothing but a definition of the nominal interest rate, it is always true. (11.54) and (11.55) – the Fisherian equations of exchanges – represent the transaction component of money demand in the two periods. Equations (11.56) to (11.61) are equilibrium conditions in the different markets, labour, output and money.

The system is closed: 18 independent equations (Walras's law) determine 18 endogenous variables. Now, the key question is to understand whether in this otherwise fully Walrasian system the introduction of the theory of liquidity preference gives aggregate demand a key role in determining aggregate supply and the volume of employment. Calculating $dL/d\alpha$ is virtually impossible – (11.43)–(11.61) is a system of fully simultaneous equations, where one cannot find any block of autonomous equations.[19] However, some economics may help us understand what happens when α increases. Look at the budget constraint (11.51). When in the first period the hoarding component of money demand goes up, the budget devoted to buy present consumption and future consumption (bonds) shrinks. If they are normal goods, the demand for both present and future consumption decreases. Aggregate demand in the first period goes down, since both C_1 and K_2 decrease due to the increase in α. As to first-period aggregate supply, it will increase provided that leisure is also a normal good.[20] So, in the first period the decision to hoard more money is likely to prompt a) an excess supply in the market for output and b) an excess supply in the market for bonds. It follows that, *ceteris paribus*, the Walrasian auctioneer will reduce P_1 and push up r.[21] These variations – look again at (11.51) – will raise the budget devoted to buying present consumption, future consumption and leisure. In other words, these variations will move aggregate demand up and aggregate supply down, until macro equilibrium is restored. However, if miracles are assumed away, the new level of aggregate demand and supply will be different from the original one. To see why, let's write aggregate demand as $D(P;\alpha)$ and aggregate supply as $S(P;\alpha)$. Let's call ε_i $(i = P,\alpha)$ and η_i $(i = P,\alpha)$, the elasticities of demand and supply, respectively, with respect to price and liquidity preference. The increase in α and the consequent reduction in P will leave D and S unaffected if and only if $(\varepsilon_\alpha/\eta_\alpha) = (\varepsilon_P/\eta_P)$. A miracle, admittedly. In any case, whatever the new levels of D and S, all those who want a job can find it. To conclude this section. One can accept the introduction in the macro system of money as a store of value. After all, giving people the possibility to express their preferences not only between present and future consumption, not only between consumption (present and future) and leisure, but also between 'extended consumption' (present, future and leisure) and real balances is acceptable within a theoretical paradigm where preferences, together with technology, are the fundamental forces at work, the engine of the economy. However, this does not invalidate the neoclassical proposition according to which the theory of unemployment requires a non-Walrasian model, where somewhat *ad hoc* assumptions on price rigidities, asymmetric information and the alike are to be introduced. Secondly, it is true that the introduction of money as a store of value gives aggregate demand some traction, but it is not necessarily true that stronger preferences for liquidity will translate into lower aggregate demand and supply. Thirdly, investments are in any case limited by the pool of available savings. Keynes's *General Theory* is nothing but a special case.

Post-Keynesians, Others and the Other Keynes

Post-Keynesians are known because of contributions they have made to the theory of price formation (the markup story and a structuralist rather than monetary theory of inflation), to the theory of firm (the idea that technology is a procedure and input–output coefficients only change over time, in an historical process which has nothing to do with well-behaved and smooth production functions) and, above all, to the theory of growth and distribution, with their attempt at moving Keynes from the short to the long run.[22] I am deeply persuaded that the origin of all these contributions is to be found, again, in a different vision of money. This vision, which concentrates on the way money is created in a capitalistic economy rather than on its functions, may be attributed to several authors. First of all, Keynes himself, in various contributions different from *The General Theory* (Keynes, 1973a, 1973b); and then Kaldor (1982, 1985), Schumpeter (1934, 1956) and others. Their vision on the process of money creation is known as the theory of endogenous money. In modern times, various post-Keynesian authors have specified the technicalities, details, subtleties and internal disagreements of the theory of endogenous money (Lavoie, 2009). The most powerful, concise and theoretically clean statement of the theory of endogenous money was not given by a post-Keynesian, but by Schumpeter (1934, pp. 73–74):

> It is always a question, not of transforming purchasing power which already exists in someone's possession, but of the creation of new purchasing power out of nothing. . . . The banker, therefore, is not so much primarily a middleman in the commodity 'purchasing power' as a *producer* of this commodity. . . . He makes possible the carrying out of new combinations, authorizes people, in the name of society as it were, to form them.

In the neoclassical world (and the neoclassical description of *The General Theory*), banks simply facilitate the transfer of resources from savers to investors (firms), but this is not the world we live in. In the world we live in banks are not middlemen of purchasing power, they are producers of purchasing power. Kaldor (1985, pp. 7–8) may help:

> the original proposition of the quantity theory of money [must be] applied to situations in which money consisted of commodities, such as gold or silver, where the *total quantity in existence* could be regarded as exogenously given at any one time as a heritage of the past; and where sudden and unexpected increases in supply could occur (such as those following the Spanish conquest of Mexico) the absorption of which necessitated a fall in the value of the money commodity relative to other commodities. . . . However, the same reasoning cannot be applied to cases where money was not a commodity like gold or oxen, but a piece of paper (bank notes) or simply a bookkeeping entry in the accounts of banks. The rules relevant to the creation of credit money are not of the same kind as those relevant to the production of gold or silver. Credit money comes into existence, not as a result of mining but of the granting of bank credit to borrowers, who use it . . . to finance expenditures. . . . This means that *in the sense required* by monetarist theory, an excess in the supply of money cannot come into existence.

Bertocco (2006, p. 7) puts very effectively what lots of entrepreneurs and borrowers know from their own experience: 'In a world in which *fiat* [bank] money is used, you need to have money in order to purchase goods, but you don't need to have goods in order to get money. . . . Rather, it is necessary to meet the criteria set by the banks for granting loans.' Clearly, the theory of endogenous money implies and requires that central banks are unable and/or unwilling to control money supply and they rather decide the level of monetary (nominal) interest rates. Essentially, central banks are always willing to satisfy commercial banks' demand for base money (borrowed reserves), either at a fixed rate ('horizontalist' version of the theory of endogenous money) or at a rate which rises with the quantity of high-powered money demanded by commercial banks ('structuralist' version). Such a vision makes sense. In the following passage quoted by Bertocco (2006, p. 20) the Bank of England does not leave many doubts on the endogenous nature of money supply:

> A central bank derives the power to determine a specific rate in the wholesale money markets from the fact that it is the monopoly supplier of 'high-powered' money, which is also known as 'base money'. The operating procedure of the Bank of England is similar to that of many other central banks. . . . The key point is that the Bank chooses the price at which it will lend high-powered money to private sector institutions. . . . A change in the official rate is immediately transmitted to other short-term sterling wholesale money-markets

> rates, such as interbank deposits . . . long-term interest rates are influenced by an average of current and expected future short-term rates, so the outcome depends upon the direction and the extent of the impact of official rate change on expectations of the future path of interest rates.

So, essentially the logical chain the theorists of endogenous money have in mind is the following: a) the central bank fixes the discount rate (either 'horizontally' or 'structurally'); b) commercial banks decide the loan rate by applying a markup to the discount rate;[23] c) entrepreneurs demand bank loans. The lower the loan rate and the better their profit expectations, the higher their demand for loans; d) 'loans make deposits': once firms get their loans, money is used to pay for productive factors and deposits are constituted; e) commercial banks borrow the required reserves (a fraction of deposits) from the central bank at the fixed discount rate. If the central bank does not want to be accommodating in the belief too much money is around, it can always push up the discount rate.

One could object that this vision is simplistic and leaves out too many aspects of the real world. Firms do not finance their investment expenditures out of bank loans only – other sources of funding are retained earnings and the securities' market. Again, commercial banks do not make loans only to firms willing to invest; they also lend money to households willing to consume, etc. . . . Solid replies to these observations may be found, for instance, in Gnos and Rochon (2006). Here, it will suffice to observe that what really matters is that firms can *also* fund their investment plans out of bank money and, in such a case, the object of the loan is not previously accumulated savings (banks as middlemen), but purchasing power created out of nothing (banks as producers of purchasing power). Literally: by a stroke of the pen. The fundamental consequence for the macro system is that in any given period investment expenditures may increase without the need for consumption expenditures to go down. '*I*' may increase at a constant or even rising '*C*', which is exactly the idea of the Keynesian 'multiplier'. Sure, it may happen that productive resources are not available to make this possible – it is not possible to produce those goods which the newly created purchasing power should buy. Still, the fact remains that the *primus* of the system is aggregate demand (the newly created purchasing power), regardless of the fact that productive resources are there or not to allow aggregate supply to follow (the reader may check this is exactly the logic applied to the BK and the SPK models above). To put it as clearly as possible: Keynes (aggregate demand governs aggregate supply via multiplier) is the general case; the neoclassicists (output is always and exclusively determined in the supply side of the system) are the special case, which corresponds to a situation in which resources are not available to produce those goods which the newly created purchasing power should buy. As to the analytics, a simple extension of the SFC model (11.22)–(11.29) gives rise to an endogenous money model. Again, let us refer to Godley and Lavoie (2007), their 'PC' (Portfolio Choice) model may serve the purpose. In its complementarity format, it may be written as:

$$C(w_t) = \mathbf{w_t b_t} \geq QV_t \tag{11.62}$$

$$V_t \geq \frac{CONS_t + GOVT_t}{QV_t} \tag{11.63}$$

$$LS_t.m_t \geq \mathbf{b_t} V_t \tag{11.64}$$

$$CONS_t = [w_t(LS_t.m_t) + r_{t-1}\mathbf{PB.BH_{t-1}}](1-\theta) + [PH(H_{t-1} - \mathbf{H_t}) + PB(BH_{t-1} - \mathbf{BH_t})] \tag{11.65}$$

$$GOVT_t = [w_t(LS_t.m_t) + r_{t-1}\mathbf{PB.BH_{t-1}}]\theta + r_{t-1}\mathbf{PB.BCB_{t-1}} - r_{t-1}\mathbf{PB.BS}_{t-1} - PB(BS_{t-1} - BS_t) \tag{11.66}$$

$$CBANK_t = PB(BCB_t - BCB_{t-1}) = PH(H_t - H_{t-1}) \tag{11.67}$$

$$CONS_t \leq \alpha_1 QV_t V_t (1-\theta) + \alpha_2(PH.H_{t-1} + PB.BH_{t-1}) \tag{11.68}$$

$$\frac{PB.BH_t}{(PB.BH_t + PH.H_t)} - \gamma_0 + \gamma_1 r_t - \gamma_2 \frac{[w_t(LS_t.m_t) + \mathbf{r_{t-1}PB.BH_{t-1}}](1-\theta)}{(PB.BH_t + PH.H_t)} \tag{11.69}$$

$$GOVT_t = QV_t G_t \tag{11.70}$$

$$CBANK_t = PB(BS_t - BH_t) \tag{11.71}$$

$$m_t \leq \overline{m} \tag{11.72}$$

Relations (11.62)–(11.64) are exactly the same as (11.22)–(11.24). (11.65) is an extension of (11.25), taking into account that households are now supposed to allocate their savings between cash (H) issued by the central bank and bills issued by the government (BH). It follows that in each period households get, on top of their wage income, also the interest payment on the stock of bills held at the end of the previous period. The nominal interest rate, r, is fixed by the central bank (the endogenous money view), whereas PB represents the (artificial) price of bills. Households allocate their savings according to (11.69) where γ_0 and γ_1 are positive parameters: the higher the interest rate paid on government bills and the lower the disposable income (a proxy for that fraction of money demand driven by transaction purposes), the higher the fraction of wealth held in the form of bills. (11.66) is an extension of (11.26). Government is now assumed to issue bills (rather than cash); in each period it has to pay interest on them (B_s is the stock of outstanding bills) and it is also assumed (following the current practice in most countries of the world) that the central bank's profits (here corresponding to the interest payments earned by the central bank on government bills in its portfolio) are transferred back to the government. (11.67) is the central bank's budget constraint and says that the variation in the stock of government bills held by the central bank is financed through money creation. (11.68) is essentially the same as (11.27), the only difference being that households' wealth is now subdivided among cash and bills. (11.70) is the same as (11.28). Finally, (11.71) says that the central bank always buys those outstanding bills which are not subscribed by the public.[24]

In this model the quantity of high-powered money (H) is clearly endogenous. Indeed, it is true that, *ceteris paribus*, the central bank may affect H by manoeuvring the interest rate r; it is also true, however, that the equilibrium value of H (both its period-by-period value and its steady-state value) is affected by households' behavioural parameters. For instance, simple simulations show that the higher γ_2 (consumption sensitivity to accumulated wealth) the lower the steady-state value of the stock of high-powered money (as well as the stock of government bills in the hands of households). Money is endogenous.

The interesting question, however, is the following: would this conclusion change when resources are not available to produce those goods which the newly created purchasing power should buy (the neoclassical, special case)? To put it formally, would our conclusions hold when, *contrary to what is usually assumed by post-Keynesians*, $m = \overline{m}$ and (11.72) is binding? In this case the model (11.62)–(11.72) might explode – when output reaches its maximum level direct taxes stop growing and therefore the government debt to GDP ratio might not reach any steady-state level – and some amendment is needed to guarantee the existence of a steady state. For instance, one could change (11.70) and assume that government expenditures follow a different rule when full capacity output has been reached. In any case, and this is what really matters from the perspective of this chapter, high-powered money remains endogenous. Changes in households' behavioural parameters affect the steady-state level of H also when $m = \overline{m}$ and some kind of fiscal discipline is to be introduced.

CONCLUSIONS

In this chapter I have argued that the most important Keynesian idea – aggregate demand is the engine which moves the economic system – is not a 'special case' as claimed by mainstream economists. On the contrary, the special case is the neoclassical one in which any increase in the investment expenditures is to be accompanied by a reduction in consumption expenditure (or some other component of aggregate demand). This conclusion may be understood if, instead of focusing on the functions of money (which is what *The General Theory* does), attention is paid to the way money is created and put into circulation (which is what Keynes does in other writings). In particular, the theory of endogenous money allows us to see that the neoclassical case only materializes when productive resources are not available to produce those goods which the newly created purchasing power should buy.

NOTES

* Special thanks to Rudiger von Arnim and Amit Bhaduri, whose comments significantly improved a previous version of this chapter. Errors are mine only.

1. Needless to say, $C(w,r)$ is the cost function 'dual' to some assumed production function with the usual properties.
2. None of the arguments developed in this chapter would be affected by the introduction of an endogenous labour supply.
3. This outcome may be easily demonstrated through total differentiation of the system (11.1)–(11.5).
4. Needless to say, labour force movements do not necessarily coincide with 'Harris–Todaro' migrations from the countryside to the city. Any movement among different locations of a segmented labour market may be represented this way.
5. A label first used by Joan Robinson (1961).
6. In both systems there are six unknowns: w, r, QV, V and $CONS$ are common to the two cases, whereas er and m are specific, respectively, to the neoclassical and the BK case.
7. The reason why (11.13) is written as a weak inequality will be clarified in a moment. This reason may also be used to rename 's': it may be called 'desired' propensity to save and when (11.13) holds as a strict inequality, it will differ from the actual saving rate.
8. Needless to say, post-Keynesian economics and structuralist economics are not the same thing. Here, however, we want to stress their common elements.
9. The markup rate is a measure of market power. If one accepts to represent market power as fully expressed by the price elasticity of demand (the standard treatment), then the markup rate is to be considered endogenous (unless constant elasticity utility functions are employed). If, as most SPK authors do, a broader perspective on market power is embraced, the markup rate may be taken as exogenous. More on this point in the text.
10. For the sake of argument we kept the models as simple as possible. However, a version of the SPK model closer to the spirit of post-Keynesian and structuralist economics should include two classes (categories of consumer) with different propensities to save. In that case, making the markup rate endogenous when full capacity has been reached would create a 'forced savings' adjustment mechanism. If, say, investment demand goes

up, then the markup rate and the price level will increase, real wages will drop and the larger share of GDP in the hands of markup incomes' earners will guarantee that total savings stay in line with higher investment.

11. Why buy machinery if not to use it or rent it out? In a neoclassical or BK framework, when there is little demand for this machinery its price, and therefore its user cost, falls so as to adjust demand and supply. In an SPK framework the machinery may simply stay idle.
12. Mathematical Programming System for General Equilibrium.
13. Two points are to be explained. First, model SIM is a fixed-price model. Secondly, however strange the introduction of a 'price of cash' may seem, this is only to pave the way to richer models where people are given the possibility to accumulate more assets.
14. When $\overline{m} = +\infty$, (11.27) holds as a strict equality.
15. If you start from a long-run equilibrium, where total output is given at the level fixed by factors' availability and productivity, monetary policies (permanent changes in money supply) only make sense in that they are supposed to work as expenditure-switching policies, more (less) net exports coupled with less (more) absorption.
16. To see this formally, just attach a shift parameter A to the production function (11.37) and modify correspondingly (11.33) and (11.35). Then calculate dr/dA and dK_2/dA.
17. 'Some even argue that we should privatize basic institutions of society, like the legal system, and subject society in its entirety to the providential harmony of "the market"; an assumed perfect insurance market would in this case guard us from any mischief caused by privatized justice' (Reinert, 2008, p. XXI).
18. In the second period, which was assumed to be the last one, money will not be hoarded at all. If you assume that $Md = M0 = 0$ – people do not wish to hoard money – you get exactly the neoclassical budget constraint (11.32), as expression (11.b) clearly shows.
19. These are exactly the cases where simulations, like those one can build through CGE models, may be helpful.
20. An increase of the hoarding component of money demand acts as an exogenous reduction in the total budget devoted to consumption (present and future). Such a reduction produces, for any standard utility function in the consumption–leisure space, lower labour supply.
21. It may be seen from (11.53) that these variations imply a higher nominal interest rate, which is exactly what we learnt from standard Keynesian textbooks.
22. A comprehensive and not too long illustration of post-Keynesian economics may be found in Lavoie (2009).
23. Needless to say, in any concrete model the markup may be taken as exogenous or endogenous – this is not really the point.
24. Obviously, this is a disputable assumption. However, it is not as strong as it might seem: the central bank can always increase the interest rate and this, *ceteris paribus*, will reduce money supply.

REFERENCES

Bertocco, G. (2006), 'Some Observations about the Endogenous Money Theory', working paper 2006/2, Università dell'Insubria, Facoltà di Economia, Varese.

Fisher, I. (1907), *The Rate of Interest: its Nature, Determination and Relation to Economic Phenomena*, New York: Macmillan.

Fisher, I. (1911), assisted by Harry G. Brown, *The Purchasing Power of Money, its Determination and Relation to Credit, Interest and Crises*, New York: Macmillan.

Fisher, I. (1922), assisted by Harry G. Brown, *The Purchasing Power of Money,*

its Determination and Relation to Credit, Interest and Crises, New York: Macmillan. New and revised Edition.
Fisher, I. (1930), *The Theory of Interest as Determined by Impatience to Spend Income and Opportunity to Invest it*, New York: Macmillan.
Foley, D.K. and T.R. Mickl (1999), 'Growth and Distribution', Harvard: Harvard University Press.
Gnos, C. and L.-P. Rochon (eds.) (2006), *Post-Keynesian Principles of Economic Policy*, Cheltenham: Edward Elgar Publishing.
Godley, W. and M. Lavoie (2007), *Monetary Economics: An Integrated Approach to Credit, Money, Income, Production and Wealth*, New York: Palgrave Macmillan.
Kaldor, N. (1982), *The Scourge of Monetarism*, Oxford: Oxford University Press.
Kaldor, N. (1985), 'How Monetarism Failed', *Challenge*, May–June, 4–12.
Keynes, J.M. (1936), *The General Theory of Employment, Interest and Money*, London: Macmillan.
Keynes, J.M. (1973a [1930]), 'A Treatise on Money', in *J.M. Keynes, The Collected Writings*, London: Macmillan Press, vols. V and VI.
Keynes, J.M. (1973b [1933]), 'A Monetary Theory of Production', in *J.M. Keynes, The Collected Writings*, London: Macmillan Press, vol. XXXIII.
Lavoie, M. (2009), *An Introduction to Post-Keynesian Economics*, London: Palgrave Macmillan.
Mathiesen, L. (1985a), 'Computational Experience in Solving Equilibrium Models by a Sequence of Linear Complementarity Problems', *Operations Research*, 33(6), 1225–1250.
Mathiesen, L. (1985b), 'Computation of Economic Equilibria by a Sequence of Linear Complementarity Problems', *Mathematical Programming Study*, 23, Amsterdam: North Holland.
Pasinetti, L. (1993), Structural Economic Dynamics: A Theory of the Economic Consequences of Human Learning, Cambridge: Cambridge University Press.
Phelps, E.S. (1968), 'Money-Wage Dynamics and Labor-Market Equilibrium', *Journal of Political Economy*, 76, No 4, Part II (July/August), 678–711.
Rayman, R.A. (1998), *Economics Through the Looking-Glass. Reflections on a Perverted Science*, Aldershot: Ashgate Publishing Ltd.
Reinert, E.S. (2008), *How Rich Countries Got Rich . . . and Why Poor Countries Stay Poor*, London: Constable & Robinson Ltd.
Robinson, J. (1961), 'Prelude to a Critique of Economic Theory', *Oxford Economic Papers*, 13:53–58.
Rutherford, T.F. (1989), 'General Equilibrium Modeling with *MPSGE*', The University of Western Ontario.
Schumpeter, J. (1934 [1912]), *The Theory of Economic Development*, Cambridge, MA: Harvard University Press.
Schumpeter, J. (1956 [1917]), 'Money and the Social Product', *International Economic Papers*, 6, 148–211.
Taylor, L. (1983), *Structuralist Macroeconomics*, Cambridge, MA: MIT Press.
Taylor, L. (1990), *Socially Relevant Policy Analysis: Structuralist Computable General Equilibrium Model for the Developing World*, Cambridge, MA: MIT Press.
Taylor, L. (2004), *Reconstructing Macroeconomics. Structuralist Proposals and Critiques of the Mainstream*, Cambridge, MA: Harvard University Press.

12. Economists on the 2008 financial crisis: genuine reflection; or constructing narratives to reaffirm the profession's authority?

Michael J. Salvagno*

INTRODUCTION

At the height of the financial crisis of 2008, Keynes was proclaimed as the economist that, to the wider peril, the profession had ignored. Now following what has been transitioning from a financial to a fiscal crisis, and from recession to depression, it seems that the project for the resurrection of a Keynes-like policy has as yet been unsuccessful. This chapter provides an analysis of a sample of initial writings by leading economists and financial journalists in the financial press, focusing primarily on their efforts to evaluate both the performance of the profession and the suitability of the project of modern economics. These writings represent an insight into the discourses that are used to shape and determine the types of knowledge and expertise that are considered appropriate for the study of the economy. They can also be interpreted to reveal how economists dismiss certain forms of empirical knowledge as irrelevant to the needs of the discipline.

The selected works by the economists are not representative of the sum of each author's serious academic works, but they are important political interventions, the majority of which were published in the leading financial press. As a sample, these writings capture a series of debates, conducted by either leading members of a discipline or leading financial commentators, in what could only be described as a period of the discipline's distress. These writings are assessed in order to determine both how each author identified the role and performance of the economics profession leading up to and during the crisis, as well as the suggested proposals for reforming the discipline. The chosen authors are: Robert Skidelsky, a pre-eminent historian and financial journalist on matters of political economy;

James Galbraith, a leading and outspoken economist; Robert Shiller, a prominent behavioural economist; and Joseph Stiglitz and Robert Lucas, both of whom are Nobel Prize-winning economists.

One of the critical findings of this chapter is that the style of theorising which a number of key economists attributed as a cause of the crisis would be directly replicated by the types of theory that in the wake of the crisis they recommended as its replacement. A number of the theorists suggest that it was the adherence to constructs such as 'rational expectations', a product of the search for psychological universal laws, that led regulators and the active participants in the markets to miss the build-up of systemic risk in the economy. A number of these theorists call for the search for 'universal' axioms of rationality, as developed in rational expectations theories, a product of an Anglo-American approach to economics, to be replaced by a search for yet more 'universal' axioms, this time amended with postulates of 'imperfect information' or differing states of 'rationality'. Rather than identify the need to study economic crises, be they financial, industrial or resource based, which would require a programme to develop institutional analyses of markets, all but the two institutionally marginal voices in this group have advocated that the discipline continue on its search for universal 'psychological axioms'. The narratives developed by economists for defining the causes of the crisis, and the immediate endorsement of a new horizon of research, are political acts: ones that should be examined and critiqued by social scientists.

THE INSTITUTIONALIST REFORMERS

Skidelsky and Galbraith are chosen as representatives of a particular type of critique of modern economics. They both adopt the argument that economics has lost its focus on, and its ability to research, 'the economy'. Skidelsky's argument is notable for its affinity with the dominant strand of American post-Keynesian economics,[1] while Galbraith's shares a heritage with the political economy championed by his father. Both writers are critical of what they interpret as a retreat by the profession from a tradition that it formerly occupied – the best sense of professional responsibility – as an actor in civil society.

Skidelsky, in *Return of the Master*,[2] attributes the failure that was the financial crisis to a complex of interconnected processes; from the inappropriate governance of the macro-economy to the ideological politics of the economics profession. In the shadow of Keynes, Skidelsky identifies the centrality of ideas for understanding the model of economic organisation in a society. Yet this assertion only leads to the need for further qualification, for what types of 'ideas' are deemed 'central'; are they theoretical, applied and/or ideological? Additionally, how is the causation from ideas to policy to be defined? Without further elaboration of these distinctions, Skidelsky wrote: 'To understand the crisis we need to get beyond the blame game. For at the root of the crisis was not failures of character or competence, but a failure of ideas.'[3] Implicitly extending the causal reach of the ideas produced by the economics profession, Skidelsky continued: 'The practices of bankers, regulators and governments', as far as they contributed to the financial crisis, were 'the fruit of the intellectual failure of the economics profession'.[4] For Skidelsky, the critical failure by the economics profession was in its inability to properly distinguish between 'risk and uncertainty', which he attributes to a reliance on models such as the 'Efficient Market Hypothesis' (EMH). It was this oversight that was said to have prevented economists and policy makers from recognising the structural imbalances in the economy. The reliance on those same types of models, based on micro-economics which utilises highly mathematical techniques, was held to have corrupted macro-economics. The problems caused by these corruptions were compounded, given the special 'division of labour' that the branches of the discipline perform. For Skidelsky, micro-economics and the use of optimisation techniques are not suited to the study of macro-economics phenomena, and should therefore be limited to the disciplines where they are useful tools of analysis: management and financial studies. These branches of the discipline should then not encroach upon macro-economics, which would provide the intellectual foundation for the governance of the economy. Skidelsky then proposed a number of reforms that would effectively aim to reverse the trend of the increasingly instrumentalist development of economic theory by reconstituting the discipline so that macro-economics involved the study of the 'real economy' as its central concern. Because he had identified the crisis as primarily an intellectual failure by economists, he developed a plan to enhance the education of the modern economist. Skidelsky's plan would require reforms to the syllabus of a modern economics education to include the study of institutions, economic history, psychology and philosophy, with mention that the PPE (Politics, Philosophy and Economics) degree at Oxford would serve as a more useful model for an economics degree.[5]

Having developed this encompassing analysis of the profession, from macro-governance to lecture hall, Skidelsky posits Keynes as the most influential economist of the 20th century. Keynes is framed as the thinker to whom we should turn for the development of new approaches to economic research and management. Yet Skidelsky's choice of title, *The*

Return of the Master, and the intervention it represents, should raise a number of questions, such as: what does the return of Keynes actually mean? Which Keynes? And what about the Keynesians?

On determining how to think of Keynes, and the difficulty of understanding the ideas of and roles performed by the great economist, Thomas Balogh, a heterodox economist and policy advisor, made a very revealing remark about the many facets of Keynes's intellectual profile:

> [T]here wasn't one Keynes; there were many 'Keyneses'. There was a 'Robertson' Keynes; there was a 'Joan' Keynes; there was a 'Kahn' Keynes, and in the end there was of course a 'Robbins–Meade' Keynes and this explains a very great many things.[6]

Identifying which Keynes to resurrect, and whether to include the Keynesians, is a vexing question. The notable absence of any mention of the Keynesians is a sure indicator that Skidelsky's Keynes is divorced from the Keynesians. Even when Skidelsky employs key arguments from the *General Theory*, the basis for many Keynesian arguments, the Keynesians are kept at a distance. Skidelsky's approach, which primarily focuses on a 'psychological' reading of Keynes's theories, and in particular on the dichotomy between 'risk and uncertainty', enables him to overlook many post-Keynesian policy debates. Yet this interpretation, part of a longer-term trend of Keynes scholarship, minimises the importance of one of the key structures in Keynes's writings. For this style of reading downplays the importance of macro-economic research and systems-level theorising – overlooking a number of the tools and techniques crucial to Keynes's work. Skidelsky, in his attempt (very much a post-Keynesian reading) to free Keynes from what he (and many others) perceive as the 'difficult' ideological baggage of the Keynesian legacy,[7] runs the risk of narrowing his reading of Keynes to one that unnecessarily overlooks the important use of empirical macro-economics.

The risk for the Skidelsky proposal is that the Keynes he seeks to resurrect, and hence the reforms to economics which would incorporate politics, history and sociology in an undergraduate degree, could lead to a Keynes (and economics) who is the champion of PPE, rather than the Keynes that combined the development of comparative macro-static analysis with national accounting. The move by Skidelsky to read Keynes through the lens of his analysis of the differences between 'risk and uncertainty' is not dissimilar to the behavioural economists who claim Keynes as a foundational thinker for their project. While Keynes anticipated many insights that have been important for behavioural economics, this reading of Keynes ignores one of his most important contributions. The macro-theorising component in Keynes's work was both directly and indirectly developed and advanced by important theorists including Richard Stone, Wassily Leontief and Wynne Godley, and is continued by theorists such as Lance Taylor. To reduce Keynes, and the potential of economics, to this psychological reading is to turn away from a rich vein of macroeconomic research, as developed by a number of the pre-eminent economists of the 20th century.

Similarly to Skidelsky, James Galbraith develops a reformist critique of the profession. Galbraith focuses on the institutional responsibilities of the economics profession, its retreat from those responsibilities and the reasons for the retreat.[8] For Galbraith, the economics profession consistent with a powerful professional body of experts that produces 'authoritative knowledge' is particularly concerned with maintaining its authority and prestige through rigorous selection processes; a characteristic of the professions. The exception of economics is that in comparison to either physics or biology, theoretical development is not checked against empirical observation.[9] This means that unless there are constraints or externally imposed regulations that seek to channel the development of the profession, its leadership is free to move in the direction that it chooses. Galbraith contends that when the filtering process became 'rigorously exclusive', with certain schools of thought championed, it was for reasons 'tribal', not 'technical'.

Galbraith acknowledges that in the heyday of Milton Friedman and Robert Lucas there was a successful ideological assault against the progressive Keynesianism of liberal democratic politics. However, he contends that when it became immediately clear that monetarism and rational expectations were untenable, theoretically and in terms of policy pronouncements, rather than return to empirical macro-analysis the economics profession moved in another direction. The shift to the analyses of multiple equilibrium, prisoner's dilemma and behavioural economics constituted the opening of more possibilities for academic applications, but crucially it also entailed a withdrawal from policy discussion to a type of work that Galbraith described as 'intellectual parlour games'.[10]

For Galbraith, a small group within the profession maintained a focus on the macro-economy, but they were informed by visions of rationally behaving individuals. This ideological perspective enabled economists to be 'non-participants or non-observers' of what he calls 'the greatest wave of financial fraud in history'.[11] He asserts that had the organisational approach of looking at firms and their relationship to the state and the market, as developed by his father, been continued, the power relations within the real economy that were the site of this fraud would have been clearly visible. Galbraith's approach, like that of Skidelsky,[12] holds the profession to account for its potential to act as an independent voice in the service of the state. Yet Galbraith is not optimistic about the potential for change unless the sole authority of the leadership of the profession could be challenged by 'universities and funders [who could] decide to create autonomous intellectual units that can promote a diversity of views and methods'. (Interview recorded for the Open Democracy.) The critiques by Skidelsky and Galbraith are united by a shared sense that the economics profession failed in its responsibility to warn the political class of the pending dangers to the economy. Their analysis and recommendations suggest that a rebalancing in the output of the profession is required – towards the study of the economy as a system, for the purposes of providing the political class with the necessary information to debate the range of policy options available for managing the economy. One of the difficulties associated with the exercise of rebalancing the output and purpose of economic research is that it immediately makes more visible the political issues that many politicians feel uncomfortable in addressing. If the financial crisis was the product of 'the greatest wave of financial fraud in history', then the Galbraith vision of economic theory would not only empower politicians with important knowledge for the prevention of such crises, but would also make clearer the limitations of their politics, for it would be more difficult to describe such crises, as argued by Skidelsky, as the product of intellectual failures.

TWO DIFFERENT ARGUMENTS THAT SUGGEST THE PROFESSION IS REFORMING: IMPERFECT KNOWLEDGE AND BEHAVIOURAL ECONOMICS

The authors who represent this centrist but reforming position suggest two revisions which could revitalise the research project of modern economics. The first is theoretical. It would require modification of the central models in economic theory, by revision of the postulates about either the degrees of knowledge, or the levels of rationality, possessed by actors in the economy as they aggregate to form a market. The second revision is of far greater political concern. It would require a lowering of the expectations of what theory can perform as a guide for developing strident policy proposals. With these two reforms, these economists contend, the constructs at the centre of the project of modern economics could continue to serve as the foundation for new theoretical discoveries.

INET: PHILANTHROPIC CAPITALISM AND THE CREATION OF A NEW HETERODOXY?

The symbolic launch of the Institute for New Economic Thinking (INET), held at King's College Cambridge, the College of J.M. Keynes, was attended by Nobel laureates and a selection of elite academics and policy officials.[13] Funded with an initial grant of $50 million from George Soros, it is envisaged that INET and its research institutes will assist (*innovative*) economic theorists to develop new insights that can challenge the ideological mantra of neo-liberalism, which, Soros believes, shares the blame for the global economic crisis.

From the conference, *The Economist* reported on two of the different visions for how the discipline might proceed.[14] The first[15] is identifiable as 'Critical Realism', and can be clearly represented by the works of Tony Lawson. The 'Critical Realists' are a small heterodox school positioned against the orthodoxy of neo-classical economics, their research focusing on the appropriate methodological aims and programmes for social and economic theorising. The second group, which is quite mainstream, is represented by Stiglitz's contribution. Effectively, this group contends that an extension or deepening of the concept of 'rationality' would be sufficient to reinvigorate the discipline.

Starting with the Critical Realists, *The Economist* reported that one group 'held that the economy is governed by historical happenstance, not timeless laws, and [is] subject to imponderable contingencies, not calculable risks'. The Critical Realists contend that the project of prediction, a failed project, prevents economists from making useful pronouncements. The suggestion is that economists 'should give up on prediction' and settle for identifying and explaining the causal mechanisms throughout the economy which in a myriad of forms link actors and institutions. To focus on the 'emergence' of institutions and networks, and by studying the range of actors and their behaviours within the economy, the 'Critical Realist' position holds that economists would be able to develop a richer understanding of the actual economy and would be better positioned to warn policy makers of developing structural imbalances. This broad approach, which is certainly not averse to the analysis of statistics, would fit within the tradition of classical political economy.

Alternatively, the centrist position of Stiglitz contends that reforms to the current theoretical paradigm can extend its usefulness. As *The Economist* reported, 'for all his radical airs, Joseph Stiglitz, who is also on the board, is keen to conserve as much of the canon as possible'.[16] Stiglitz would state that, in spite of 30 years' worth of theoretical and empirical critiques of the claims concerning market efficiency, 'the efficient market hypothesis has played a central role in the development of economic theory and policy'.[17] He argued that a rational expectations model could explain much of what went wrong during the crisis if 'common knowledge' was denied. This would require the inclusion of a set of assumptions that describe a distribution of knowledge so that all actors would know how the economy works, on the condition that not every actor would know that everyone knows. Countering the detractors of this research programme, who interpret the crisis as confirming its deficiencies – of particular interest here Skidelsky – Stiglitz writes:[18]

> Skidelsky makes much of the distinction between risk and uncertainty. . . . But much of the behaviour that led to the crisis (the irrational and sometimes predatory lending, the excesses of leverage and other forms of risk-taking) did not depend on this distinction. . . .The distinction between risk and uncertainty, unfortunately, gives us little insight into the failures in the labour market: why the usual laws of supply and demand, which should result in full employment, have failed to work.

One difficulty with Stiglitz's analysis is that the distinction between 'risk and uncertainty' on which Skidelsky draws is not intended to be a catch-all insight that can explain failures of the labour market. Rather, the distinction is intended to shift the focus of macro-governance so that policy makers have a greater sense of alertness to the dangers wrought by structural imbalances in the economy. While Stiglitz espouses a richer role for the incorporation of analyses from sociology and behavioural psychology, he does so within a framework that only allows a narrow reading from those disciplines. To acknowledge that agents possess different types of rationality, that switch at various points of the economic cycle, might incline some to believe that the discipline would by necessity have to support a rich pluralistic view of human behaviour. But the switching referred to, taken as representative of the inclusion of sociological and psychological postulates, does not unify theoretical advance with empirical research and would be of questionable benefit were the economics profession to fail in its quest to prioritise its responsibilities of providing guidance to policy makers.

SHILLER

For Shiller, a pioneer of Behavioural Economics, 'faulty models' were at the root of the widespread failure of economists to forecast the 2008 financial crisis.[19] Poor-quality models meant that economic policy makers and central bankers received no warning of what was to come. Referring to *Animal Spirits*,[20] his book with Akerlof, Shiller reiterates that the global financial crisis was driven by speculative bubbles in the housing, stock, energy and commodity markets. A newly rediscovered concept, he states that the subject of speculative bubbles had been largely absent from most economics textbooks, treatises and central bank research papers. Effectively, economists had abandoned the idea that not just the economy, but bubbles, too, were phenomena worthy of research. To this, Shiller essentially frames a response to the rhetorical question of why did the market respond to Greenspan and moral hazard – doesn't this argument just further undermine the authority or credibility that economists deserve?[21]

This question can be reworded as: why did the market exploit the moral hazard, high-risk opportunities for supra-natural profits caused by Greenspan's indications that firms which were too large to fail would be rescued by the Federal Reserve. This two-part question warrants two answers. The second part to this question is answered first. While economists deserve severe sanction for their failures, and while their popular legitimacy may have been undermined, their capacity to exert policy influence has arguably increased.

The market responded to the moral hazard created by Greenspan because the agents in the market (e.g. the traders and the firms they represent) have no trouble in perceiving the definitions of rationality, as defined in an academic theorem, as just that. Shiller conflates different conceptions of rationality, from the type used in normative models to the sort that could be employed by a trader, and concludes that on the basis of a revised conception of rationality the profession has started to reform itself. In a process of selective retrospection, Shiller invokes the authority of the statistician Leonard 'Jimmie' Savage who, in 1954, theorised that 'if people follow certain axioms of rationality, they must behave as if they knew all the probabilities and did all the appropriate calculations'. Shiller interprets Savage's theoretical work with a particularly tight causality, implicitly holding the assumption that from those theoretical insights the mainstream of economists and policy makers would infer the truth.

Shiller identifies that 'the core element of the behavioural economics revolution' of the last decade has provided a sufficient quantity of research to refute Savage's 'scientific fact'. He states: 'Abundant psychological evidence has now shown that people do not satisfy Savage's axioms of rationality.' Invoking the work of neuroscientists, and the technology of functional magnetic resonance imaging experiments, he states it has been discovered that 'bull markets are characterized by ambiguity-seeking behaviour and bear markets by ambiguity-avoiding behaviour'.[22] While Shiller adds that 'these behaviours are aspects of changing confidence, which we are only just beginning to understand', a sceptic might contend that these new insights offer little more than the common understanding that in bull markets, traders aggressively seek opportunities for arbitrage.[23]

Shiller is an optimist; for despite the oversight of the economics profession, he believes the financial crisis can serve as a turning point on the road to professional renewal. Accordingly, he interprets that the profession has already begun the process of broadening its research efforts, as economists come to pay more attention to 'scientists with different expertise'. Such a move is critical, writes Shiller, for 'Only then will monetary authorities gain a better understanding of when and how bubbles can derail an economy, and what can be done to prevent that outcome.'[24]

The analyses of the positions advocated by Joseph Stiglitz and Robert Shiller share in common the view that with a number of theoretical and practical revisions the intellectual project of modern economics need not be substantially reconstructed. There are two difficulties with this position. The first is that it is not practical, and is without recent precedent, to expect a downgrading over the long term of the certainty that economic analysis provides either academics or policy makers. It is when political actors believe in the certainty of the market analyses that useful postulates turn into highly ideological devices. This pattern of behaviour is unlikely to change, although this is a question for the political psychologists. The second difficulty is that the switch from a profession focused on the search for axioms of rationality, to one modified by its inclusion of axioms of imperfect knowledge or different types of rationality, does not entail a transformation of the research focus that would facilitate an analysis of when an economy was entering a period of systems-level risk. The revised theory may bring to attention the concepts and models required to discuss such phenomena in either the classroom or in the press. But for the profession to provide actionable research that would be of value to the political class, it cannot avoid the process of generating empirical research. The difficulty for this alternative project is how, or whether it is even possible barring a major political change, to substantially shift the direction of the profession, when its leaders are committed to a project premised on an exploration for positivist 'universal laws'.

DEFENDERS OF THE ORTHODOXY THAT 'ECONOMICS IS A SCIENCE'

Robert Lucas, a defender of the 'economics as science' vision, develops a powerful critique of the integrity of the models used by economists. Describing the caricature of economic theory as described in an editorial in *The Economist*[25] as 'nonsense', Lucas delves to the core of the theoretical economist's central defence.[26] He raises two questions: 'What can the public reasonably expect of specialists in these areas, and how well has it been served by them in the current crisis?' These questions reflect a vision and strategy that locates the authority of the economist in the expertise required for and derived from using particular technical models. Yet it also limits their responsibility for what one might reasonably know from their models. Effectively the economist is not at fault for what a model is unable to predict, but if one does not use the model, the economist's claims to knowledge can be denied and his or her work determined as devoid of rigor or scientific authority.

Responding to the 'widespread disappointment' with economists for their inability to forecast or even prevent the financial crisis, a well-rehearsed but powerful argument is developed: 'there are no models that can forecast sudden falls in the value of financial assets'. Lucas asserts that this limitation should not be of surprise, as it is a basic condition of the EMH. In a telling passage that reflects the technical ethos of many economists and the usefulness of 'un-realistic' models, Lucas had previously stated:

> One of the functions of theoretical economics is to provide fully articulated, artificial economic systems that can serve as laboratories in which policies that would be prohibitively expensive to experiment with in actual economies can be tested out at much lower cost. . . . Any model that is well enough articulated to give clear answers to the question we put to it will necessarily be artificial, abstract, patently 'unreal'.[27]

It is from this position of using theorems and models for 'scientific experiments' that Lucas defends the EMH as 'a law of nature', even if he is prepared to concede that Fama may have been wrong to use the adjective 'efficient'.[28] The main lesson for policy makers is that the EMH, which Lucas describes as 'a law of nature', should inform regulators of the futility of attempting to anticipate the market. Not only is it impossible to predict sudden falls in financial assets, but the central bankers and regulators with the responsibility to identify and puncture bubbles are not supposed to exist. Lucas contends, 'If these people exist, we will not be able to afford them', for, as the argument holds, they would choose to optimise their rent-seeking capacity by entering the business world.[29]

In answer to his second question – have economists served the public well? – Lucas asserts that both Mr Bernanke and Mr Mishkin of the Federal Reserve, taken as representing the elite in the profession, were adept in responding to the changing events during the financial crisis. Having exempted economists from any responsibility for 'predicting' the date of the collapse of financial markets, Lucas claims that the actions of those at the Federal Reserve helped avoid the depression scenario. Moreover, he asserts that their performance is representative of the health of the profession.[30] Lucas's response to *The Economist*[31] is a stern defence of the intellectual rigour of macro-theorising, yet in an alternative and extended interview he acknowledged that macro-economists had been cavalier. Admitting that some economists overestimated their abilities, he stated: 'You had a bunch of guys who thought they knew a lot. It turns out we didn't know a damn thing about the stability of the banking system, so it's back to the drawing board and we'll see what comes out of it.'[32]

That confidence may have been well served by the prestige associated with the mathematisation of economics. But Lucas is quick to dismiss the reliance on mathematics as the cause of the crisis. He says: 'It's nonsense. A lot of people hate maths. They're missing the boat and they've been missing it for centuries. You don't need modern maths to have a financial crisis.'[33] Lucas makes an important point: the use of modern mathematics in economics is not the problem. The problem is the ends to which modern maths is used in economics. Economists are adept at developing tools that have been deemed useful in the economic management of the state, but as the specificity of their tools has increased there has been a concomitant increase in the 'hyper-contextuality' of that knowledge. The theories have revealed more about an increasingly abstract set of experimental scenarios. But this has not weakened the authority of the profession. And very few economists would disagree with this. Defining how mathematical reasoning is to be employed by economists is the critical and difficult question. An example of how economists perceive the technical nature of their discipline, and its authority as a form of reasoning for policy makers, is revealed in a fascinating statement by Dasgupta, when he wrote:

> Economics is a quantitative subject. When the Chancellor of the Exchequer asks his expert advisers to tell him of the fiscal advantages and disadvantages of an increase in the tax on petrol, he does not want a philosophical discourse, nor a lecture on what Marx would have thought about the matter. . . . He wants to know how much revenue he would be able to raise, what effects its imposition would have on other sectors of the economy, . . . mathematical modelling is essential and is here to stay.[34]

It is curious that Dasgupta interprets that it is mathematical modelling that the Chancellor or other policy makers require, when the combination of statistical analysis of time series data, and comparative analyses of similar policy scenarios – drawing on different types of reasoning – could provide policy makers with a very rich form of analysis; the type of which a chancellor would more likely understand. Mathematical modelling is important for economists, but it need not be employed without consideration for questions of institutional significance. Mathematical modelling presents the economist with a set of tools, optimally, to be employed in a range of analyses that serve particular purposes. Yet, despite the technical facility that mathematical reasoning gives an economist, Lucas humbly reveals that he did not think the fragility of the US financial system to be anything 'worth thinking about'. To his defence though, he adds, 'neither did anyone else'.[35] The 'anyone else' refers to a small macro-economics profession that excludes economists who use different techniques and investment managers who sensed trouble from structural imbalances. Those economists who predicted the crisis fall outside Lucas's category of relevant theorists, as their style of research is non-mathematical and would fail to *predict the timing* of the crisis. Their research belonged to literatures which are too often deemed inconsequential. This argument retreats to the position that the people who mattered did not study the banking system, and those that studied the banking system did not matter.

CONCLUDING ANALYSIS

The financial crisis of 2008 represents the type of complex political and economic phenomenon that, one might hope, would lead to a questioning of the function, responsibility and performance of the wider social sciences, and in particular economics. Spurned by a combination of both a severe credibility deficit and the opportunity to engage and respond to important public debates, the interventions that were detailed in this chapter represent attempts that otherwise seem to offer a genuine reflection on the state of the profession. While these writers take differing stances on the degree of responsibility to be placed on the economics profession, in general questions of responsibility are subtly minimised. Note their attempts to define how certain models were responsible for the crisis – in the main, making the models at fault, rather than the profession's ethos. The economists would then identify new theories that were not supposed to suffer the same deficiencies. This time the models were to be attuned to market psychology. This has the effect of lending an air of responsiveness to these developments, yet the proposed theories are not new, and models alone are unable to prevent crises or ensure responsible economic management. To argue that the unreal assumptions of the leading models, the efficiency of the market or the rationality of individuals led to a poor understanding of the economy and therefore inadequate policy management can paradoxically serve to reaffirm the authority of empirically divorced theoretical ideas. For it is held that it was not the empirically divorced and technical nature of those ideas as such that was the problem, but rather the unreal assumptions particular to some specific models. Empirical realism is not perceived to be of primary importance. To infer that the inclusion of new assumptions, which only under some conditions could be considered more realistic, would ensure that theorists and therefore policy makers would be more astute to the threat of crises, is unfounded.

There is a complex interplay between the modelling assumptions of rational expectations theorising and the ideological ends to which it has been used at different times, in the advocacy of free market politics. But the question remains, how to develop the analyses of the economy so that the future collective of economists, the political classes and the wider business community can shift the debate from the rationality of individuals and markets to the range of signals for identifying new risks to both the economic system and the financial sovereignty of states. This transformation would require a new foundation for economic theory. It would require that the discipline move beyond the search for psychological universals and instead focus on the interconnectedness of networks across the different sectors of the economy. Importantly, this search for networks could co-exist with the search for psychological universals – it is just that matters of economic management should not be primarily informed by the search for the latter.

Here we might reflect on the writings of the brilliant economist and critic of modern economics, Wassily Leontief, who discussed the problems facing the economists of the 20th century. Focusing on the increasing complexity of the markets, and the stock of knowledge that had already been captured by the foundational analytic assertions of the discipline, Leontief was led to the position that further scientific advance would require increasingly sophisticated data about the activities in the economy, to be coupled with advances in research integration, ultimately connecting the theorists with the empiricists. To extend the frontiers of research would require the successful combination of financial and organisational assistance from the state and private sector. Leontief wrote:

> The great nineteenth century economists were in the enviable position of being able to theorise about the general, well known, some called them obvious, aspects of economic life. By now these ubiquitous raw materials of economic knowledge have been fairly well exhausted; the advanced, more refined analysis requires special kinds of detailed factual data that just do not lie around. Because of the resulting chronic raw material shortage a large portion of the processing, i.e., of the model building capacity of modern economics is used mainly to regrind at high speed the same old stuff. Vertical integration of economic inquiry from the abstract-analytical down to the empirical-raw-material-extracting state seems to offer the only effective remedy against the perpetuation of its present imbalanced state.[36]

The research methodology that was advocated by Leontief, if properly carried out, would not enable economists to predict the date of a financial crisis. But it would certainly serve to inform economists and policy makers about systems-level instabilities. The vision that economics as a social science can build up a store of axioms based on psychological universal truths, starting from the individual and aggregating until an analysis of the functioning of an economy could be developed – is beyond the current capabilities of the discipline. Even with time it may be discovered that the project is not 'solvable'. But even if it is, it may not be the most efficient method of conducting economic research designed to prevent or minimise the severity of economic crises.

The financial crisis was, after all, the crisis of an economic system. Rather than focus the central efforts of the discipline on aiming to build theoretical knowledge on the basis of universal axioms, a richer understanding of the economic system's weaknesses could be generated by focusing on an empirically driven network analysis of the different commercial and resource sectors throughout the international economy. It would require analysis of the powerful and emerging economies at the level of the nation state, but also of the connections between centres of finance and industry with developed and emerging markets.

It would be the study of the capitalist system that we live in, but which we reproduce. It is a vision for economics that could be an institutionally focused discipline. But it would require a shift from the trajectory of its own path and of the other social sciences. In an increasingly globalised economy, with the opportunity for more truly global projects in the social sciences, while there are ever greater complex pressures on the economic system, be it resource scarcity or the shifting balance of economic and political power, it would be a study of the richness and complexity of the capitalist system that could integrate analyses from the commercial world with the study of eco-systems, history, psychology and sociology. Economics, or the social science that is bold enough to seize this initiative, could then become the discipline of our global capitalist society.

While it may seem that genuine reform or a critical review of the profession's performance is taking place, the analysis presented in this chapter contends that from the authors listed, and with the exception of the institutionalist reformers, this process has barely begun. To describe the financial crisis as a result of the intellectual error of economists and policy makers who mistakenly believed in faulty models – before identifying the new economic theorems, which are worryingly similar – underestimates the seriousness of the intellectual crisis which has beset the economics profession and the political class. Given the political importance of what is called 'economic theory', this debate requires the addition of at least one more important question:

> What type of politics would be required for the development and transformation of the discipline of economics so that it could accommodate into its project, empirically grounded institutional analyses of the economy?

NOTES

* The author would like to thank Prof. Andrew Gamble and Prof. John Dunn.
1. See Davidson (2007).
2. Skidelsky (2009).
3. Ibid., p. 28.
4. Ibid.
5. PPE is a popular interdisciplinary undergraduate/graduate degree which combines study from the three disciplines. According to the journalist Jon Kelly, it 'dominate[s] public life' (in the UK). See Kelly (2010).
6. Balogh (1982), pp. 71–72.
7. For instance, see Skidelsky (1977).
8. See Galbraith (2010a, b).
9. Ibid.
10. Ibid.
11. Ibid.
12. This is particularly in keeping with the tradition of Keynes.
13. Kaletsky (2010).
14. *The Economist* (2010).
15. The arguments that can be attributed to the Critical Realists were reported, but neither the school nor Tony Lawson was named.
16. *The Economist* (2010).
17. Stiglitz (2010a).
18. Stiglitz (2010b).
19. Shiller (2009).
20. Akerlof and Shiller (2009).
21. Shiller, Robert. 'Time for a more realistic approach'. The International Economy, Fall 2009, p. 48.
22. Ibid, p. 49.
23. Ibid.
24. Ibid.
25. *The Economist* (2009), pp. 70–72.
26. Lucas (2009), p. 67.
27. Lucas (1981) cited in Hamouda (1991), p. 161.
28. See Islam (2010).
29. Ibid.
30. Lucas (2009), p. 67.
31. *The Economist* (2009), pp. 70–72.
32. See Islam (2010).
33. Ibid.
34. Dasgupta (2002), p. 81.
35. See Islam (2010).
36. Leontief (1958), p. 106.

BIBLIOGRAPHY

Akerlof, G.A. and R.J. Shiller (2009) *Animal Spirits: How Human Psychology Drives the Economy, and Why it Matters for Global Capitalism*. Princeton, NJ; Woodstock: Princeton University Press.

Balogh, T. (1982) *Keynes as a Policy Adviser: The Fifth Keynes Seminar held at the University of Kent at Canterbury 1980*, Ed, A.P. Thirlwall, London, Macmillan, p. 71.

Dasgupta, P. (2002) 'Modern economics and its critics', in U. Maki (ed.), *Fact and Fiction in Economics: Models, Realism and Social Construction*. Cambridge: Cambridge University Press.

Davidson, Paul, (2007) *John Maynard Keynes*, Basingstoke: Palgrave Macmillan.

The Economist (2009), Briefing: 'The state of economics', *The Economist*, 18 July, pp. 70–72.

The Economist (2010) Economics focus: 'George Soros has left his mark on many economies. Can he do the same for economics?' 15 April, online version from the print edition, accessed 26 March 2013 at http://www.economist.com/node/15908207.

Frean, A. (2010) 'George Soros backs Oxford to refresh economics', *The Times*, 5 April.

Galbraith, J. (2010a) Interview with Open Democracy, www.opendemocracy.net/audio/interview-with-james-galbraith, last accessed 14 September 2010.

Galbraith, J. (2010b) Written statement to members of the Senate Judiciary Committee delivered on May 4, http://utip.gov.utexas.edu/Flyers/GalbraithMay4SubCommCrimeRV.pdf, last accessed 12 April 2010.

Hamouda, O. (1991) *Verification in Economics and History: A Sequel to Scientifization*, London: Routledge.

Islam, Faisal (2010) Transcript of an interview with Robert Lucas, http://blogs.channel4.com/snowblog/2009/09/08/chicago-defends-itself-against-keynesian-attacks/, last accessed 14 July 2012.

Kaletsky, A. (2010) 'Academics ready to crush old economic theories with a new reality', *Economic View*, *The Times*, 6 April.

Kelly, John (2010) 'Why does PPE rule Britain?', BBC News, 31 August.

Leontief, W. (1958), 'The state of economic science', *Review of Economics and Statistics*, 40(2), 103–106.

Lucas, Robert (2009) 'In defence of the dismal science', *The Economist*, 8 August, p. 67.

Open Democracy, interview accessed 14 September 2010 at http://www.opendemocracy.net/audio/interview-with-james-galbraith.

Shiller, R. (2009) 'Time for a more realistic approach', *International Economy*, Fall, 48–49, http://www.international-economy.com/TIE_F09_Shiller.pdf, last accessed 27 August 2012.

Skidelsky, R. (Ed.) (1977) *The End of the Keynesian Era: Essays on the Disintegration of the Keynesian Political Economy*, London: Macmillan.

Skidelsky, R. (2009) *Keynes: The Return of the Master*, London: Penguin.

Stiglitz, J. (2010a) (Preliminary and incomplete) paper, 'An agenda for reforming economic theory', prepared for session on, 'What Kind of Theory to Guide Reform and Restructuring of the Financial and Non-Financial Sectors?' INET conference, Cambridge, 9 April.

Stiglitz, J. (2010b) 'The non-existent hand', *London Review of Books*, 32(8), 22 April, http://www.lrb.co.uk/v32/n08/joseph-stiglitz/the-non-existent-hand, last accessed 27 August 2012.

Index